Collector's Guide To

Inkwells

Identification & Values

BOOK II

Veldon Badders

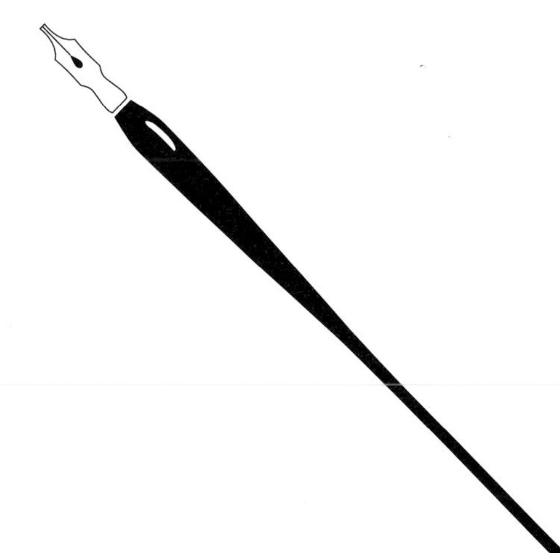

COLLECTOR BOOKS

A Division of Schroeder Publishing Co., Inc.

The current values of this book should be used only as a guide. They are not intended to set prices, which vary from one section of the country to another. Auction prices as well as dealer prices vary and are affected by condition as well as demand. Neither the Author nor the Publisher assumes responsibility for any losses that might be incurred as a result of consulting this guide.

Searching for a Publisher?

We are always looking for knowledgeable people considered to be experts within their fields. If you feel that there is a real need for a book on your collectible subject and have a large comprehensive collection, contact Collector Books.

On the Cover:

Clockwise, from top left:
Silver-plated, hinged silver cover with pomegranate on top, $175.00 – 225.00.
Porcelain, white with hand-painted decoration and gold trim, German, $130.00 – 150.00.
Bronze finish pot metal gentleman's high-top shoe, hinged flat lid, $160.00 – 200.00.
Traveler, red Morocco cover, brass interior fittings, $100.00 – 125.00.

Cover design by Michelle Dowling
Book design by Holly C. Long

Additional copies of this book may be ordered from:
Collector Books
P.O. Box 3009
Paducah, Kentucky 42002-3009

@$19.95. Add $2.00 for postage and handling.

Contents

Dedication

We respectfully dedicate this book to Edward Cornwell, Jr. His gifts are many — his charms and wit have made the hours seem like minutes and the days seem like hours. His far-reaching knowledge of antiques keeps us in a perpetual state of enlightenment. Our education continues under his expert (and exceptional) tutelage. A great deal of his knowledge, and a little bit of his soul, show up on each and every page.

Special Thanks

To my loving wife Gail who has poured her heart and soul into this book. Without her at my side working tediously to keep things on track, it would have been impossible. To Gail I convey a very special thank you. You truly are my "Honey Bee."

Acknowledgments

We would like to thank the following people for allowing us the privilege of photographing their collections and/or furnishing photos of their inkwells. The lengthy communications before, during, and after the photo sessions mean as much to us as the photographs themselves and to those who entertained our stay at their homes, what wonderful times and memories we have.

Scott & Dixie Rodkey
Houston, Texas

John & Mickie Wherry
Cape Cod, Massachusetts

Marilyn Herr-Gesell
Executive Director
E. Bloomfield Historical Society
E. Bloomfield, New York

John Hummer & Doris
Akron, Pennsylvania

Tom & Gina Thorp
Utica, New York

Hester Smith
North Chili, New York

Matthias Meyer
Alfter, Germany

The George E. Ohr
Arts and Cultural Center
Biloxi, Mississippi

We would also like to thank the following for their continuing support and generous contributions:

Windsweep Antiques
Brockport, New York

Janis Franco
History Librarian
Meriden Public Library
Meriden, Connecticut

Mary Smith
"Our own wonderful historian"
Hamlin, New York

Betty D. Goldman
Historical Collections Dept.
Bridgeport Public Library
Bridgeport, Connecticut

Photo Processing Technicians
Renee Povio
Rochester, New York
Marj Smith
Brockport, New York

Biloxi Public Library
Biloxi, Mississippi

Richard & Evelyn Vacca
Mt. Morris, New York

Amy Holland
(helpful daughter)
Rochester, New York

The Strong Museum
Rochester, New York
Christopher Bensch
Curator of Furnishings
Carol Sandler
Librarian

Photography
Veldon Badders
Hamlin, New York
Matthias Meyer
Germany

Introduction

We find it extremely rewarding that so many people are eager to have *still* more background information on inkwells. In the beginning it was our intention to furnish just this type of material. As we became further immersed in the research process, we discovered that there are several fine sources of material already available. The integrated network of both public and private libraries makes it relatively easy to obtain such wonderful books as:

Inkstands and Inkwells, Betty and Ted Rivera

Ink Bottles and Inkwells, William Covill

Doulton Ink Wares, available from Bee Publications, 39 Half Moon Lane, London SE24 9JX UK

(This is an excellent source of material about the beginnings and extremely successful life of the Doulton Pottery, complete with photos and details.)

Walkers Inkwells of 1885 catalog

Walkers provides thorough detail on inkwells and standishes of that particular time period. Walkers, unfortunately, is not as readily available as most of the other sources.

1892 Tower Manufacturing and Novelty Co. catalog

This catalog provides a vast array of photos representing the various styles of inkwells offered for sale at the time of publication.

The A.C. McClurg & Co. of Chicago Price List, c. 1893 – 94

The price list offers an excellent photographic representation of inkstands sold during that time period.

McGraw's Book of Antique Inkwells, available from The Society of Inkwell Collectors, 5136 Thomas Avenue South, Minneapolis, MN 55410

One may also wish to consider becoming a Society member. One of the benefits of membership in the Society is a quarterly publication, *The Stained Finger,* which contains important and interesting information for the antique collector and the antique dealer alike.

On a more global scale, one may also wish to consider membership in Writing Equipment Society of London, c/o Mr. Kevin Prime, 75 Elmwood Crescent, Flitwich, Beds, MK45ILJ UK

In the following, we offer our readers additional information on the various companies which manufactured and distributed some of the more desirable inkwells and collectibles of today.

BRADLEY & HUBBARD MFG. CO., MERIDEN, CONNECTICUT

Nathaniel L. Bradley and Walker Hubbard co-founded the business in 1854. It was formally organized on January 1, 1875, as the Bradley Hubbard Mfg. Co.

Production primarily focused on metal-based goods, including brass, bronze, and iron. Local sales offices were located in Boston, Chicago, and New York City. The company began with a factory consisting of one wooden structure which employed six people. At the height of production, it encompassed several sturdy brick buildings and employed over 1,100 people.

Like so many companies of this time period, little reference has been made in historical literature with regard to the manufacture of inkwells and desk accessories. The early twentieth century

saw a line of desk appointments, book ends, and architectural bronze and iron produced, although this was a relatively minute portion of their business. Bradley and Hubbard strived to maintain their position as forerunner in production of inkwells and desk accessories during the Victorian, Art Nouveau, Arts and Crafts, and Art Deco time periods. By staying up-to-date with the latest developments in the manufacturing environment and by listening to what it was that the public wanted and/or needed, Bradley and Hubbard was able to carve out an important niche for itself in this area.

Bradley and Hubbard products remain very collectible.

Bradley and Hubbard Mfg. Co. factory

The Tower Manufacturing and Novelty Co.

Tower sold figural and novelty inkstands in the early twentieth century. The more common items included dogs, horses, and deer.

Meriden Britannia Co., Connecticut

Meriden produced elegant, beautifully detailed silver-plated designs, similar to those produced by Sheffield and Gorham.

S. Benedict Mfg. Co., Easy Syracuse, New York

The latter part of the nineteenth century and the early part of the twentieth century saw the production of a wide variety of white metal or pot metal inkstands. Typical designs included an inkwell shaped like a head with removable top to reveal the insert. In 1904, Benedict produced an inkwell to resemble a scantily clad lady lying on a horse.

The George E. Ohr Arts and Cultural Center, Biloxi, Mississippi

The Center was established in George's home town of Biloxi on October 22, 1994, to celebrate his contribution to the art of pottery.

George E. Ohr, nicknamed "The Mad Potter of Biloxi," was born on July 12, 1857, in Biloxi, Mississippi. He proclaimed himself to be the "Greatest Potter on Earth." His pottery shop, aptly

George E. Ohr, 1857 – 1918

named "Pot-Ohr-E," became a well-known workshop by 1894. Ohr's creations include children's piggy banks, plaques of Southern buildings, and ceramic hats. His most famous work were his so-called "Mud Babies."

Ohr's work continues to receive much recognition to this day. Some of his inkwells are featured in our *Collector's Guide to Inkwells* (1995) (see Plates 152 – 155). Some of his pieces have sold for prices in excess of $60,000.

John Round & Son, Ltd., Sheffield, England

During the late 1800s, Round produced a vast array of figural inkwells which were electroplated on Britannia metal.

Homan Silver plate Co., Cincinnati, Ohio

Homan was know for producing many novelty inkstands, the most famous of which is the head of Pierrot, the French clown.

Roycroft Shops, East Aurora, New York

Elbert Hubbard was born on June 19, 1856, in Bloomington, Illinois. He later relocated to East Aurora, New York, where he established the Roycroft Shops in 1895. Roycroft was renowned for its selection of books, magazines, leather novelties, artistic iron work, and its hammered brass, copper, and silver. At the height of its popularity, Roycroft employed approximately 500 people, all of whom were allowed creative freedom, a rare gift during this time period. Elbert and his wife Alice both lost their lives on board the *Lusitania* when it sank on May 7, 1915. Roycroft was led by Elbert Hubbard II until 1938, when it declared bankruptcy. The inkwells produced by Roycroft during its tenure make very worthy collectibles.

Zephyr American Corp., New York

Alfred Neustadtter invented the Swivodex which was made and sold by Zephyr American Corp. In the 1940s, it was an inkwell widely used by the U.S. military, acclaimed to be non-spilling, evaporation proof, and resistant to temperature changes, with position for the pen always out of the ink. It was used by Shigemitsu at the peace signing of the end of WWII.

Zephyr American Corp. Swivodex inkwell used by military

JENNINGS BROS. FACTORY, BRIDGEPORT, CONNECTICUT

Originally listed in 1892 as the American Jewelry Co., the company became Jennings Bros. Mfg. in 1893. They produced silver-plated ware, casket hardware, and novelties*. During this time it manufactured a large array of inkwells, desk sets, etc. Its very prominent mark is J.B.

*Bridgeport Public Library

Jennings Brothers factory

Porcelain & Pottery

Plate 1
Porcelain, footed well with transfer floral decorations, loose matching dome cover, Rococo influence, 2⅝" square x 3⅛" high, c. 1900, $85.00 – 95.00. Hummer collection.

Plate 2
Porcelain, iridescent light gray dome shape, transfer printed, claret and gold decoration, picture in Adam manner, brass hinged dome-shaped matching cover, Kauffmann style, 4" diameter x 3⅜" high, c. 1900 – 1910, $150.00 – 180.00. Hummer collection.

Plate 3
Porcelain, one piece with eight-sided gold trimmed base and cylindrical well and loose cover with finial, marked "Royal Copenhagen Denmark" surrounding an insignia plus "792-3334" in script, 3¾" wide, c. early twentieth century, $150.00 – 175.00. Hummer collection.

Plate 4
Porcelain base and loose well container, polychrome floral garlands, trimmed in gold, loose gold trimmed cover with finial, porcelain insert, marked on base "Ursula GES-GESCH" plus "903" and "B" in crown insignia, 6⅛" diameter, c. 1910 – 1920, $140.00. Hummer collection.

Plate 5
Porcelain, transfer printed, Rococo in form, trim is hand-painted, loose porcelain wells and covers, marked "7137," 7¼" x 6", c. 1910 – 1920, $185.00. Hummer collection.

Plate 6
Porcelain, classical ancient Roman sham (urn), eagle with thunderbolts on front, brass hinged cover with finial, porcelain insert, marked "MADE IN FRANCE-HAND-PAINTED," 5¾" x 3", c. 1910 – 1920, $150.00 – 175.00. Hummer collection.

Plate 7
Porcelain, figural dogs with loose head cover, children with hair wigs, hand-painted, both marked "GERMANY – 1359," 3¼" wide base x 2½" high, c. 1890, $250.00 each. Hummer collection.

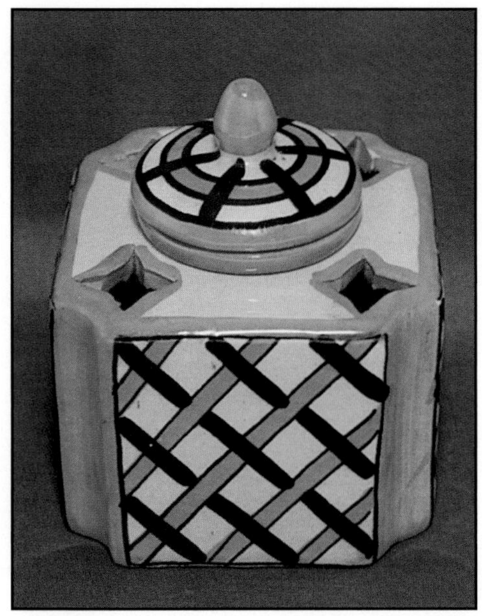

Plate 8
Tin glazed pottery, loose matching cover with finial, basket weave design in black and caramel, four quill holes, pottery insert, marked "H and D–1270" plus "MADE IN FRANCE," 2⅝" square x 3" high, c. 1900, $115.00 – 130.00. Hummer collection.

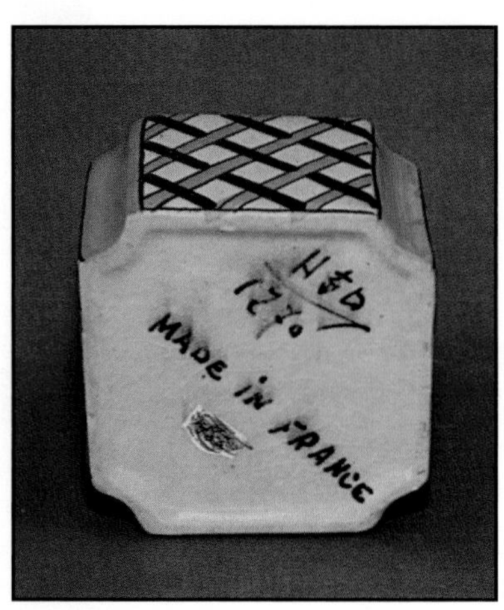

Plate 9
Bottom of Plate 8.

Plate 10
Pottery, rural French, hand-painted cockerel, polychrome, loose matching cover, four quill holes, 2⅝" square x 2⅞" high, c. 1900, $120.00 – 150.00. Hummer collection.

Plate 11
Porcelain, six-sided, off-white with bird and fruit transfer decoration, quill hole, loose cover, marked "LIMOGES FRANCE," 3" wide x 2" high, c. twentieth century (modern), $90.00 – 110.00. Hummer collection.

Plate 12
Earthenware, transfer printed, gilt embellishments, chrysanthemum pattern, French, mushroom-shaped matching cover, porcelain insert, marked "CHRYSANTHEME – LUNEVILLE, KG R," 3" diameter x 3½" high, this probably had a hinged collar, c. 1880 – 1890, $80.00 – 100.00. Hummer collection.

Plate 13
Majolica (earthenware) building with pen channel, roof missing, glass insert, marked "BLACK FOREST PEASANT HOUSE, ERPHILA, GERMANY – 997A," 4⅝" x 4⅞" x 1½" high, c. 1900, $20.00 – 25.00 as is. Hummer collection.

Plate 14
Porcelain with quill hole and quill rest, hand-painted floral design, loose porcelain sander and well inserts, loose covers, German, marked "V," 3¼" wide x 1¼" high, c. 1860 – 1870, $150.00 – 175.00. Hummer collection.

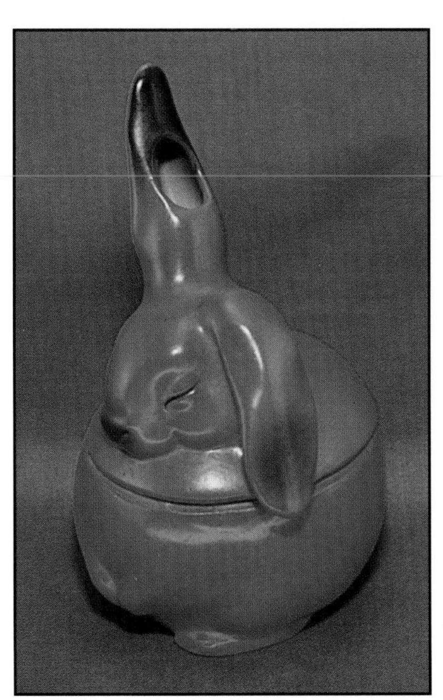

Plate 15
Porcelain, orange with black trim, loose rabbit's head cover with quill hole in ear, porcelain insert, base impressed "X.S., 432 DEP," German, 2½" diameter x 4½" high, c. early twentieth century, $300.00 – 400.00. Hummer collection.

Plate 16
Porcelain, hand-painted blue and gold luster, lady in 1840s dress with asters on skirt, loose figural woman cover, marked "NORITAKE — HAND-PAINTED MADE IN JAPAN," 3¼" diameter x 4⅜" high, c. 1920, $150.00 – 175.00. Hummer collection.

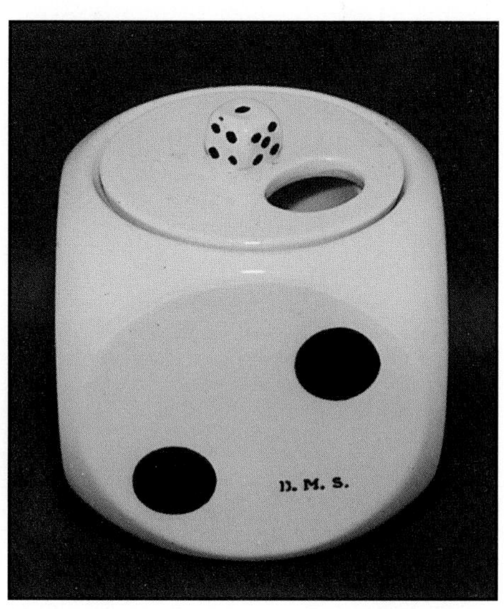

Plate 17
Porcelain, dice shape, loose sliding cover with dice finial, porcelain insert, marked "D.M.S." plus marked on base "2777-V," 2¾" square x 2¾" high, c. 1910 – 1920, $80.00 – 100.00. Hummer collection.

Plate 18
Art pottery, mushroom-shaped with loose mushroom-shaped cover, mottled brown, ocher, and green, American, marked "CC," 3¹⁄₁₆" diameter x 1⅞" high, c. early twentieth century, $80.00 – 100.00. Hummer collection.

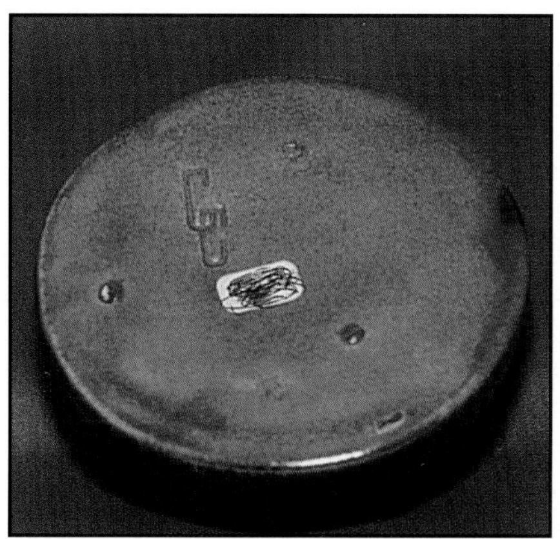

Plate 19
Bottom of Plate 18.

Plate 20
Stoneware, tapered body with blue hand-painted bands, cork closure, American, c. mid-19th century, \$85.00 – 125.00. Rodkey collection.

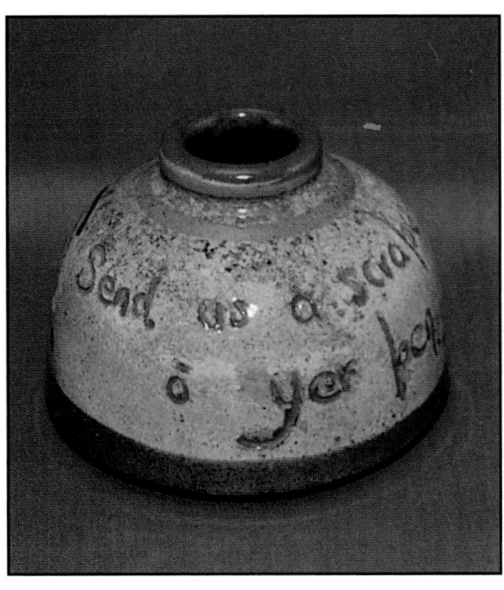

Plate 21
Pottery, dome-shaped, tan and gray with hand-painted floral design, gold and blue trim, all under glaze, marked on base "WATCOMB TORQUAY – MADE IN ENGLAND," plus incised around well "SEND US A SCRAPE Ō YER PEN," $2\frac{13}{16}$" diameter base x $1\frac{7}{8}$" high, c. 1910 – 1915, \$200.00. Hummer collection.

Plate 22
Art pottery, Moorcroft, silver-plated brass, hinged collar, pomegranate and leaves decoration, marked "ENG. MAKE," c. late nineteenth century, \$350.00. Smith collection.

Plate 23
Stoneware, salt glazed, gray, American, $2\frac{1}{4}$" dimeter x $1\frac{1}{8}$" high, c. 1850 – 1860, \$75.00 – 85.00. Hummer collection.

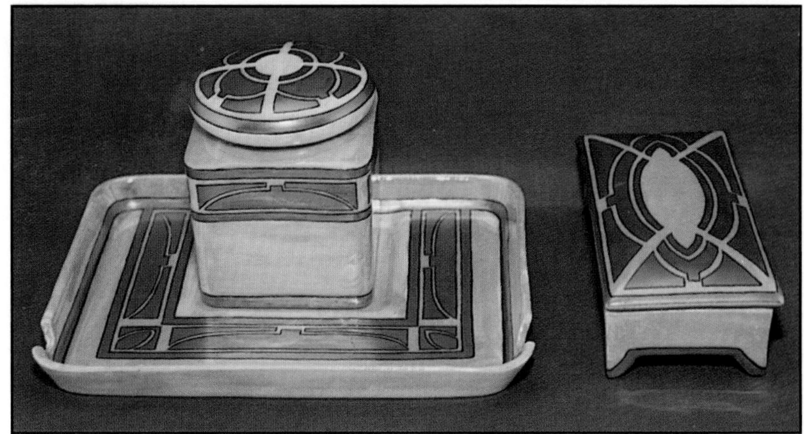

Plate 24
Japanese export porcelain tray and well, Arts and Craft movement influence, green iridescent glaze, loose well and cover, porcelain insert, four-footed stamp box with matching cover, marked on well NORITAKE – NIPPON," 5½" x 4¼" tray, c. 1915, $175.00 – 200.00. Hummer collection.

Plate 25
Pottery, white with blue decoration, loose matching cover, pottery insert, Art Deco influence, marked "G.D. PARIS FRANCE" plus "DEPOSE," 4⅝" diameter x 2⅞" high, c. 1920, $125.00 – 150.00. Hummer collection.

Plate 26
Porcelain with stepped pen rest base. Art Deco influence, hand-painted trim in orange, blue, and yellow, loose cover with figural duck finial, porcelain insert, marked "GERMANY – 4826," 4⅜" x 4⅛" x 3⅝", c. 1920 – 1930, $100.00 – 125.00. Hummer collection.

Plate 27
Porcelain, children in 18th century costumes, polychrome, loose sander and well insert, loose covers, 3½" octagonal base x 3⅛" high, c. 1850 – 1860, $300.00 – 360.00. Hummer collection.

Plate 28
Porcelain, white with transfer floral decoration, pen channel, loose matching cover, marked "R.S. GERMANY" in a green wreath insignia, 5¼" wide x 1⅜" high, c. 1900, $75.00 – 95.00. Hummer collection.

Plate 29
Porcelain, white with gold trim and hand-painted floral decoration, pen rack, cover is overturned flower, Rococo style, possibly German, 3½" x 3¼" x 2¾" high, c. 1890 – 1900, $150.00 – 175.00. Hummer collection.

Plate 30
Porcelain, six-sided with quill channel and quill hole, transfer print pastoral couple in eighteenth century costume, porcelain insert, possibly American, marked "HAND DECORATED" plus an insignia plus "FINE CHINA" (cover missing), 4⅛" wide x 2⅝" high, c. 1930 – 1940, $85.00 – 95.00 as is. Hummer collection.

Plate 31
Porcelain, violet and butterfly transfer decoration, bowed sides, one quill hole, loose matching cover, marked "LIMOGES, FRANCE," 4" wide x 3¼" high, c. 1900, $140.00 – 150.00. Hummer collection.

Plate 32
Porcelain, ovoid urn shape, white with hand-painted decoration and gold trim, five quill holes, loose matching cover and insert, marked "LIMOGES – HAND-PAINTED," 6⅝" x 3½" high, c. 1900 – 1910, $150.00 – 175.00. Hummer collection.

Plate 33
Porcelain with attached well, hand-painted floral decoration with gold trim, loose cover with finial, pure Rococo form, marked "GERMANY" plus "GES GESCHUTZT" plus crossed swords with an "S," 6⅝" x 4¾", c. 1890 – 1900, $175.00 – 200.00. Hummer collection.

Plate 34
Porcelain, dome-shaped, orange iridescent, loose cover with quill hole, Arts and Crafts influence, marked "26," 3½" diameter base x 3" high, c. 1915, $90.00 – 100.00. Hummer collection.

Plate 35
Porcelain, white with hand-painted decoration and gold trim, loose dome-shaped matching cover, scroll feet, acanthus leaf on shoulder, marked "MADE IN GERMANY" plus "SCHUTZ-MARKE-DEP" with insignia, 2⁹⁄₁₆" square, c. 1910 – 1920, $130.00 – 150.00. Hummer collection.

Plate 36
Porcelain scalloped shell, cone-shaped opening on font with one quill hole on each side, classical human face, well forms cap on head, Blanc de Chaine style, (possibly missing lid), French, c. 1860 – 1870, $200.00. Smith collection.

Plate 37
Old Paris porcelain, shaded pink with gold striping, flower is highlighted in cobalt blue, leaf and fruit design, one quill hole, marked on base "M-8," flower petal repaired, cover missing, 3" wide, c. 1850 – 1860, $150.00 as is. Hummer collection.

Plate 38
Porcelain base with two wells recessed, ivory with hand-painted floral decoration and gold trim, finials on pots are fruit and leaves, marked "KPM," German, Kaiser Porcelain Mfg., 9¾" x 6⅞", c. 1860 – 1870, $500.00 – 600.00. Hummer collection.

Plate 39
Porcelain base with recesses for loose well, pounce pot and covered seal wax container, white with hand-painted floral decoration and remnants of gold trim, European, 12⅜" x 7⅞" base, c. 1860, $200.00 – 225.00. Hummer collection.

Plate 40
Pottery, Rockingham glazed, three front open compartments and back well ledge, two quill holes, matching funnel type wells, base impressed with oval shield insignia, 6⁵⁄₁₆" x 4¾" x 2½" high, c. 1850 – 1900, $300.00 – 400.00. Hummer collection.

Plate 41
Porcelain, transfer printed with hand-painted gold trim, loose matching cover and porcelain insert, marked "OSCAR SCHLEGELMILCH" plus "HANDGEMALT," 7⅝" wide x 2⅛" high, c. 1920 – 1930, $150.00 – 175.00. Hummer collection.

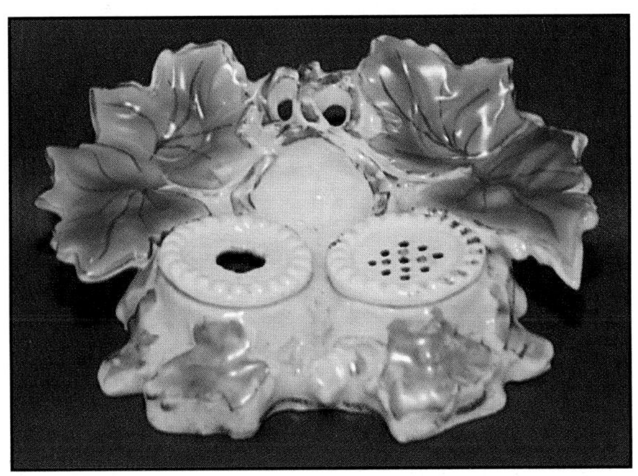

Plate 42
Porcelain, white with green and gold trim, rustic style, foliate base and feet, small nib dish, loose well and pounce pot, possibly German, 5½" wide x 2" high, c. mid-nineteenth century, $130.00 – $150.00. Hummer collection.

Plate 43
Wedgwood, Jasperware, classical Roman form, pale blue with relief acanthus leaf decoration in white, saucer base, two quill holes, loose lid with acorn-shaped finial, 7¼" x 5⅝" x 3½", c. 1900. $300.00 – 350.00. Wherry collection.

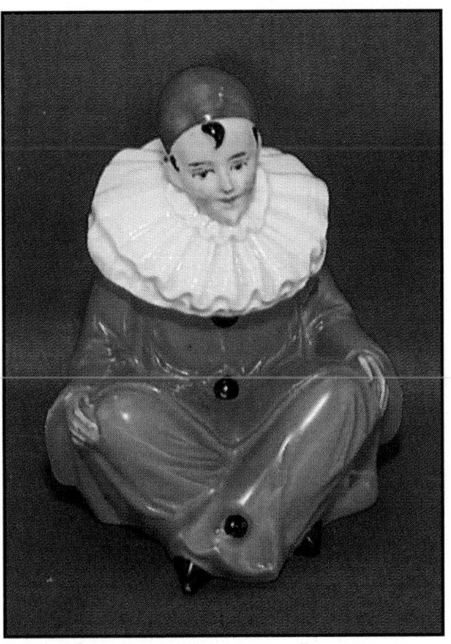

Plate 44
Japanese export porcelain, loose white collar and head cover, "Pierrot," 3$\frac{3}{16}$" wide x 3¾" high, c. 1920, $125.00 – 150.00. Hummer collection.

Plate 45
Pottery, bell-shaped, black with gold band trim, matching stopper, marked on front "WILLIAM'S INK POT, RD NO 331808," $3\frac{5}{8}$" diameter base x $4\frac{1}{4}$" high, c. twentieth century, $150.00. Hummer collection.

Plate 46
Porcelain, transfer printed, stylized floral design, brass hinged mushroom-shaped matching cover, $2\frac{9}{16}$" x $4\frac{1}{8}$" high, c. late nineteenth century, $110.00 – 125.00. Hummer collection.

Plate 47
Porcelain, six-sided, tapered base, white with hand-painted gold relief decoration, Rococo style, loose matching cover, porcelain insert, marked "T & V LIMOGES FRANCE" plus "MS" in gold script, $3\frac{3}{8}$" hexagon x $3\frac{3}{8}$" high, c. 1900, $125.00. Hummer collection.

Plate 48
Matching bone china well and straight pen, well is bulbous contour with transfer printed roses and gilt trim, well is marked on bottom "BONE CHINA MADE IN ENGLAND," c. 1910 – 1915, $185.00 – 200.00. Thorp collection.

Plate 49
Yellow ware porcelain figural with original matching double inserts, mid-Victorian child playing with a drum and a rabbit on elaborate Baroque trim stand with masks and acanthus leaves, scrolled feet, marked on base "CJ 23," c. 1850, $350.00 – 400.00. Thorp collection.

Plate 50
Same as Plate 49.

Plate 51
Porcelain dish, one-piece, white with blue hand-painted decoration trimmed in black and gold, brass hinge and snap type collar assembly attached to neck of well with attached matching porcelain cover, marked "ENCRIER A PRESSTON, PARIS, VIENNE TROIS MEDAILLES A.D. PARIS" plus incised on base "160-4," 4⅛" diameter x 3" high, c. 1850 – 1860, $200.00 – 300.00. Hummer collection.

Plate 52
Pottery, bulbous with three quill holes, hand-painted blue trim, possibly ironstone, relief foliate design, 2¾" diameter x 2⅛" high, c. mid-nineteenth century, $85.00 – 125.00. Hummer collection.

Plate 53
Porcelain (hard paste), hinged bronze collar and cover, hand-painted, Rococo influence, dome has acanthus leaf decoration, German, c. 1890, $110.00 – 150.00. Thorp collection.

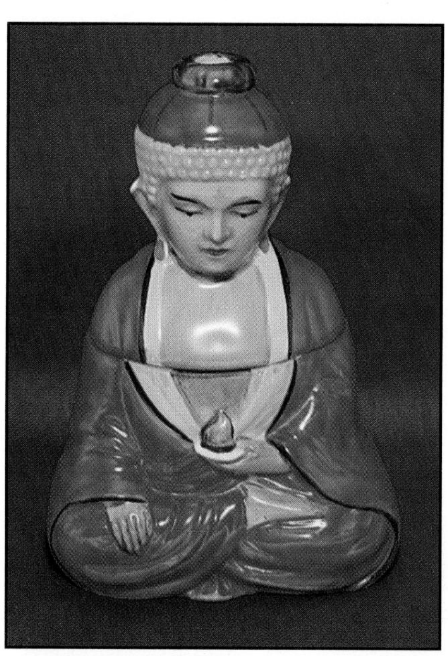

Plate 54
Japanese export porcelain, deep orange Buddha, one quill hole on top of head, loose matching cover, porcelain insert, 3⁹⁄₁₆" x 5" high, c. 1920, $100.00 – 125.00. Hummer collection.

Plate 55
Porcelain bulbous well sitting in saucer base, hand-painted floral with gilt embellishment, Rococo style, loose cover with finial, matching pen, c. early twentieth century, $200.00 – 250.00. Thorp collection.

Plate 56
Same as Plate 55.

Plate 57
Porcelain (hard paste) tray with double matching wells, matching inserts and covers, Dresden, neo-Japanese style with Rococo influence decoration, prunis flowers, gold embellishment, 9" long x 6¾" deep x 3" high, c. 1890 – 1900, $250.00 – 300.00. Thorp collection.

Plate 58
Hard paste porcelain, painted in Chinese export classical style with garlands and lattice work, gilt bronze mounts with rope trim, two pen holders, marked with red seal "FRANCE," c. 1900, $185.00. Thorp collection.

Plate 59
Hard paste porcelain with wood grain painted decoration, Venetian gondola form, cabin is well, hinged lid, possibly European, c. early twentieth century, $150.00 – 200.00. Thorp collection.

Plate 60
Porcelain German U-boat, mottled green trim, applied high relief flower with gold embellishment, mounted gun, novelty, 4½" x 2" x 2", c. 1900 – 1910, $200.00 – 300.00 (rare). Rodkey collection.

Plate 61
Porcelain with brass hinged matching cover, souvenir of Wales, transfer printed, hand-colored print of ladies in Welsh national costume, gold embellishment, printed "WELSH COSTUMES" under the art work, 6¼" long x 2⅝" high, c. early twentieth century, $150.00 – 200.00. Thorp collection.

Plate 62
Porcelain (hard paste) tray with two matching wells and covers, hand-painted, polychrome flowers with ribbons and scrolls, Rococo style, German, marked on base "SWAINE & CO HUTTENSTENACH," 8⅛" wide x 5 13/16" base, c. early twentieth century, $200.00 – 250.00. Thorp collection.

Plate 63
Porcelain (hard paste) figural of three pirates with treasure chest, polychrome, marked "MADE IN JAPAN" on bottom, c. 1930, $225.00 – 275.00. Thorp collection.

Plate 64
Pottery, green glazed, figures of angels in relief (some with dogs' heads), separated by classic columns, Gothic style, two loose lids with knob finials on well and pounce pot, Arts and Crafts movement, possibly American, poor condition, 7⅛" x 4¾" x 4", c. 1910, $150.00 as is, $300.00 – 350.00 if perfect. Wherry collection.

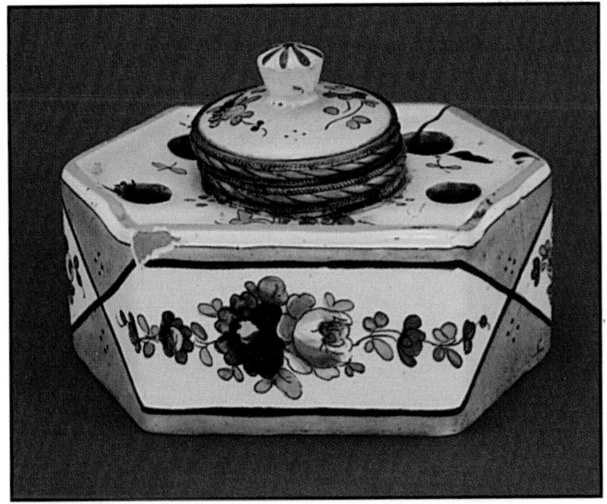

Plate 65
Faience, blue and gray, hand-painted with polychrome flowers, ocher striping, six-sided, braided design brass mounts, pottery insert, hinged brass collar, 4½" x 3" x 3", c. 1900, $70.00 – 90.00 (slight damage). Wherry collection.

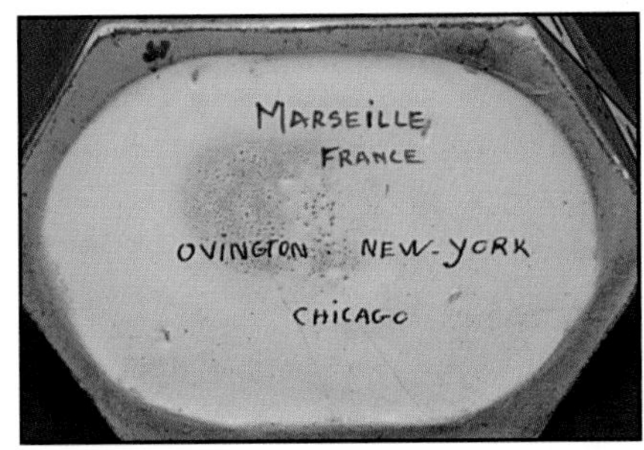

Plate 66
Same as Plate 65.

Plate 67
Porcelain, shape of Maltese cross, hand-painted rose decoration with blue striping around color panels, 3¼" square x 1¾" high, c. 1900, $95.00 – 110.00. Wherry collection.

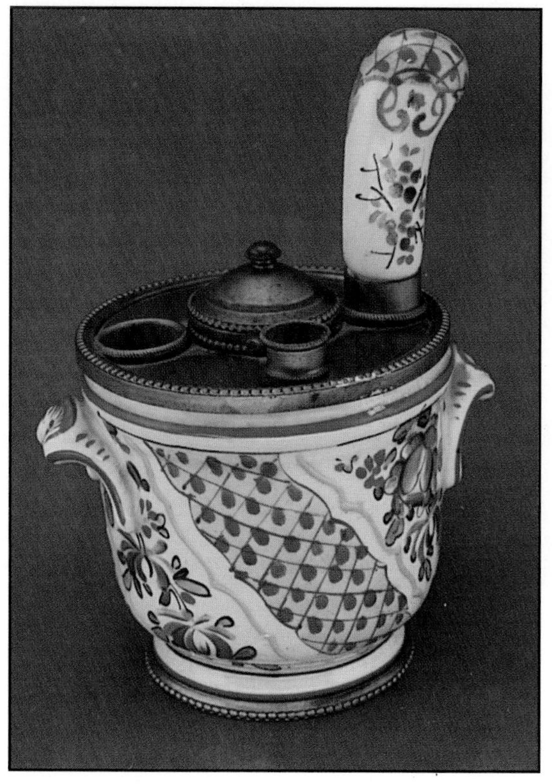

Plate 68
Porcelain, hand-painted, nineteenth century in eighteenth century style, rose pompadour, brass mounts with bead trim, has seal for sealing wax, French, Rococo style, $500.00 – 600.00. Wherry collection.

Plate 69
Japanese export porcelain with ornate gilt brass mounts, has side handles and seal for sealing wax, Famille Verte pattern, has reserve panel with ducks and flowers and allover ivy design, three pen holes, center wafer box, and two seal holes (appears to be missing one seal), early nineteenth century, $400.00 – 500.00. Wherry collection.

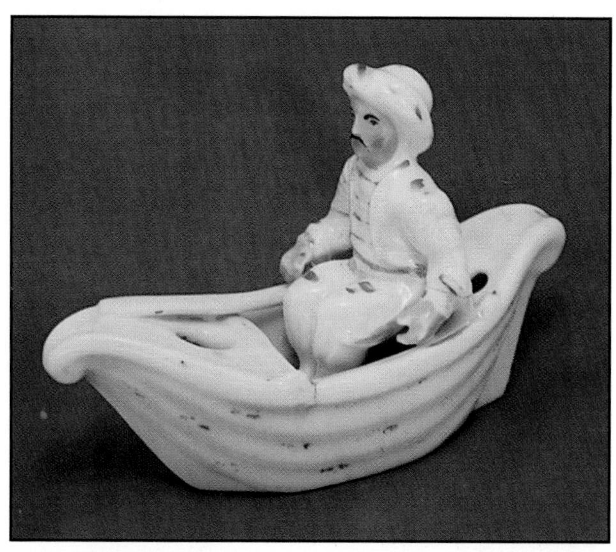

Plate 70
Porcelain from Old Paris factory, gentleman wearing turban in a boat (boat originally had more gold embellishment), 5" x 2" x 3", c. 1840 – 1850, $300.00 – 400.00. Wherry collection.

Plate 71
Porcelain, transfer printed with pastoral scene, maid milking a cow, hand-painted over transfer print, Nippon, 2¾" x 2" high, c. 1910, $130.00 – 150.00. Wherry collection.

Plate 72
Porcelain, possibly from Rockingham factory, lady playing a lute, polychrome decoration and gold embellishment, English, Staffordshire, 4" x 4½", c. 1830, $400.00 – 500.00. Wherry collection.

Plate 73
Porcelain, boat with courting couple, sailor and his lady, primary color is rose pompadour, inside is well and pounce pot, relief decoration on base, possibly English, flag has repair, 3½" x 5½", c. 1860 – 1870, $400.00 – 450.00. Wherry collection.

Plate 74
Art pottery, saucer base with attached eight-sided well, hand-painted, Dutch Gouda, loose cover, c. 1900 – 1910, $250.00 – 300.00. Smith collection.

Plate 75
Japanese export porcelain, yellow with concave sides, transfer printed flowers and gold trim embellishment, marked "7924," 2⁵⁄₁₆" x 2¼" high, c. twentieth century, $55.00 – 65.00. Hummer collection.

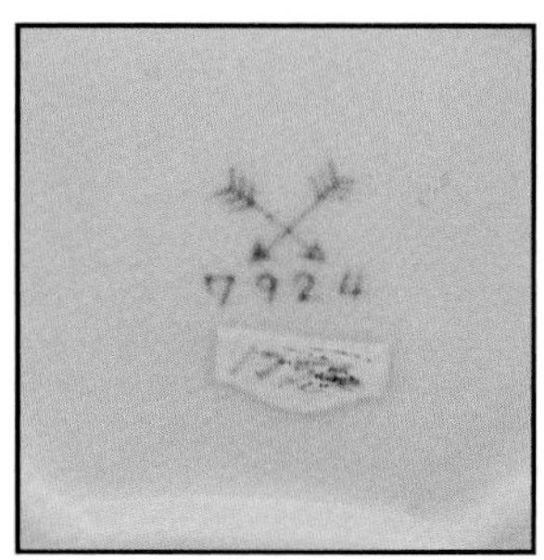

Plate 76
Bottom of Plate 75.

Plate 77
Ceramic miniature, hand-painted floral design, called "World's Smallest Inkwell," possibly European, c. 1900 – 1910, $100.00. Rodkey collection.

Plate 78
Porcelain, transfer printed, Dutch metal gold sponged on surface, Rococo style, hinged brass collar, scroll feet, Germany, 3½" square, c. 1890 – 1900, $150.00 – 180.00.

Plate 79
Porcelain, "Erphila Ink Girls" stamped on base, frontal pen rest, porcelain insert, Germany 2¼" square, c. 1920, $140.00 – 160.00.

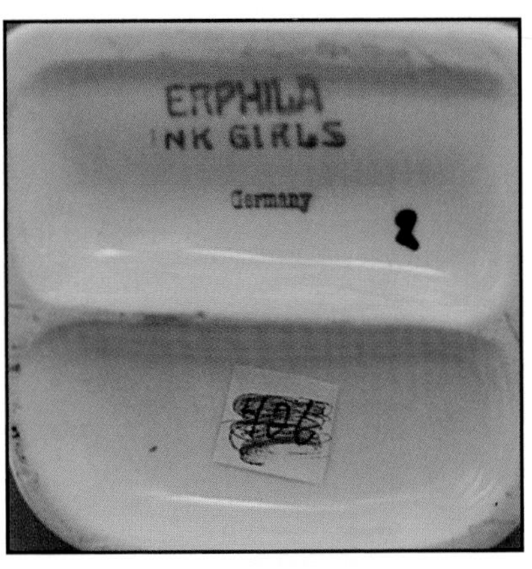

Plate 80
Base of Plate 79.

Plate 81
Pottery, yellow ware with applied gold decoration, well and pounce pot, Lion of St. Mark in center, England, 5¾" x 5" x 3", c. 1860 – 1870, $250.00 – 275.00.

Plate 82
Porcelain, transfer printed with hand-painted embellishment, saucer base with central well and pen holder, Limoges, French, 3⅛" x 1½" high, c. early twentieth century, $140.00 – 160.00. Wherry collection.

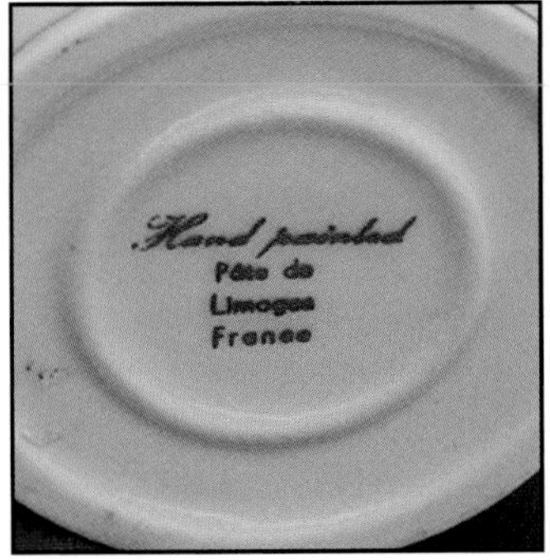

Plate 83
Bottom of Plate 82.

Plate 84
Porcelain, loose mushroom cover, transfer printed flowers with hand-painted gold embellishment, glass insert, Japanese Nippon, 4" square x 4" high, c. 1905 – 1910, $130.00 – 160.00. Wherry collection.

Plate 85
Bottom of Plate 84.

Plate 86
Porcelain, hand-painted, ground color is rose pompadour with hand-painted flowers, brass hinged cover, separate insert, Dresden, 3" x 2½", c. 1860, $200.00 – 250.00. Wherry collection.

Plate 87
Bottom of Plate 86.

Plate 88

French faience in Chinese Hawthorne style (emblem of spring), brass mounts, bead trim with acorn finial, c. 1890 – 1900, $250.00 – 300.00. Wherry collection.

Plate 89

Bottom of Plate 88.

Plate 90

Left: Porcelain with Adam influence, transfer printed flowers, brass hinged collar, c. 1870 – 1880, $80.00 – 100.00. Right: Porcelain, Old Paris type, hand-painted with little roses on blue/green background, eight-sided top with brass hinged collar, c. 1860 – 1870, $100.00 – 120.00. Wherry collection.

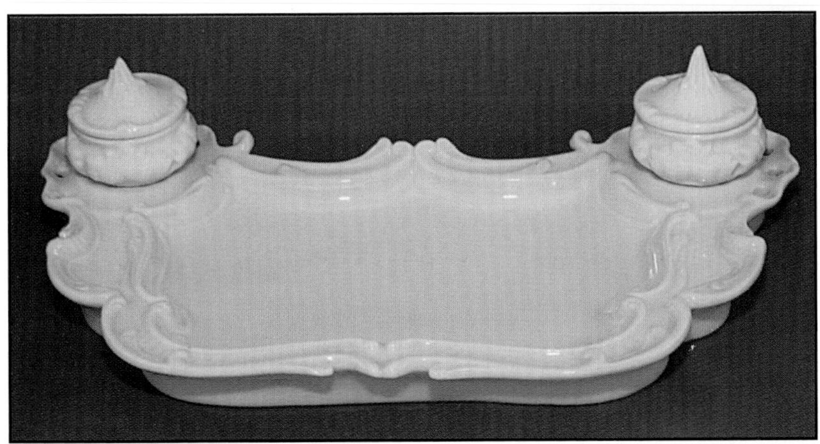

Plate 91

Porcelain, Rococo style scroll work embellishment around central tray, loose covers, European, c. 1890 – 1900, $150.00. Wherry collection.

Plate 92
Porcelain, French Empire style, lion's paw feet, olive green body, relief bands in an egg and dart motif surmounted by a classical lyre, possibly French, 3¾" x 5", c. 1900, $200.00 – 300.00. Wherry collection.

Plate 93
Porcelain, hand-painted floral design with gold embellishment, loose covers with flower bud finials, Rococo influence, German, 8⅞" x 6⅞" x 3⅜", c. 1890 – 1900, $160.00 – 200.00. Wherry collection.

Plate 94
Porcelain (Old Paris) snail well with saucer base, hand-painted, ancient Greek style, cast brass mounts and pen rest, 4" x 6", c. 1870, $300.00 – 350.00. Wherry collection

Plate 95

Porcelain (Old Paris), saucer base with quill holder, reservoir type with threaded tinware cover, 4" x 6", c. 1850, $200.00 – 250.00. Wherry collection.

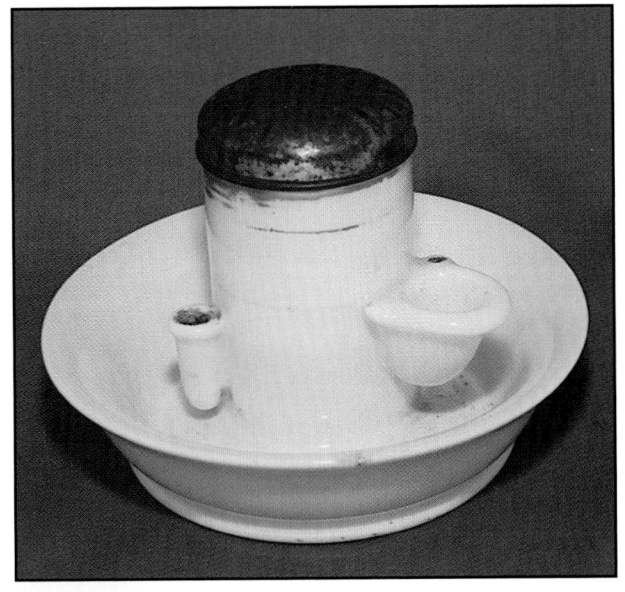

Plate 96

Porcelain, gravity feed type, hand-painted floral design, tinware lids, damaged wood base, 8½" x 5¾" x 5¾" high, c. 1850 – 1860, $160.00 – 200.00. Wherry collection.

Plate 97

Porcelain, neo-Oriental style, Famille Verte palettes, pale blue cracked ice background, upright seal, hinged brass collar with matching cover and finial, c. 1890 – 1900, $200.00 – 250.00. Wherry collection.

Plate 98
Ceramic, transfer prints of birds and flowers with hand-painted accents, hinged brass collar, neo-Japanese, marked "G.D. PARIS, DEPOSE," 4" x 3" high, c. 1880, $150.00 – 160.00. Wherry collection.

Plate 99
Porcelain with elaborate figural cover, mother and father showing baby to grandmother, pounce pot and well inside, German, 6½" x 4⅝" x 6¼" high, c. 1850, $600.00 – 700.00. Wherry collection.

Plate 100
Same as Plate 99.

 **Plate 101**
Porcelain, two hunters fighting over a hare, polychrome, base contains two wells, 7¼" x 4¾" x 6¼" high, c. 1860 – 1870, $500.00 – 600.00. Wherry collection.

Plate 102
Porcelain, claret ground, hand-painted central depression, two ladies with parasols in a field, gilt Rococo embellishment, two wells with loose covers, European, c. 1890, $250.00 – 325.00. Wherry collection.

Plate 103
Ceramic world globe on tiered circular base, transfer printed, polychrome, two ceramic wells inside, Japanese, 3" x 3⅞" high, c. early twentieth century, $100.00 – 125.00. Rodkey collection.

Plate 104
Japanese folk art pottery, "Hear no evil, see no evil, speak no evil," polychrome, medallions between monkeys, concave loose pottery insert, c. 1900 – 1910, $200.00 – 250.00. East Bloomfield collection.

Plate 105
Porcelain (hard paste), hand-painted with gilt embellishment, brass hinged collar, floral design, German, 3¾" x 2½" high, c. 1870 – 1880, $80.00 – 100.00. East Bloomfield collection.

Plate 106
Art pottery, hand-painted crowing rooster on one side, incised motto on other side, c. 1905, $200.00 – 250.00. East Bloomfield collection.

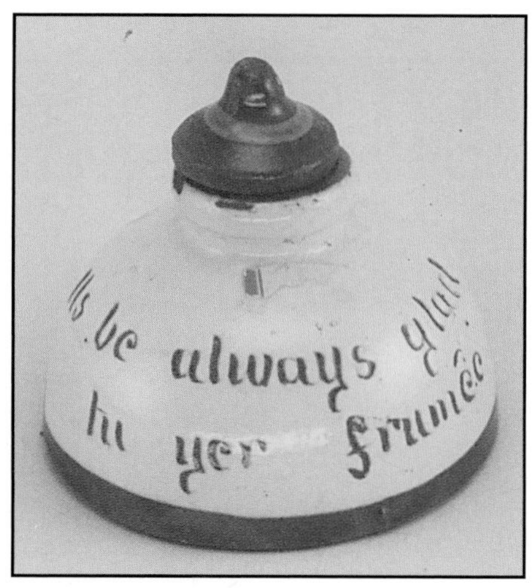

Plate 107
Same as Plate 106.

Plate 108
Porcelain, standish with rectangular deep base, scroll feet, elaborate hand-painted decoration — roses and morning glories etc., well and pounce pot and central flower shaped candle holder, c. 1850, $450.00. Smith collection.

Plate 109
Bottom of Plate 108.

Plate 110
Porcelain with Rococo style base, hand-painted with scrolls on pot and surrounding area, raised paste turquoise gemstones on pot, well is urn-shaped with loose lid and scrolled finial, French, c. 1900, $160.00 – 200.00. Smith collection.

Plate 111
Porcelain, oval in contour, relief figures of cupids on sides, two quill holes, Capo-di-Monte, c. early twentieth century, $300.00. Smith collection.

Plate 112
Japanese art pottery, three applied masks of elderly Japanese people, dripped glazed shoulder mottled in black, white, and gray, lower body is earth red, glazed insert, ornamental circular openings in body, c. 1900, $200.00 – 220.00. Smith collection.

Plate 113
Porcelain, transfer printed rose and ribbon pattern, gold rimmed saucer base with matching cover, Dutch metal gold embellishment, possibly German, c. early twentieth century, $120.00 – 150.00. Smith collection.

Plate 114
French faience (pottery), hand-painted polychrome, octagonal body, four quill holes, loose pottery insert (possibly missing cover), seventeenth century style, c. 1900, $80.00 – 110.00. Smith collection.

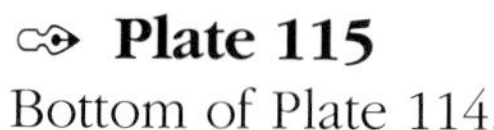

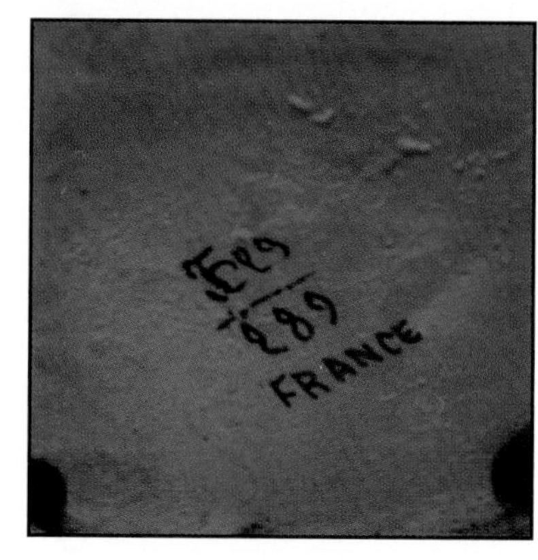

Plate 115
Bottom of Plate 114.

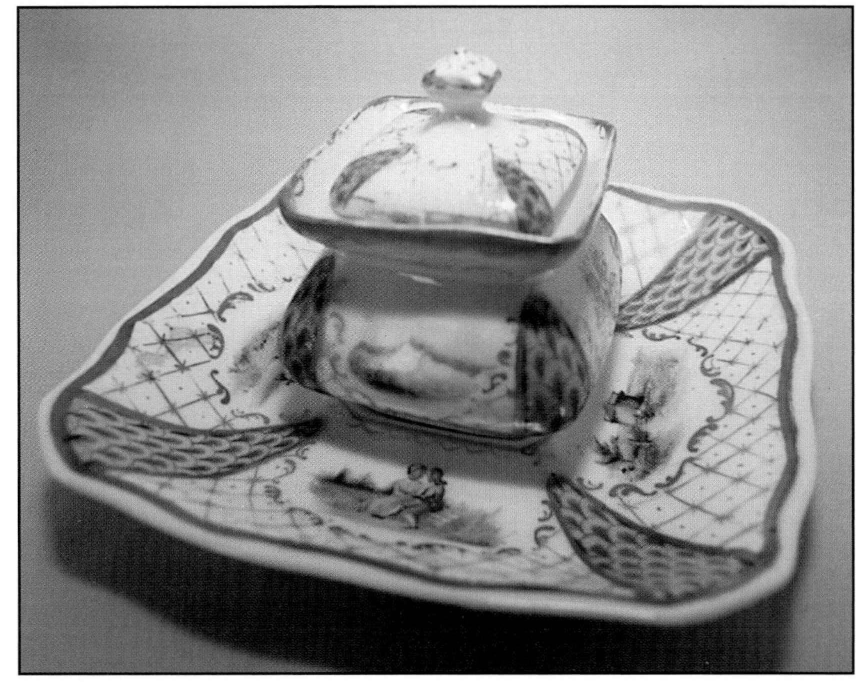

Plate 116
Porcelain, panels of French pastoral scenes of the eighteenth century, scale motif on corners in blue/gold, lattice between panels, Rococo revival, loose cover with finial, c. 1900, $200.00 – 225.00. Smith collection.

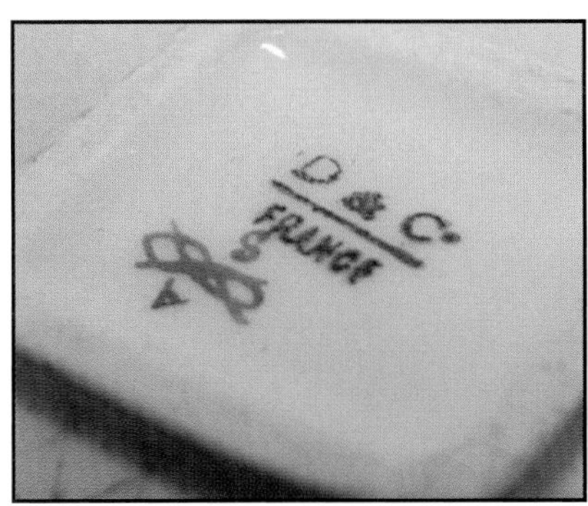

Plate 117
Bottom of Plate 116.

Plate 118
Porcelain, base with attached well, cobalt blue with applied decoration of cherubs, Rococo style, loose cover with finial, c. 1890 – 1900, $190.00 – 220.00. Smith collection.

Plate 119
Hard paste porcelain, transfer printed, neo-Oriental design, matching individual mushroom covers, pen rest, base oval in contour, German, 8" x 5½" x 2¾", c. 1900, $150.00 – 200.00.

Plate 120
Hard paste porcelain, Rococo style, hand-painted cobalt blue with gold leaf decoration, two quill holes, white pounce pot and one white well, loose cover with finial, French, 5½" x 3¼" x 3½" high, c. 1850, $200.00 – 250.00.

Plate 121
Ceramic "Snoopy" dog, novelty, 2½" x 3¾" x 4¼", c. 1958 – 1966, $40.00 – 45.00.

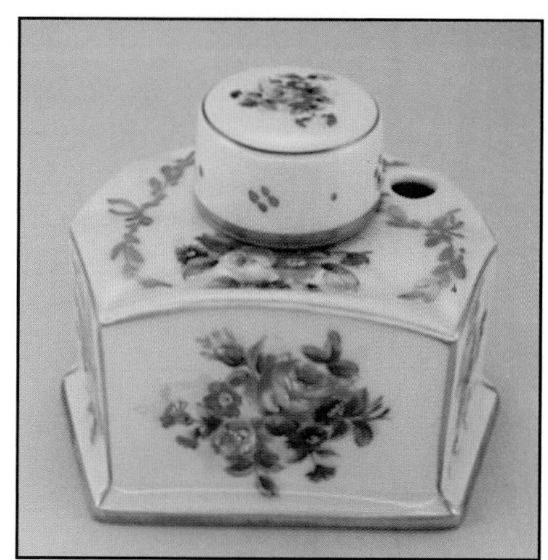

Plate 122
Porcelain, transfer printed with applied painting, naturalistic flowers, classical style, porcelain insert, French, 4" x 2¼", c. early twentieth century, $110.00 – 120.00.

Plate 123
Stoneware, cubed contour, brown and off - white, round glass individual insert, American, 2¾" high, c. 1900, $30.00 – 45.00.

Plate 124
Japanese export porcelain with reticulated lattice design on two sides, chrysanthemum and bird foliage on body, transfer printed, loose cover with finial, c. early twentieth century, $95.00 – 125.00. Smith collection.

Plate 125
Porcelain, applied transfer print, cobalt blue and Dutch metal gold floral design, double pen rest, picture of Meriden High School on front, stamped on base "GLOCK CO OF MERIDEN, CONN.," American, 2¼" square, $40.00 – 65.00.

Plate 126
Porcelain, transfer printed design, embellished with Dutch metal gold, six-sided, porcelain insert, loose matching cover, made in Limoges district of France, 2⅝" x 2", c. early twentieth century, $60.00 – 90.00.

Plate 127
Porcelain, transfer printed floral design, domed lid with finial, individual porcelain insert, 5¾" x 2½" high, c. 1930, $90.00 – 110.00.

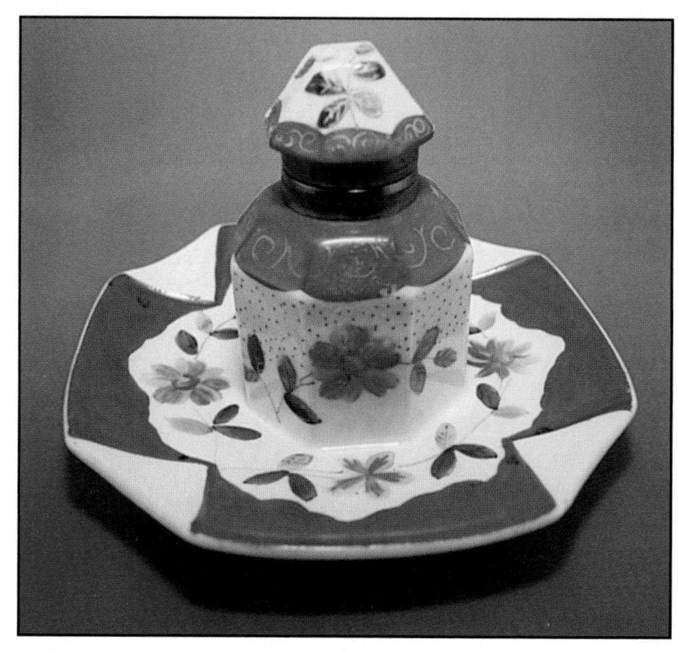

Plate 128
Porcelain, folded napkin design, saucer base with attached well, earth red and blue, silver colored metal hinged collar with eight-sided top, c. 1870 – 1880, $100.00 – 140.00.

Plate 129
Porcelain figural, polychrome, mother and female child, hand-painted, interior compartment holds porcelain sander and well, Germany, c. 1860, $500.00 – 600.00. Smith collection.

Plate 130
Porcelain figural, polychrome, base trimmed with relief fruit and leaves, relief flower motif on sander and well, German, c. 1860, \$450.00 – 550.00. Smith collection.

Plate 131
Porcelain figural, polychrome, three adults in mid-eighteenth century costume playing chess, marbleized base with sander and inkpot in interior, Germany, 10½" x 10" x 9", c. 1860, \$600.00 – 700.00. Smith collection.

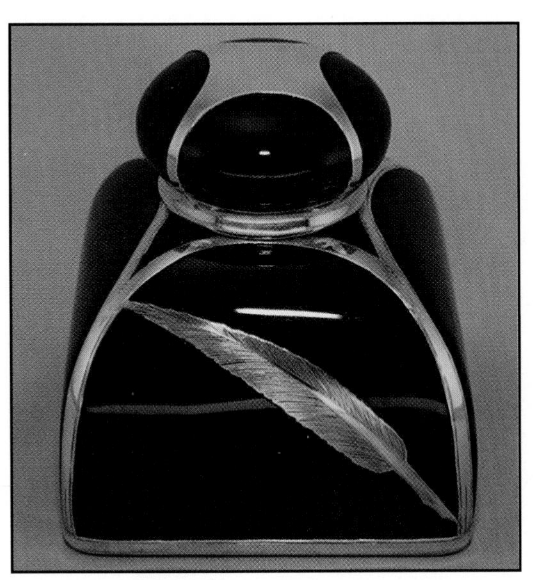

Plate 132
American Belleek, cobalt blue, Lennox with silver overlay, Art Noveau influence, quill pen decoration, mushroom-shaped cover, Gorham, 3¾" x 4", c. 1889, $700.00 – 800.00. Wherry collection.

Plate 133
Bottom of Plate 132.

Plate 134
Tin glazed pottery, polychrome, Gouda, Delft, six-sided design with raised panels, made in Holland, 3" x 3", c. 1910 – 1915, $185.00 – 195.00. Wherry collection.

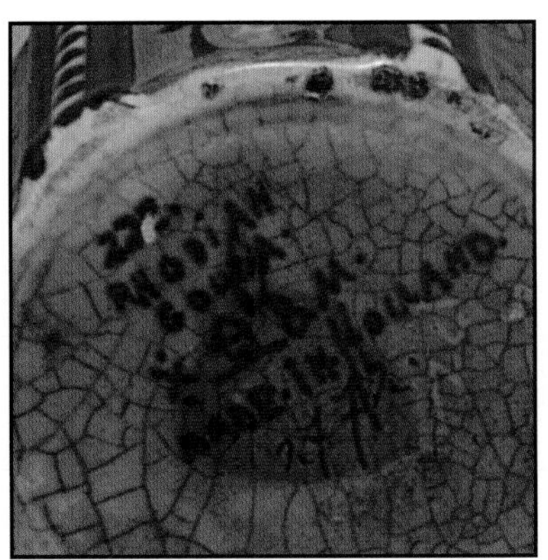

Plate 135
Bottom of Plate 134.

Crystal & Glass

Plate 136
Opaque glass with double rack and hand-painted forget-me-nots, rectangular form with cut corners, loose matching cover with blue trim, 4" x 3⅞" x 3⅝" high, c. 1880, $85.00 – 115.00. Hummer collection.

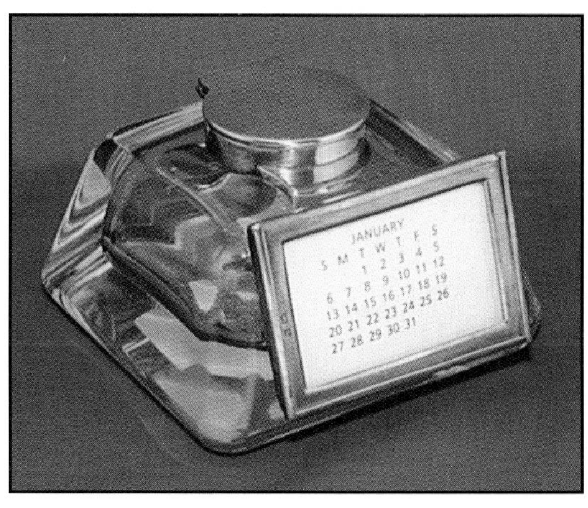

Plate 137
Pressed glass well, silver-plated, has frontal calendar with silver-plated frame, hinged top, early twentieth century, $90.00 – 100.00. Wherry collection.

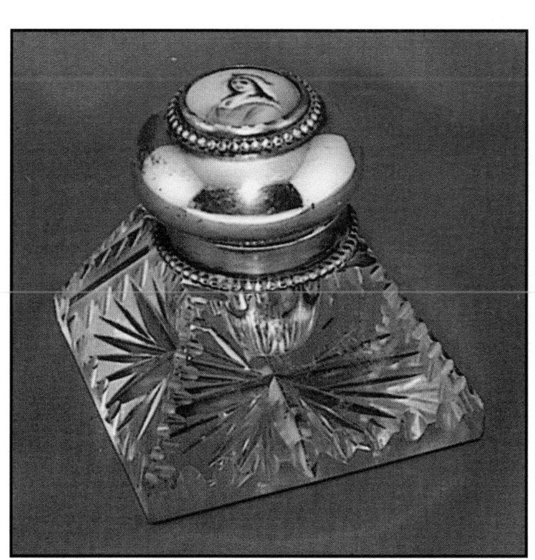

Plate 138
Cut glass pyramidal base, silver-plated cover with inset porcelain hand-painted Victorian lady, bead bezel, 3" x 3" square, c. 1880 – 1890, $185.00 – 200.00. Wherry collection.

Plate 139
Polished crystal, angled, fluted design, silver-plated hinged lid, lid has monogram, Lewis Comfort Tiffany, c. 1890 – 1910, $200.00. Wherry collection.

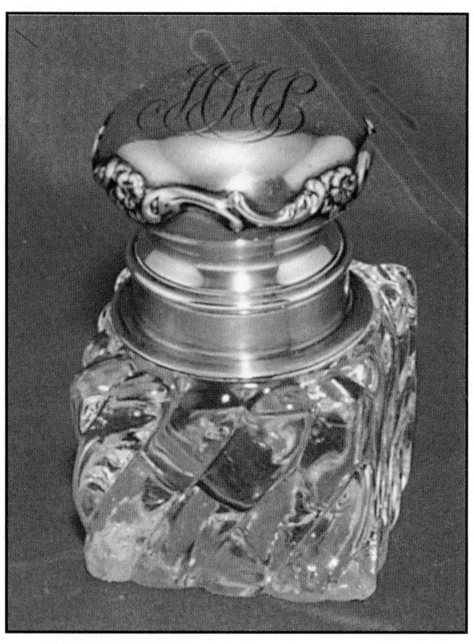

Plate 140
Pressed glass, Baccarat type swirl, Rococo embellishment on monogrammed sterling hinged lid, lid has floral motif, c. 1890 – 1900, $200.00 – 250.00. Wherry collection.

Plate 141
Pressed glass, scuttle shape, hinged cover with miniature print in color of gentleman on horseback outside of English inn, pen rest on back, 2" x 2¼", x 2¼", c. 1900 – 1910, $85.00 – 125.00. Wherry collection.

Plate 142
Pressed glass, bulbous, diamond point design, funnel opening, bracket feet, American, 2¾" diameter x 1¾" high, c. 1880, $80.00 – 90.00. Wherry collection.

Plate 143
Cobalt blue glass, molded, brass hinged lid, 3" square x 2¾" high, c. 1880 – 1890, $125.00 – 150.00. Wherry collection.

Plate 144
Clear cut glass, hand polished base, brass hinged collar, wood cover lid with lion design in relief, 2" square x 2½" high, c. 1900, $75.00 – 85.00. Hummer collection.

Plate 145
Crystal, intense cobalt blue and hand cut, brass hinged collar, hand cut domed top in honeycomb design, 1¾" diameter x 3½" high, c. 1890, $275.00 – 300.00.

Plate 146
Hand faceted pressed glass, hinged brass plated cover, 1½" square x 1¾" high, c. 1900 – 1910, $65.00 – 75.00. Hummer collection.

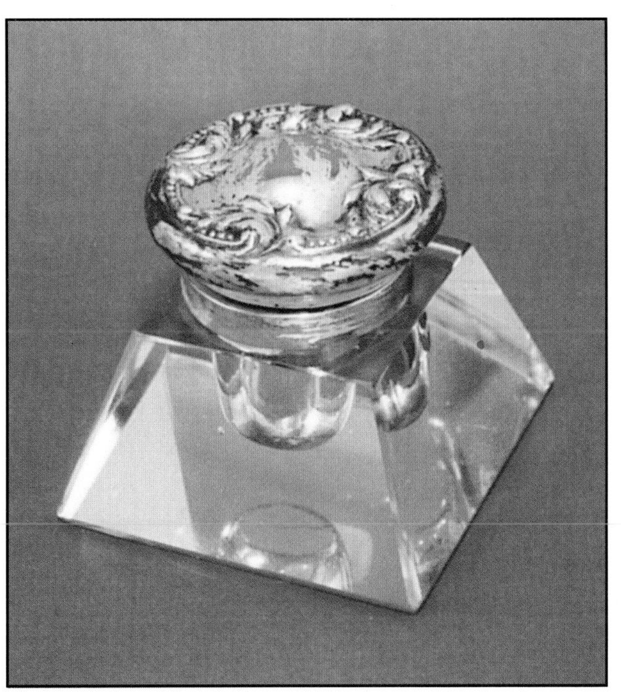

Plate 147
Clear cut glass, trapezoidal shape, hinged silver cover with scroll work in relief, marked "STERLING-7955" plus hallmarks, 2³⁄₁₆" square x 2⅛" high, c. 1890 – 1900, $150.00 – 200.00. Hummer collection.

Plate 148
Pressed glass, cane pattern, hinged brass mounts, blue glass cover with polychrome enamel floral design, 2⅝" square x 3⅛" high, c. 1890, $150.00 – 200.00. Hummer collection.

Plate 149
Clear cut glass, diamond shape, brass hinged collar, faceted octagonal cover, 2⅞" x 2" x 3" high, c. 1890 – 1900, $120.00. Hummer collection.

Plate 150
Crystal, cube-shaped with beveled edges, brass hinged lid, possibly French, 1⅝" x 2" high, c. late nineteenth century, $90.00 – 110.00. Rodkey collection.

Plate 151
Pressed glass cylindrical shape, swirl design, possibly European, 2" diameter x 1⅞" high, c. 1890 – 1900, $60.00 – 80.00.

Plate 152
Pressed glass, dome-shaped body with diamond pattern, polished brass screw-on cover, open type, stamped on cover "STERLING PAT'D DEC 8, 1891," 3½" diameter base x 2⅞" high, c. late nineteenth century, $80.00 – 100.00. Hummer collection.

Plate 153
Pressed glass, cane pattern, black Bakelite funnel insert assembly, 2¼" square, c. 1900 – 1910, $85.00 – 100.00. Hummer collection.

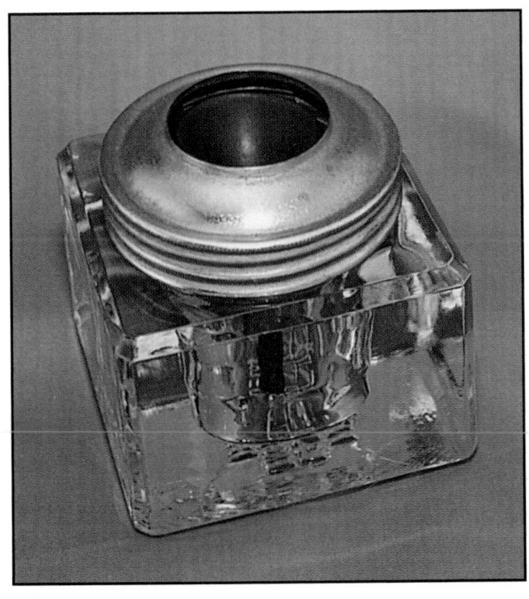

Plate 154
Pressed glass, beveled cube base, brass finish screw-on cover with Bakelite open type insert, marked on base of well "PAT'D U.S. JULY 17, ENG. APR. 14, 1894," 3" square x 2⅝" high, c. 1890 – 1900, $70.00 – 90.00. Hummer collection.

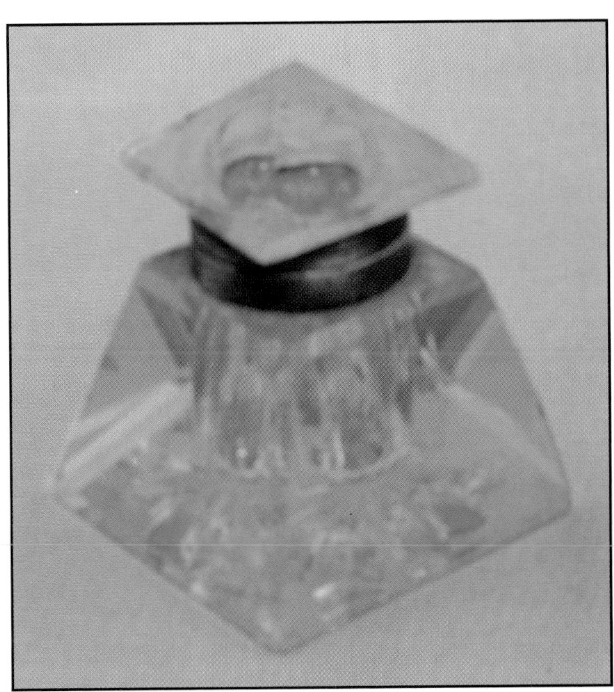

Plate 155
Cut, pyramidal, vaseline color crystal, star cut, pyramidal lid has hinged collar, French, 2" square x 2½" high, c. 1890, $350.00 – 400.00. Wherry collection.

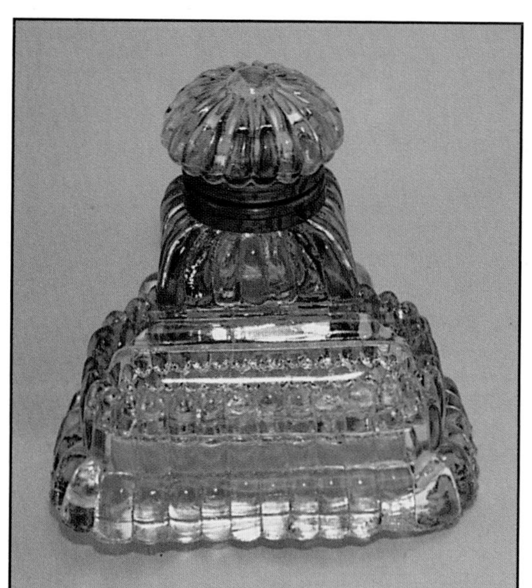

Plate 156

Clear pressed glass with quill channel, vertical lobed design, brass hinged matching cover, possibly French, 4⅜" square x 3½" high, c. 1890, $100.00 – 125.00. Hummer collection.

Plate 157

Pressed glass, silver finish hinged collar, matching cover, marked on base "DEPOSE PARIS" plus "CH" insignia (C is crossing the H), 6¼" square x 3½" high, c. late nineteenth century, $100.00 – 125.00. Hummer collection.

Plate 158

Cut glass with pen channel, cane and four-leaf pattern bottom with vertical ribbing around base, hinged silver-plated mushroom cover, 3¼" x 5¼" x 3⅛", c. 1900, $150.00 – 175.00. Hummer collection.

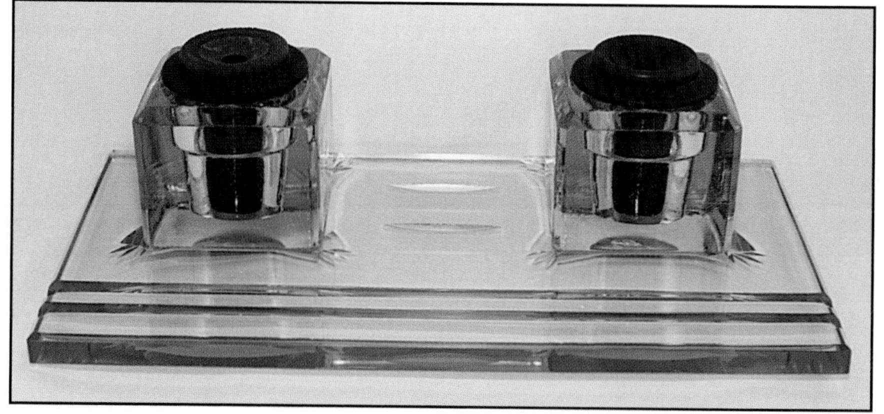

Plate 159

Cut glass light green base with two pen channels, recessed for wells, clear pressed glass wells with Bakelite cover and insert assemblies, crow's foot cutting at corners of wells in base, covers marked "Sengbusch Self Closing Inkstand Co, Milwaukee Wisc. Pat Apr 21, 03, Aug 23, 04; Jan 15, 07," 12⅞" x 6⅝" base, 3" square wells, $90.00 – 120.00. Hummer collection.

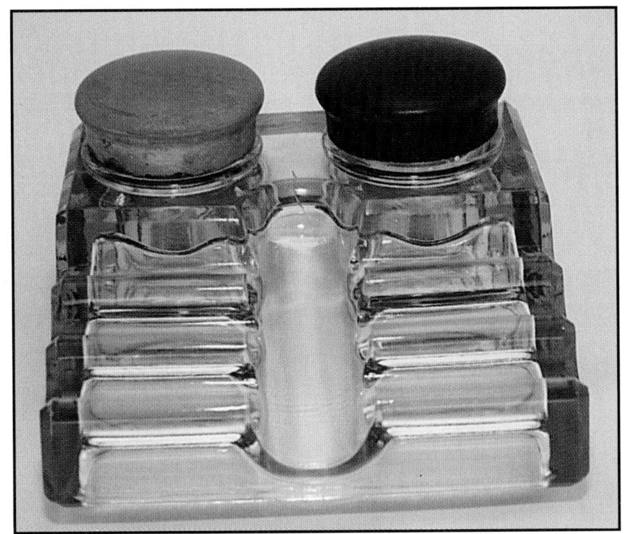

Plate 160
Pressed glass with three-tier pen ledge, brown and black loose covers, flanged glass inserts, base marked "FRANK A WEEKS MFG CO, 50 PARAGON PAT. PENDING," covers marked "PARAGON 1256," inserts marked "PARAGON," 5" x 4¾" x 3" high, c. 1915, $50.00 – 60.00. Hummer collection.

Plate 161
Pressed glass with vertical ribbing design and pen rack, silver finish metal cover assembly with glass automatic closure, marked on top of base "NOVELTY P.N. MFG CO PATENTED NOV. 11, 1884," 3¾" x 2¾" base, $65.00 – 90.00. Hummer collection.

Plate 162
Clear glass, 12-sided body, pewter cover holding a screw-in glass funnel insert, screws to an attached pewter collar, loose pewter cap with finial, marked on cover "DRAPER'S PATENT JAN.7.1851" plus "IMPROVED," 4" diameter x 3¼" high, $250.00 – 275.00, rare. Hummer collection.

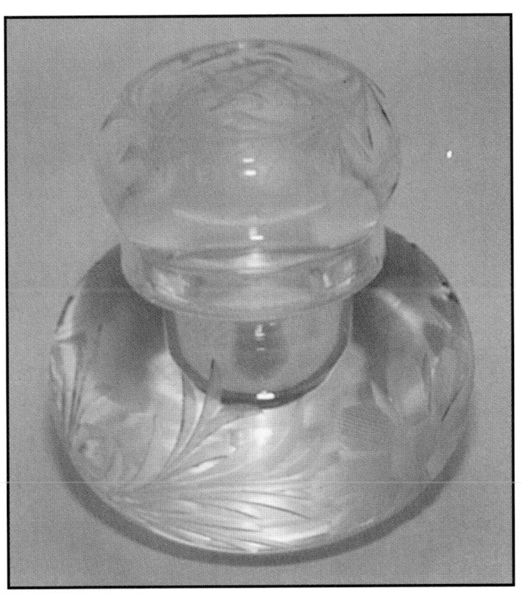

Plate 163
Cut glass paperweight type, bulbous with cut etched design, loose matching monogrammed cover, copper wheel engraved decoration, American, 3¼" diameter, c. 1910 – 1915, $85.00 – 95.00. Hummer collection.

Plate 164

Cut glass with pen channel and cut etched design, loose cut matching cover, matching cut etched rocker blotter with polished brass rocker, late Georgian style, copper wheel engraved, 5⅞" x 3½" x 2½" high well, c. 1910 – 1920, $150.00 – 175.00. Hummer collection.

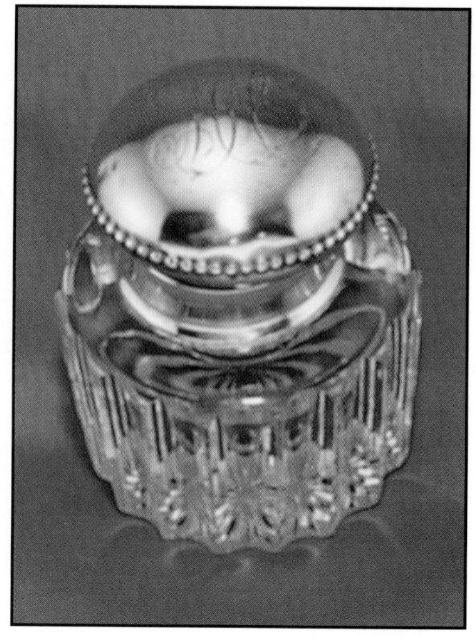

Plate 165

Clear cut glass with 24-point star pattern on base and vertical concave channel design, hinged silver monogrammed and beaded rim cover, Georgian style, marked "STERLING-S-1830" plus hallmarks, 2 9/16" diameter x 3½" high, c. 1890 – 1900, $150.00 – 200.00. Hummer collection.

Plate 166

Clear cut glass with 16-point star pattern on base and gold hand-painted decoration, convex shape front and back, hinged hammered brass mushroom cover, 3" square x 2½" high, c. 1900 – 1910, $75.00 – 90.00. Hummer collection.

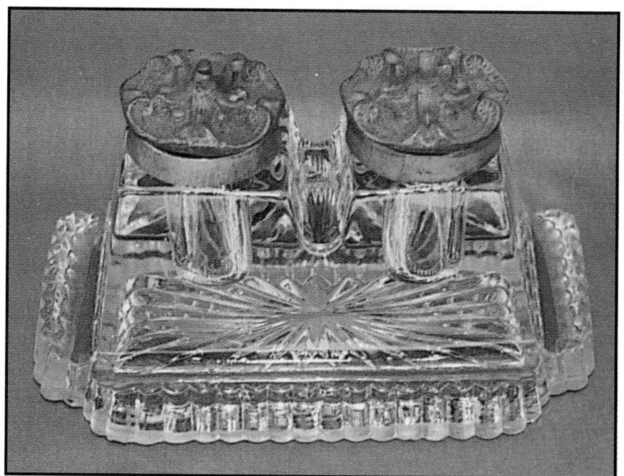

Plate 167

Pressed glass, one-piece with pen channel on all sides, vertical ribbing design around base and sunburst design on base, Rococo scrolls, hinged brass covers, with finials, marked inside back channel "R" within a diamond and crown-shaped insignia, 5" x 3¼" x 2⅞" high, c. 1900, $85.00 – 95.00. Hummer collection.

Plate 168
Pressed glass swirl well with brass hinged dome-shaped swirl cover, encased in lead filigree, 2¼" square x 3" high, c. 1900, $90.00 – 125.00. Hummer collection.

Plate 169
Pressed glass with loose round cover with boy and girl design in relief, beveled edges, American, 2⅜" square x 2" high, c. 1900 – 1915, $55.00 – 60.00. Hummer collection.

Plate 170
Clear cut glass with three-tier pen ledge, brass hinged collars, cut faceted covers, possibly French, 2⅝" x 2¾" x 2¼" high, c. 1900, $130.00. Hummer collection.

Plate 171
Crystal, square in contour, sterling mushroom-shaped hinged cover with Rococo scroll work, monogram in center, American, c. 1890 – 1900, $85.00 – 95.00. Hummer collection.

Plate 172
Clear cut glass, trapezoidal shape, hinged silver cover with floral design in relief, marked on top of cover "STERLING," American, 2" square x 2" high, c. 1910 – 1920, $150.00 – 180.00. Hummer collection.

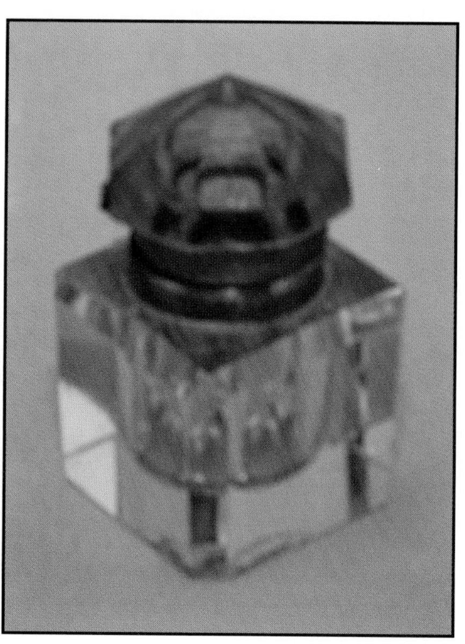

Plate 173
Clear cut glass with brass hinged mount, electric blue cut octagonal pyramidal cover, possibly French, 1¼" square x 2" high, c. 1890 – 1900, $145.00 – 160.00. Hummer collection.

Plate 174
Opaque glass, green enamel decoration on brass cover with finial, marked on base "ANCHOR S.P. CO.," American, 2" square x 2⅞" high, c. late nineteenth century, $85.00 – 95.00. Hummer collection.

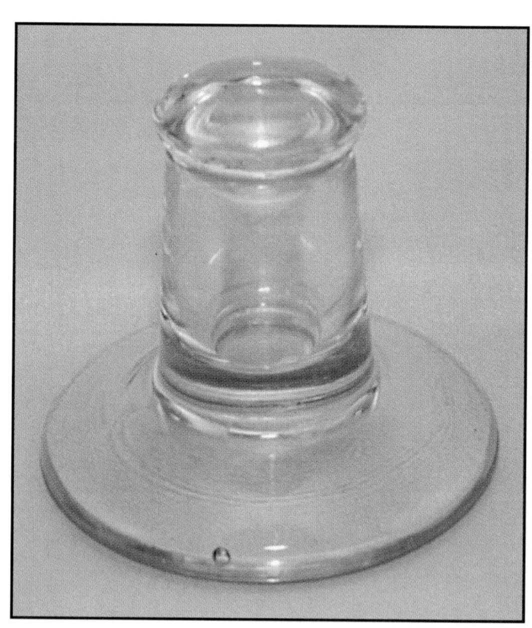

Plate 175
Pressed glass, one-piece with loose glass cover, mold blown, American, 3½" diameter x 3⅛" high, c. 1900 – 1910, $125.00 – 150.00. Hummer collection.

Plate 176
Cut glass, vaseline, hinged brass mount, matching pyramid cover, French, 2 7/16" x 3 1/8" high, c. 1890, $300.00 – 400.00. Hummer collection.

Plate 177
Clear cut glass, four-footed, brass hinged cut faceted cover with enameled floral motif, French, 1 1/2" square x 2 3/8" high, c. 1890s, $100.00 – 150.00. Hummer collection.

Plate 178
Clear cut glass with brass hinged faceted cover, elephant in relief on recess of body of well, French, 1 3/4" square x 2 1/2", c. 1890, $150.00 – 175.00. Hummer collection.

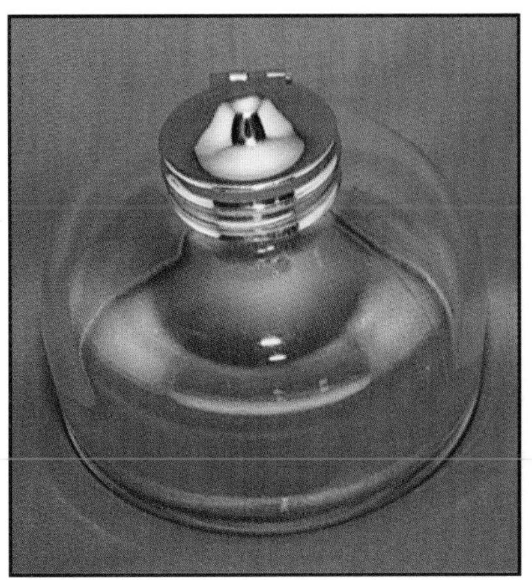

Plate 179
Clear glass, dome-shaped, hinged nickel-plated screw-on cover assembly, 3 1/2" diameter x 3" high, c. 1930, $75.00 – 85.00. Hummer collection.

Plate 180
Pressed glass, 10-panel sides, attached glass cover with a fill and dip hole, American, 2⅜" wide x 1 9/16" high, c. 1870 – 1880, $60.00 – 70.00. Hummer collection.

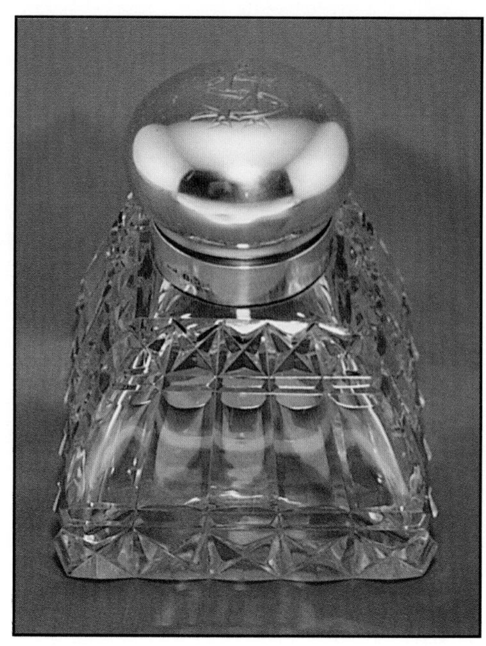

Plate 181
Cut glass with vertically cut sides and triangular design around base and top of well, hinged silver monogrammed mushroom cover, glass insert, Sterling-English Birmingham region, marked on collar "G & S" plus hallmarks, 4" square base x 4½" high, c. 1910 – 1920, $225.00 – 250.00. Hummer collection.

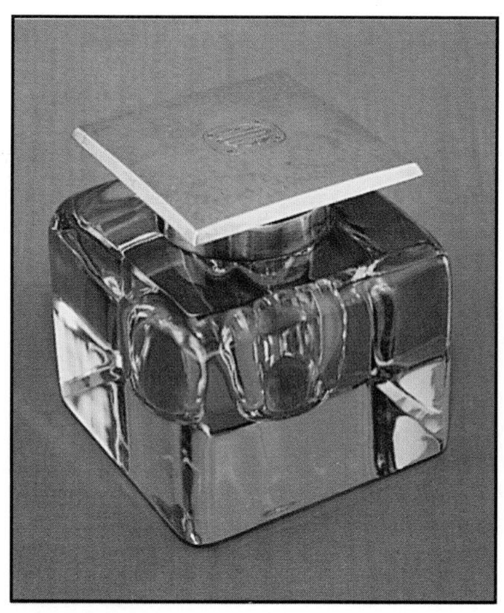

Plate 182
Hand polished cut glass, hinged silver flat cover with monogram in an insignia, Art Deco design, marked "STERLING-44291-1.H.M.D.," 3" square x 3 1/16" high, c. 1930, $225.00 – 250.00. Hummer collection.

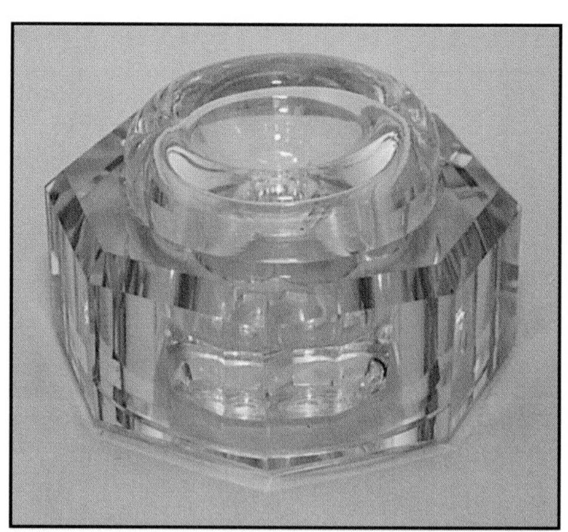

Plate 183
Clear glass funnel with paneled base, funnel well sets into clear cut base, 3¾" wide x 1⅝" high, c. 1880 – 1890, $90.00 – 120.00. Hummer collection.

Plate 184
Clear cut glass, swirl, bulbous with 24-point rayed base, Baroque style, hinged silver electroplated monogrammed cover, marked "TIFFANY & CO–E.P.," 5½" diameter x 3⅜" high, c. 1900, $300.00 – 400.00. Hummer collection.

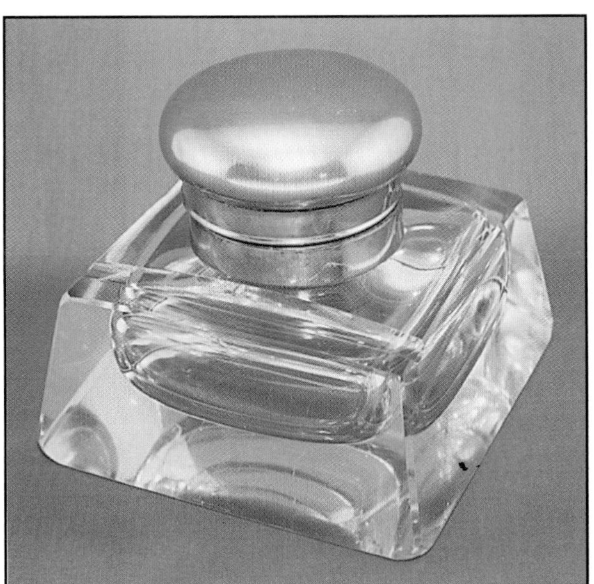

Plate 185
Clear cut glass with pen channel, hinged silver-plated mushroom cover, 4½" square x 3¾" high, c. 1900, $120.00 – 150.00. Hummer collection.

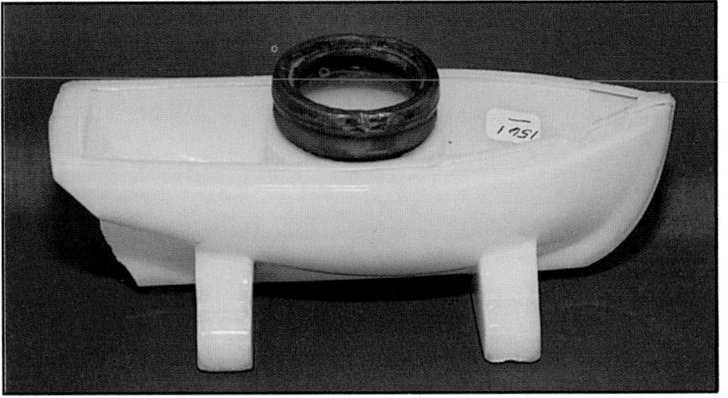

Plate 186
Opaque glass (opal or milk type) boat-shaped with pewter collar, marked inside rear of boat "PAT'D AUG. 9, 1870," cover missing, 5 7/16" wide, $85.00 – 95.00 as is. Hummer collection.

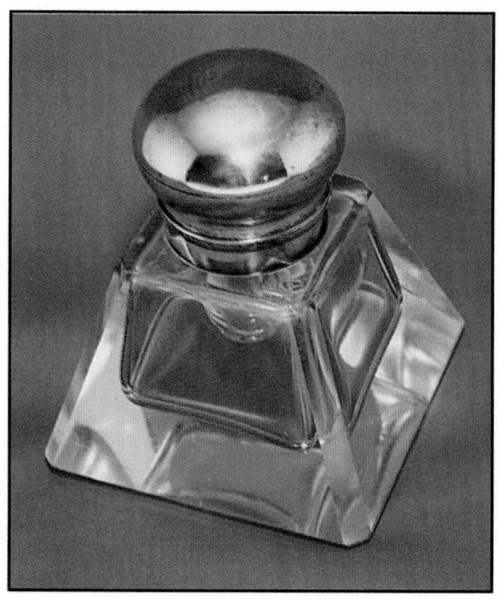

Plate 187
Clear cut glass, trapezoidal shape with beveled edges, hinged silver-plated cover, glass insert, 3⅝" x 4¼" high, c. 1900 – 1910, $90.00 – 120.00. Hummer collection.

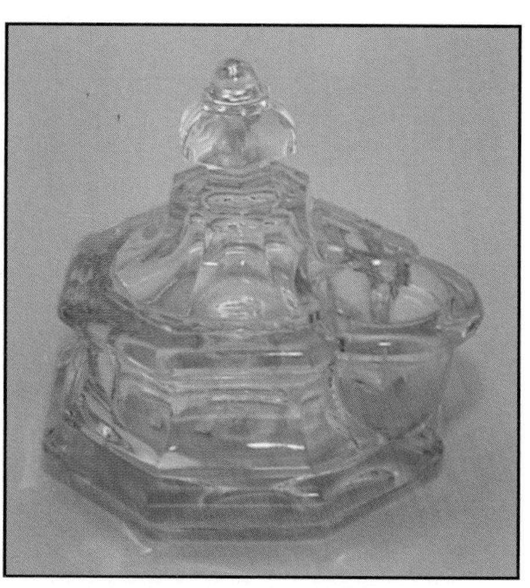

Plate 188
Clear glass fountain with eight-sided base and finial, mold blown, American, 3⅝" x 3¾" high, c. 1860 – 1870, $125.00. Hummer collection.

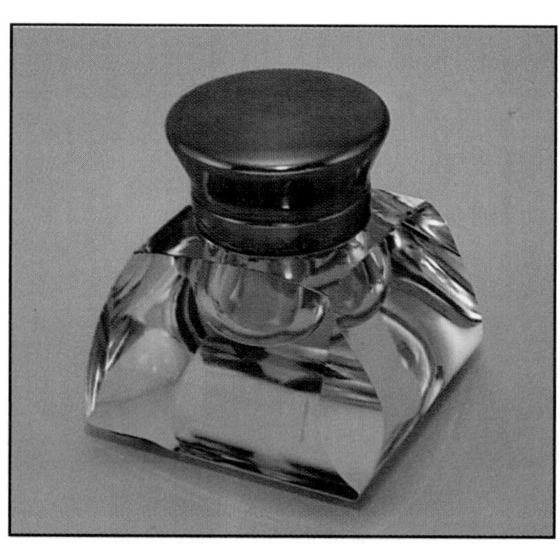

Plate 189
Clear cut crystal with rounded sides and cut corners, hinged brass cover, French, possibly Baccarat, 3" square x 3" high, c. 1900, $120.00 – 140.00. Hummer collection.

Plate 190
Clear cut glass, hexagon, tapered with hand-painted floral decoration, brass hinged cut matching cover, French, 2$\frac{1}{16}$" hexagon x 2⅛" high, c. 1890 – 1900, $140.00 – 190.00. Hummer collection.

Plate 191
Pressed glass, probably French, relief flowers and scrolls, Baccarat type swirl well with matching lid, 4⅞" diameter, c. 1880, $150.00 – 200.00. Hummer collection.

Plate 192
Vaseline crystal, trapedoizal, loose silver cover with design and monogram, possibly not original cover, 3¹⁄₁₆" square x 2¹⁄₁₆" high, c. 1890, $200.00 – 225.00. Hummer collection.

Plate 193
Emerald green hand cut crystal well, brass base with well holder and green enamel decoration, corners of base are crimped points, loose brass cover with finial, 4⅜" square, c. 1890 – 1900, $400.00 – 500.00. Hummer collection.

Plate 194
Clear cut glass with vertical and horizontal cut slots on each side, brass hinged mounts, dome-shaped cut cover, French, 2" square x 3⅛" high, c. 1890, $100.00 – 125.00. Hummer collection.

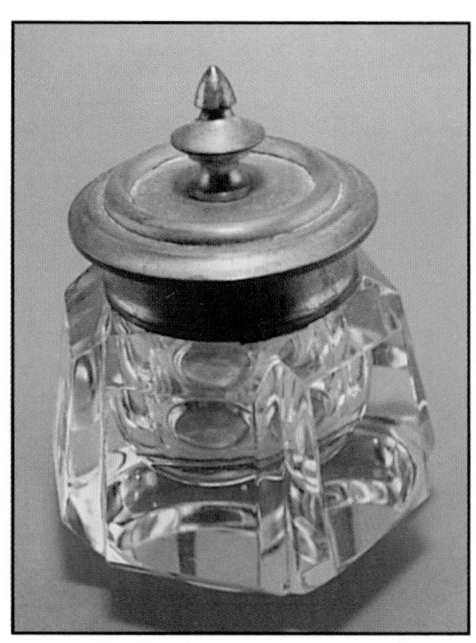

Plate 195
Pressed glass, cut and hand polished, six-sided, fluted corners, hinged plated brass cover with finial, American, c. 1900 – 1910, $80.00 – 100.00.

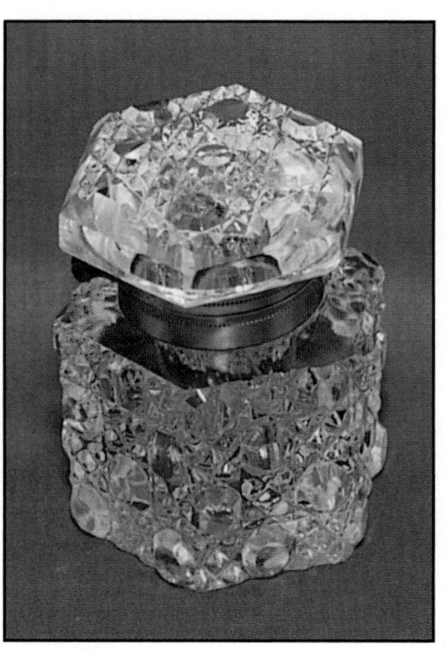

Plate 196
Pressed glass, cane pattern, six-sided, brass hinged matching cover, American, 1¹⁵⁄₁₆" wide x 2½" high, c. 1890 – 1900, $95.00 – 125.00. Hummer collection.

Plate 197
Clear cut cylindrical with diamond point pattern, brass hinged insert and collar assembly, matching cover with sunburst pattern top, possibly European, 2⅜" diameter x 3¾" high, c. early twentieth century, $90.00 – 110.00. Hummer collection.

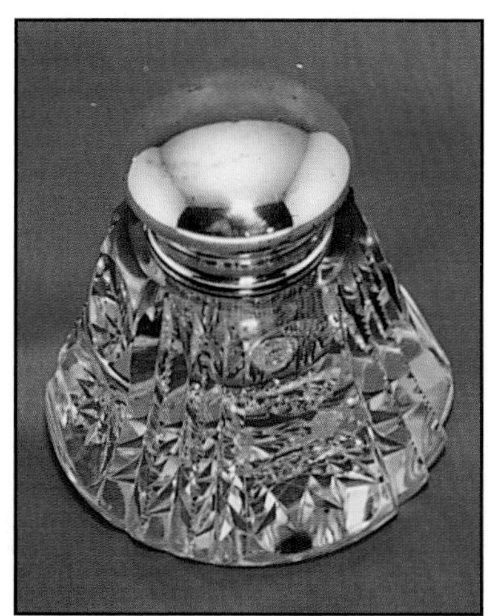

Plate 198
Clear cut glass, conical shape with alternating vertical rib sawtooth and thumbprint design, fancy star cut design base, hinged silver-plated dome-shaped cover, 3⅛" diameter x 3⅛" high, c. 1890 – 1900, $90.00 – 125.00. Hummer collection.

Plate 199
Pressed vaseline glass, daisy and button variation, American, possibly New England Glass Co., loose cover, c. 1880 – 1890, $150.00 – 200.00. Wherry collection.

Plate 200
Ruby cased glass with vertical ribbing, blown ground, hinged brass flat cover, 1¾" diameter x 2⅛" high, c. 1890 – 1900, $85.00 – 110.00. Hummer collection.

Plate 201
Clear cut glass with hinged silver mushroom-shaped cover, marked on cover "WOMAN'S TRAPSHOOTING LEAGUE SEASON 1931 – 1933" plus marked on collar "STERLING 2934," trophy well, 2⅛" square x 2½" high, $150.00 – 175.00. Hummer collection.

Plate 202
Clear cut glass with cane pattern base, hinged silver cover with Art Nouveau design, marked on collar "STERLING" plus "1670-1" plus a hallmark, $2\frac{5}{16}$" square x 3½" high, c. 1900, $175.00 – 200.00. Hummer collection.

Plate 203
Pressed glass, starburst on bottom, reeded decoration around base, lids are overturned sunflowers, hinged, Heisey, 5" x 3¼", c. 1910, $300.00 – 400.00. Wherry collection.

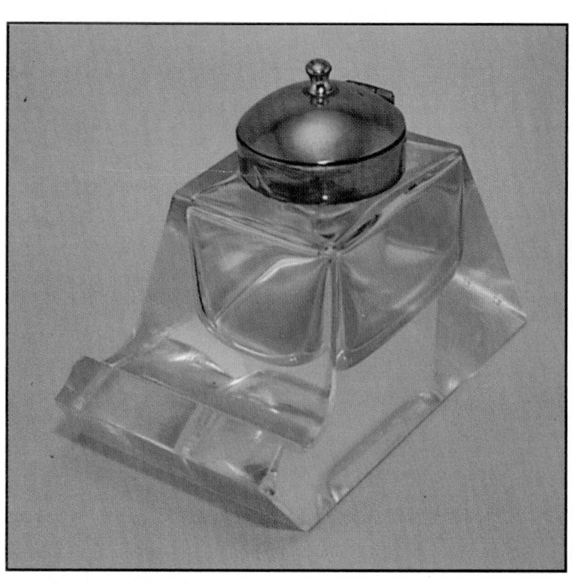

Plate 204
Cut glass with hand polished finish, Art Deco influence, hinged brass domed cover with finial, 2⅝" x 4⅛" x 3¼" high, c. early twentieth century, $85.00 – 95.00. Hummer collection.

Plate 205
Blown-in-mold crystal, hand polished, electroplated nickel silver mushroom-shaped hinged cover, frontal pen rest, 2½" x 4½" x 3⅝" high, c. 1900 – 1910, $85.00 – 125.00. Wherry collection.

Plate 206
Pressed glass arm chair, daisy and button design, cover and well missing, 2½" wide x 4½" high, c. 1890, $125.00 – 160.00. Hummer collection.

Plate 207
Art glass, dome-shaped with overlay, red and white ribbed body, hinged flat brass cover, American, 3$\frac{3}{8}$" diameter x 1$\frac{3}{4}$" high, c. 1890, $150.00 – 175.00. Hummer collection.

Plate 208
Glass, bun-shaped with hinged brass screw-on cover assembly with pen rack, green felt base with gold-filled impressed lettering, marked "CHARNOCK BROS. & CO — SCRABO ST BELFAST 01L DISTILLERS & GREASE MANUFACTURERS — EST'D OVER A CENTURY," 4" diameter base, c. 1895 – 1905, $125.00 – 135.00. Hummer collection.

Plate 209
Art glass, dome-shaped with overlay, blue and white ribbed body, brass collar and hinged lid, relief Deco on lid, c. 1890 – 1900, $150.00 – 175.00. Wherry collection.

Plate 210
Black glass well with black screw-type top with center opening for dip pen, stepped circular base, graduated cone shape, Art Deco influence, 3$\frac{15}{16}$" high x 3$\frac{3}{16}$" diameter, c. 1930, $80.00 – 90.00. Thorp collection.

Plate 211
Pressed glass, dome top reservoir with Bakelite pen receiver, original label on back (Sengbusch), c. 1920 – 1930, $85.00 – 95.00. Thorp collection.

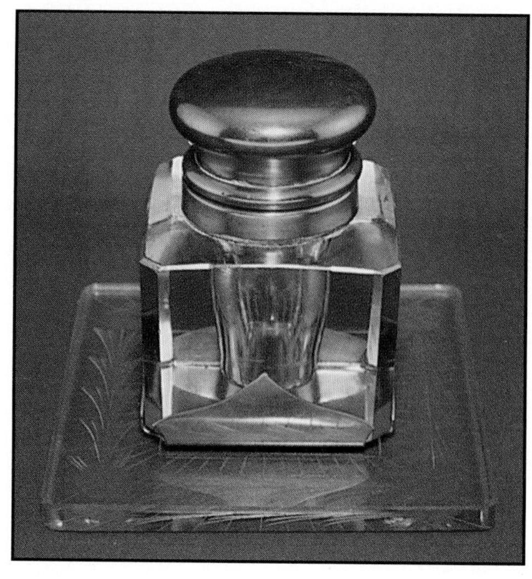

Plate 212
Crystal, green tablet base with copper wheel engraved foliage design, square crystal well has beveled edges, brass mounts and hinged brass lid, c. 1920, $150.00 – 160.00. Thorp collection.

Plate 213
Pressed glass, recessed columns and corners, fluted mushroom top, brass hinged collar, c. 1890 – 1900. $80.00 – 85.00. Thorp collection.

Plate 214
Blown and cut six-sided electric blue crystal, sterling hinged mounts and faceted domed top, French, c. 1890, $375.00 – 425.00. Thorp collection.

Plate 215
Crystal, blown, cut, and faceted, hinged brass fitting, dome-shaped lid, 2¼" square base x 3½" high, c. 1890 – 1900, $125.00 – 150.00. East Bloomfield collection.

Plate 216
Crystal, blown and polished, plinth-shaped, faceted domed lid with brass hinged collar, concave pen rests, possibly French, c. 1890 – 1900, $125.00 – 150.00. East Bloomfield collection.

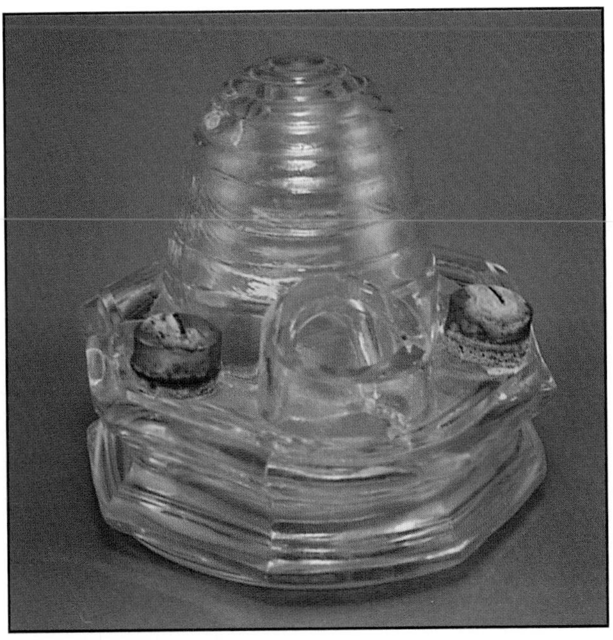

Plate 217
Pressed glass, eight-sided, beehive-shaped reservoir, gravity feed, brass fittings, American, "PAT'D AUG 9, 1870," $150.00 – 170.00. East Bloomfield collection.

Plate 218
Pressed glass, lobed body, enameled green cast iron swivel service lids, double pen rest and nib tray, American, 6" x 4¼" x 3" high, c. 1880 – 1890, $140.00 – 160.00. East Bloomfield collection.

Plate 219
Pressed acid etched glass, six-sided tapered shape, triple pen rest, dome cover, relief decoration on lid, 4½" x 4" x 2½", c. 1880, $150.00 – 180.00. East Bloomfield collection.

Plate 220
Deep amethyst cut glass, front to back taper, faceted lid, frontal pen rest, matching blotter, 4¼" x 3⅛" x 2½" base, 1¼" square cut glass well, c. 1900 – 1910, $150.00 – 190.00. Wherry collection.

Plate 221

Pressed glass, sandwich star pattern, hinged brass collar and matching cover, 3" x 3½, c. mid to late nineteenth century, $100.00 – 125.00. Wherry collection.

Plate 222

Polished cut glass, Gothic style, lancet-shaped motif on base, brass hinged collar and cut dome top, 3¾" x 5¼", c. 1880, $145.00 – 185.00. Wherry collection.

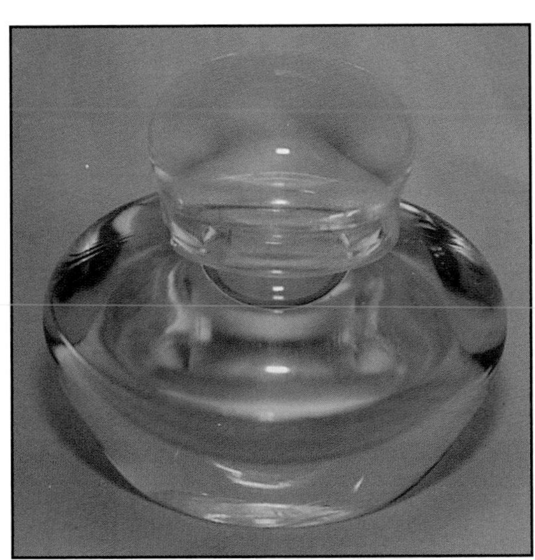

Plate 223

Crystal, bulbous shape, blown in mold, Art Deco influence, loose mushroom-shaped cover, 3" x 3¾", c. 1910, $150.00 – 175.00. Wherry collection.

Plate 224

Crystal, hand polished, octagonal, loose bronze cover with crown finial, Renaissance style, c. 1890, $85.00 – 100.00. East Bloomfield collection.

Plate 225
Flint glass, documented Sandwich pattern from factory of Sandwich, Mass., loose cast iron cover with finial, American, 3" diameter x 3⅛" high, c. 1850 – 1860, $200.00 – 250.00. Hummer collection.

Plate 226
Clear cut glass with triangular faceted corners, cut eight-sided cover with brass hinged mounts, French, 1 7/16" square x 2⅛" high, c. 1890 – 1900, $120.00 – 150.00. Hummer collection.

Plate 227
Pressed glass, bulbous, with heavy vertical ribbing, crown-like top, silver finish hinged matching glass cover, 3½" diameter x 4¼" high, c. 1910 – 1920, $75.00 – 85.00. Hummer collection.

Plate 228
Pressed clear glass, Baccarat type swirl, loose umbrella style cover with finial, possibly French, 2" square x 3⅜" high, c. 1890, $95.00 – 110.00. Hummer collection.

Plate 229
Amber cut glass, eight-sided with matching pyramidal cover, missing brass hinged collar, French, 2½" x 3⅛" high, c. 1890, $200.00 – 350.00, scarce. Hummer collection.

Plate 230
Hand cut and polished crystal, electric blue, brass hinged collar and faceted cover, French, 2⅜" x 3⅛" high, c. 1890, $400.00 – 450.00. Wherry collection.

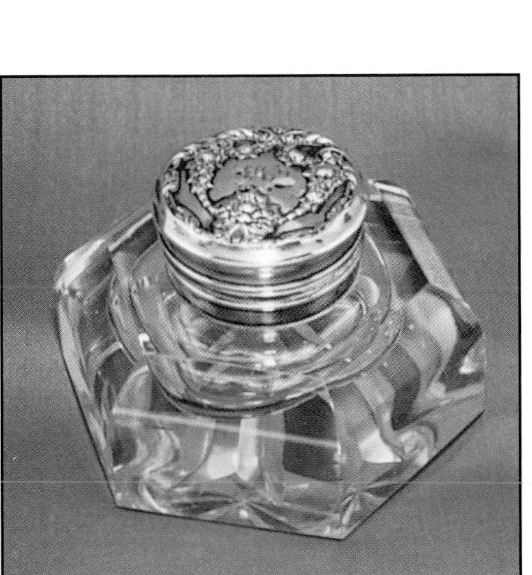

Plate 231
Clear cut glass, six-sided with rounded shoulders and eight-point star pattern on base, hinged silver cover, monogrammed design in relief with Repousse floral work in Georgian manner, marked on collar "STERLING PAT'D 1377" plus "F & B" within an insignia, 3⅜" hexagon x 2¼" high, c. 1890 – 1900, $175.00 – 225.00. Hummer collection.

Plate 232
Electric blue cut glass, two-tier pen ledge, brass hinged cut clear glass faceted cover, 1½" x 3" x 3" high, c. 1890 – 1900, $350.00 – 400.00. Hummer collection.

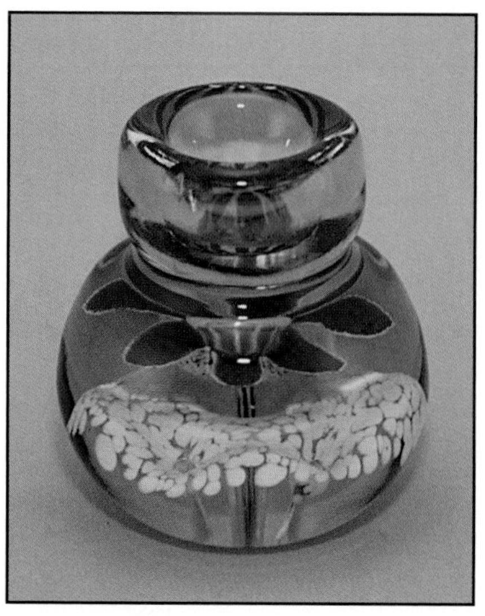

Plate 233
Blown, ground, and hand polished paperweight type glass, clematis flower design, white spangled cushion, American, 3" diameter x 3¼" high, $250.00. Hummer collection.

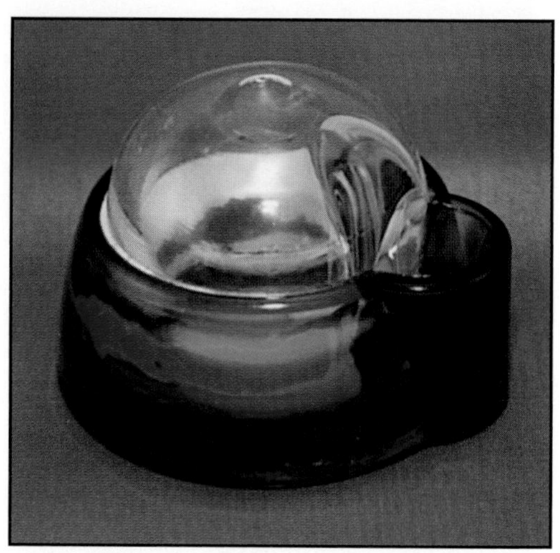

Plate 234
Pressed glass, emerald green base with clear glass dome-shaped cover, marked "GENERAL SUPPLY CO. DANIELSON, CT — JACOBUS PAT. NO. 879470" plus "ECLIPSE" in an insignia, 2⅞" diameter x 2¼" high, c. 1910 – 1920, $80.00 – 90.00. Hummer collection.

Plate 235
Cut glass inset type with block and triangle faceted panels, set in fruitwood base, hinged brass mounts, hinged matching cut glass pyramidal cover, 1½" diameter base x 3⅛" high, c. 1900, $90.00 – 100.00. Hummer collection.

Plate 236
Clear cut glass with faceted waffle body and waffle bottom, hinged silver cover with low relief floral design, marked "STERLING — S2586" plus hallmarks, 2½" square x 2½" high, c. 1900 – 1910, $125.00 – 150.00. Hummer collection.

Plate 237
Left: Pressed glass comic cat, had enameled decoration, nickel-plated brass collar, Czechoslovakian, "Ooloo," 3½" high. Right: Pressed glass terrier dog, nickel-plated brass collar, Czechoslovakian, 3¾" high, c. 1920, $185.00 – 200.00 each. Rodkey collection.

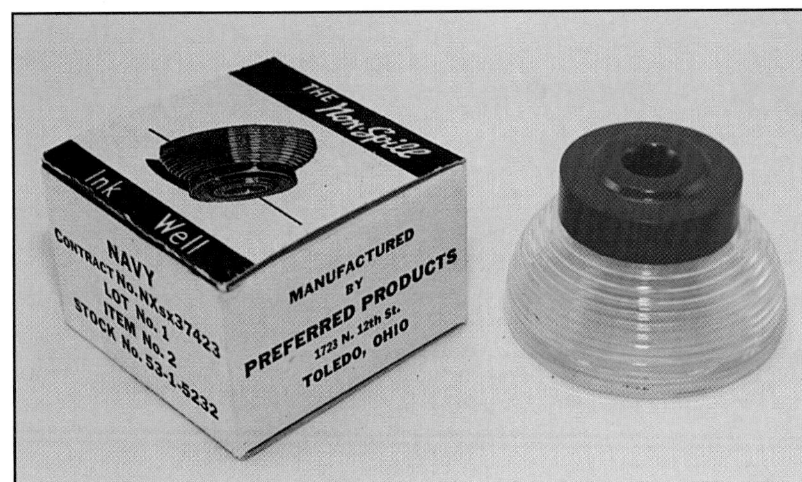

Plate 238
Pressed glass, red plastic top, horizontal ribs, Art Deco influence, made for Navy by Preferred Products, original box, c. 1930, $40.00 – 50.00. Rodkey collection.

Plate 239
Pressed glass base, stepped, triple frontal pen rest with central recessed receptacle, stamp receptacle in center between wells, Bakelite well, left black, right red, Art Deco, "Frank A. Weeks Mfg Co, Pat'd Dec 23, 1919, #549," 8½" x 5½" x 1½" high, $85.00 – 125.00. Rodkey collection.

Plate 240
Black glass base with cut edges, pen holder and wells are brown grained plastic, frontal receptacle, swivel pen holder, Art Deco influence, American, Sengbusch, 7" x 4$\frac{1}{2}$" x 2$\frac{5}{8}$" high, c. 1910, \$80.00 – 90.00. Rodkey collection.

Plate 241
Pressed glass rectangular base, frontal pen rest, central sponge holder has cast iron open-work, domed top with silvered finial, goats in relief on pot metal lids, 7$\frac{5}{8}$" x 4$\frac{5}{8}$" x 4$\frac{1}{8}$" high, c. 1890 – 1900, \$150.00 – 175.00. Rodkey collection.

Plate 242
Pressed glass stepped rectangular base, dome lid, pen insert, and original pen, Art Deco influence, American, Sengbusch, 3$\frac{1}{4}$" x 4$\frac{3}{4}$" x 3$\frac{1}{2}$" high, c. 1920 – 1930, \$85.00 – 95.00 each. Rodkey collection.

Plate 243
Polished crystal well, cube-shaped, concave pen receiver, marked "The Davis Automatic Inkwell, Pat'd 188901993," 3" square x 2⅝" high, $60.00 – 70.00 each. Rodkey collection.

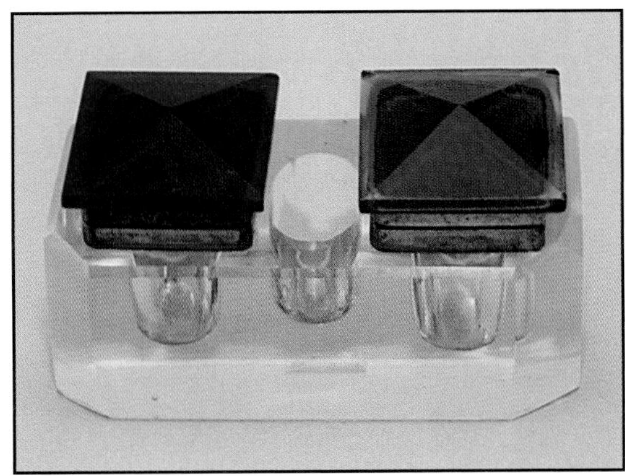

Plate 244
Double crystal wells on sled-shaped rectangular base, hinged stamped collars, cut crystal covers, one amber and one cobalt blue, 3¾" x 1⅝" x 2⅛" high, c. 1900 – 1910, $200.00 – 250.00. Rodkey collection.

Plate 245
Frosted pressed glass (acid etched), Art Nouveau influence, gilt brass lids are flower forms, possibly French, right: 5⅛" x 2¾" high; left: 5" x 2½" high, c. late nineteenth century, $200.00 each. Rodkey collection.

Plate 246
Crystal with brass trim on base and brass hinged collar, relief grape cluster on closure, 2⅜" x 3½" high, c. 1890 – 1900, $85.00 – 125.00. Rodkey collection.

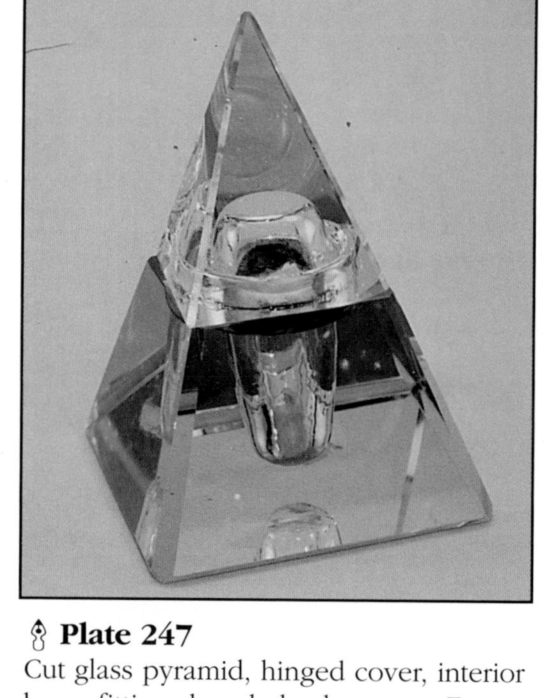

Plate 247
Cut glass pyramid, hinged cover, interior brass fitting, beveled edges, neo-Egyptian, possibly American, 3" square x 4½" high, c. 1825, $200.00 – 225.00. Rodkey collection.

Plate 248
Pressed glass, hobnail (dewdrop) pattern, American, 2½" square x 2¼" high, c. 1890, $80.00 – 90.00. Rodkey collection.

Plate 249
Pressed glass, circular, rayed bottom, hinged roll top brass cover, lid stamped "PROV. PAT," c. 1900, $85.00 – 95.00. Rodkey collection.

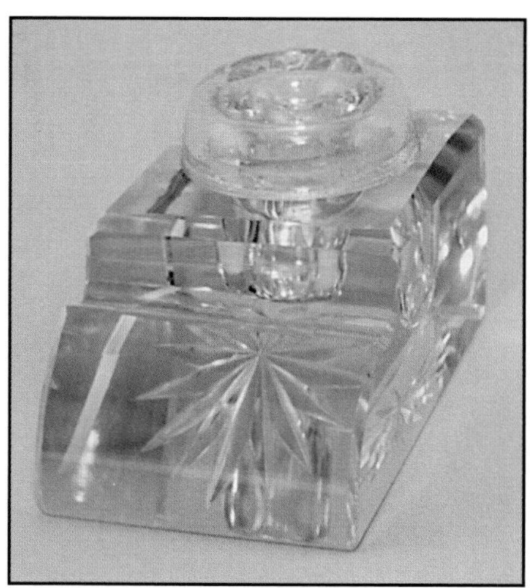

Plate 250
Cut crystal with star on base, pressed glass funnel top, frontal pen rest, 2¼" x 3½" x 2¼", c. 1900 – 1910, $85.00 – 95.00. Rodkey collection.

Plate 251
Opaque opalescent blown glass (art glass), soft jade green, hinged brass mushroom cover, 3½" diameter x 3¾" high, c. 1900 – 1910, $500.00 – 600.00. Rodkey collection.

Plate 252
Crystal, hand faceted, ten-sided rose, tapered body with paneled sides, cylindrical thimble-shaped crystal top with hinged brass collar, possibly Czechoslovakian, 1⅛" base x 3¼" high, c. 1900 – 1910, $400.00 – 500.00, rare. Rodkey collection.

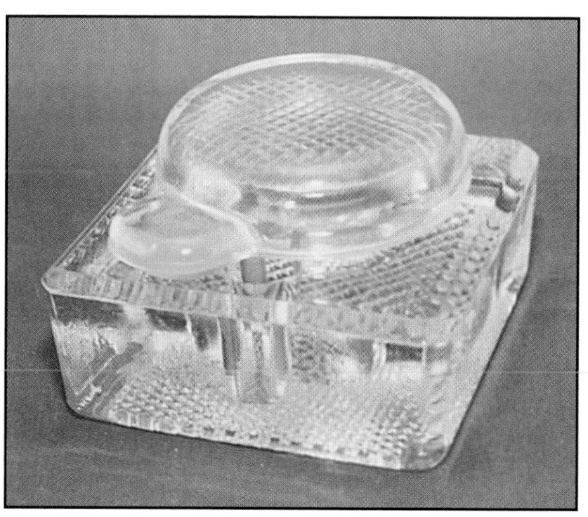

Plate 253
Pressed glass crystal with diamond point design on base and on loose swivel lid, 2⅞" square x 2" high, c. early twentieth century, $45.00 – 60.00. Rodkey collection.

Plate 254
Pressed glass, daisy and button variation, amber tone, loose domed foliage metal cover, American, 2" square x 2¼" high, c. 1880 – 1890, $200.00 – 250.00. Rodkey collection.

Plate 255
Amber crystal, hand polished and cut, hexagonal, hinged brass lid with faceted gemstone top, possibly French, 1⅞" diameter x 2⅜" high, c. 1890 – 1900, $200.00 – 250.00. Rodkey collection.

Plate 256
Glass Army hat, World War I, relief tassels, crown of hat is lid, American, 4" x 2¼", c. 1915 – 1920, $95.00 – 110.00. Rodkey collection.

Plate 257
Polished crystal, electric blue, pyramidal with faceted domed lid, hinged brass collar, four pen rests on base, French, 3" x 3" high, c. 1890, $475.00 – 500.00. Rodkey collection.

Plate 258
Glass, intense blue, lighthouse shape, brass collar, ball finial, concave circular base, possibly American, 2¾" x 4" high, c. 1890 – 1900, $350.00 – 450.00. Rodkey collection.

Plate 259
Polished crystal well with red enamelled base and matching cover, Art Deco, American, 1¾" square well, 4" square base, c. 1910 – 1915, $150.00 – 170.00. Rodkey collection.

Plate 260
Pressed glass crystal with brown Bakelite swivel lid, stamped "MADE IN ENGLAND" on bottom, 2½" x 1¾" high, c. early twentieth century, $45.00 – 60.00. Rodkey collection.

Plate 261
Pressed glass, square with beveled edges, relief decorated hard rubber insert (one chipped corner), printed on cover "THE GARDNER INKSTAND, C.H. NUMAN CO, NY SEPT 8, 1896," 2½" square x 2½" high, $65.00 as is. Rodkey collection.

Plate 262
Pressed glass, ribbed body, eight-sided funnel screw top, American, 3" x 2½" high, c. early twentieth century, $45.00 – 50.00. Rodkey collection.

Plate 263
Pressed glass, square with beveled corners, Art Deco influence, hard rubber lid with retracting closure, printed "PRESTO INKWELL NO. 1, PATENTED JAN. 1922," 3¼" x 3½" x 1¾" high, $110.00 – 140.00. Rodkey collection.

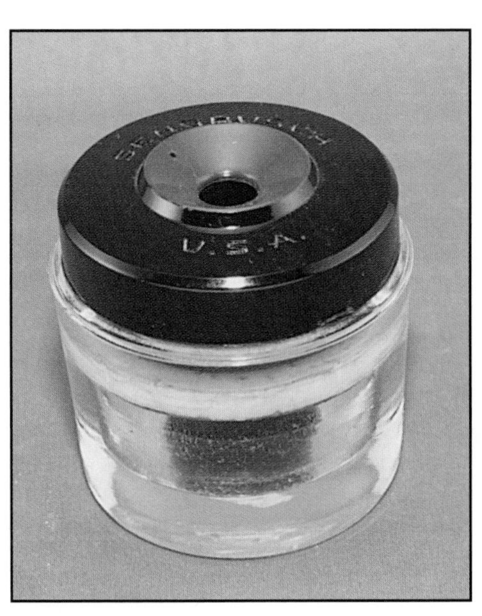

Plate 264
Pressed glass, cylindrical well, Bakelite top, printed "SENGBUSCH #62, SELF-CLOSING," c. early twentieth century, $35.00 – 45.00. Rodkey collection.

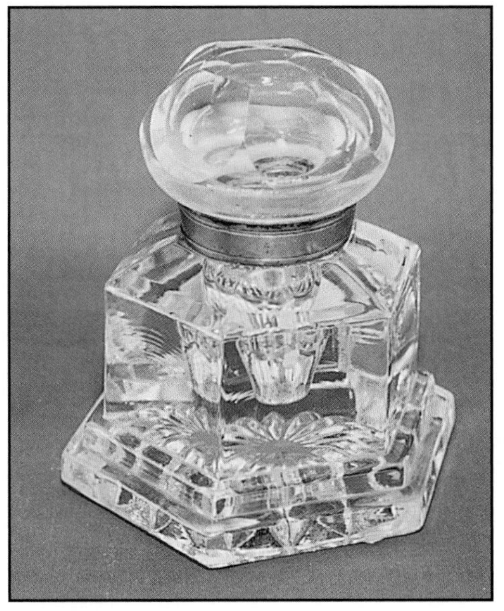

Plate 265
Pressed glass hexagonal with stepped base, domed lid with hinged brass collar, 3⅝" diameter x 4½" high, c. 1900, $125.00. Rodkey collection.

Plate 266
Pressed glass, lobed body, ball trimmed recessed tray, hinged brass collars, center nib container, 6⅛" x 5" x 3¼" high, c. 1900 – 1910, $110.00 – 125.00. Rodkey collection.

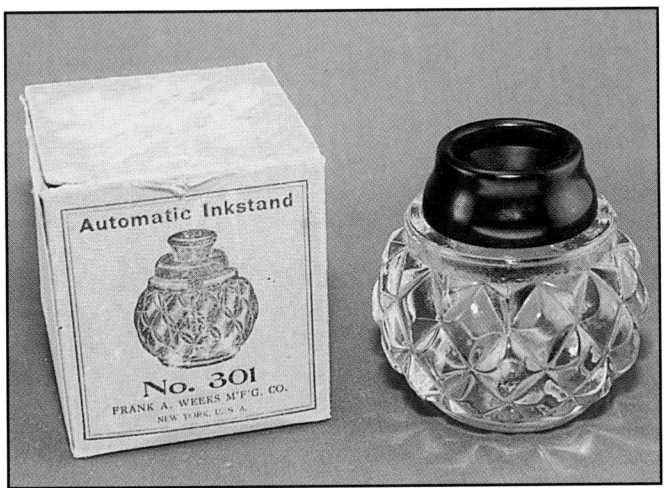

Plate 267
Pressed glass with diamond point design, floating hard rubber receiver top, American, original box, c. early twentieth century, $60.00 – 90.00. Rodkey collection.

Plate 268
Pressed glass, reeded body, saucer base with scalloped rim, pen receiver on base, gutta-percha regulator top, 4¾" diameter x 3⅞" high, c. early twentieth century, $110.00 – 150.00, Rodkey collection.

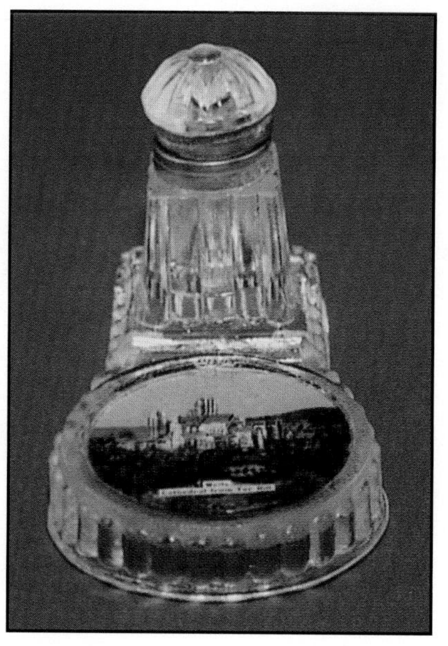

Plate 269
Pressed glass, circular base with square well, hinged collar, domed lid, souvenir, "WELLS CATHEDRAL FROM TOT HILL," 2" x 3⅜" x 2¼", c. late nineteenth century, $130.00 – 140.00. Rodkey collection.

Plate 270
Pressed glass base, clover-shaped, lobed wells with domed lids, picture of Crystal Palace, souvenir, 4" x 3¾" x 2¼", c. late nineteenth century, $150.00 – 190.00. Rodkey collection.

Plate 271
Pressed glass, lobed base, pressed glass well, well has hinged collar with bead trim, souvenir, "WREXHAM CHURCH, ENGLAND," floral motif, 3⅞" x 2¾" x 2¼", c. late nineteenth century, $130.00 – 140.00. Rodkey collection.

Plate 272
Pressed glass, rectangular base with sepia tone picture of cathedral, square well with hinged collar and domed lid, souvenir, English, 1¼" x 2¾" x 2⅜", c. late nineteenth century, $100.00 – 125.00. Rodkey collection.

Plate 273
Pressed glass, dome-shaped gravity fed reservoir with Greek key motif, body of well is fluted, bronze finish pot metal hinged lid, 2⅜" x 3¾" x 2½" high, c. 1890 – 1900, $150.00 – 175.00. Rodkey collection.

Plate 274
Pressed glass, Baccarat type swirl, emerald green, black glazed conical pen receiver, 2⅜" sq x 2¾" high, c. 1890, $250.00 – 275.00. Rodkey collection.

Plate 275
Pressed glass, cube-shaped, daisy and button pattern, vaseline color, silver colored metal top with Rococo influence, 2" square x 2¼" high, c. 1890 – 1900, $200.00 – 225.00. Rodkey collection.

Plate 276
Pressed glass, beaded quilt design, ruby red, hard rubber funnel top, 2¼" x 2⅛", c. 1890 – 1900, $300.00 – 400.00. Rodkey collection.

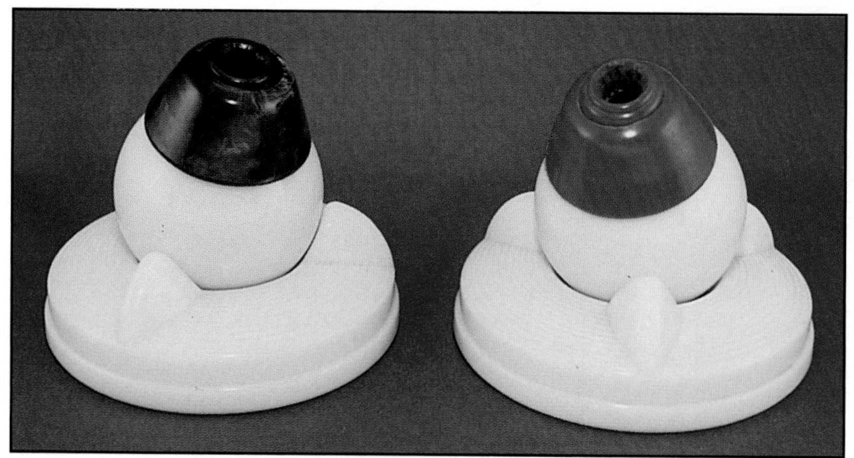

Plate 277
Opaque glass (milk) circular bases, left has a black pen receiver and right has a red pen receiver, Art Deco, American, "Swiv-o-dex," 3⅜" x 3¼", c. 1930, $85.00 each. Rodkey collection.

Plate 278
Pressed glass, light amber, lobed contour.
Right: Has Rococo mushroom-shaped brass top, 1¾" x 2⅜", c. 1900 – 1910, $300.00, scarce. Rodkey collection.
Left: Has black glazed porcelain funnel top receiver, 1⅞" x 1⅜", c. 1900 – 1910, $275.00, scarce. Rodkey collection.

Plate 279
Left: Purple glass, controlled air bubbles, hinged brass cover, Art Deco influence, c. 1920 – 1930, $300.00.
Right: Crystal, controlled air bubbles, nickel-plated hinged cover with spring loaded closure, c. 1920 – 1930, $150.00. Rodkey collection.

Plate 280
Pressed vaseline glass, two-tiered design (waisted), nickel-plated cover, 3" x 2¾", c. 1890, $300.00 – 350.00. Rodkey collection.

Plate 281
Pressed vaseline glass, cube form, daisy and button variation, sterling silver cover, floral design, American, 2" square, c. 1890 – 1900, $250.00 – 300.00. Rodkey collection.

Plate 282
Pressed glass, domed lid, flower-shaped finial, side reservoir, hexagon base, c. mid-nineteenth century, $100.00 – 140.00. Smith collection.

Plate 283
Molded European art glass, shaped for pen rest, hinged brass collar with dome top, confetti design, Loetz type, c. late nineteenth century, $375.00 – 385.00. Smith collection.

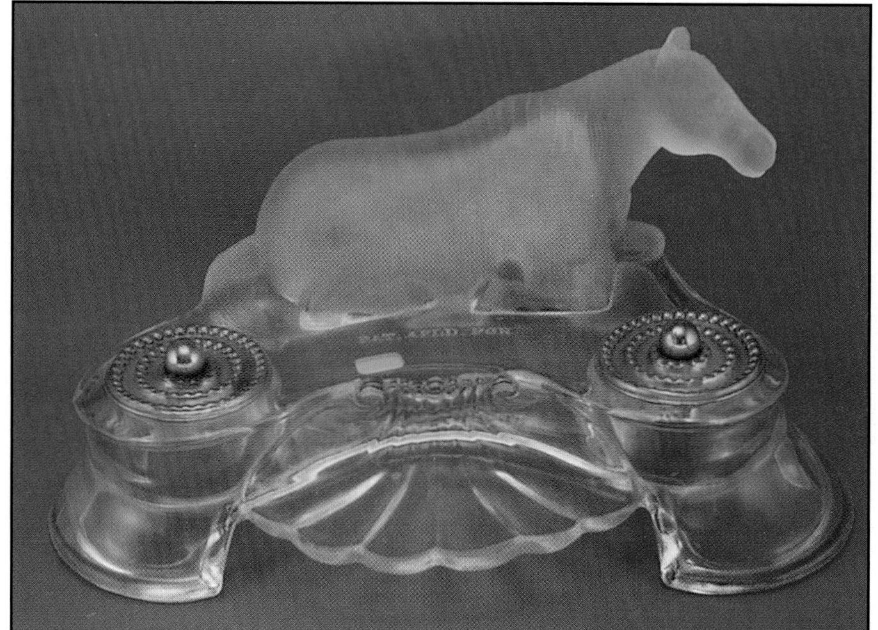

Plate 284
Pressed glass standish, surmounted by acid etched horse figure (reclining), two fonts with stamped brass lids, lids have bead design and ball finials, scallop shell center, "PAT APPLIED FOR MADE FOR 1888 WORLD'S FAIR IN PHILADELPHIA," $230.00 – 250.00. Smith collection.

Plate 285
Blown glass with shallow floral cutting, lobed body with Rococo collar and bulbous lid in sterling silver, marked "WILLIAM CRIORS, LONDON 1743," c. 1915, $275.00 – 285.00. Smith collection.

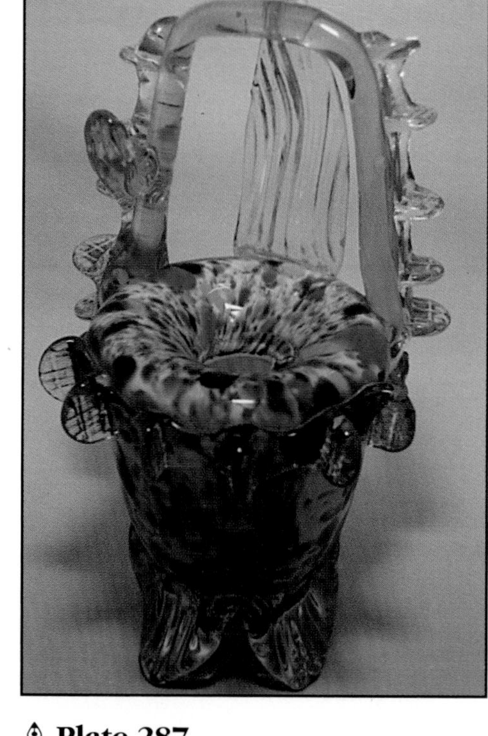

Plate 287
Hand blown art glass, basket-shaped with foliate feet, applied tabs around flange, Venetian style spangled body (end of day glass), one pen rest missing on handle of basket, c. late nineteenth century, $90.00 – 120.00 as is. Smith collection.

Plate 286
Pressed glass, Brittania cast lid, hobo bunny in relief on cover, c. 1860, $120.00 – 140.00. Smith collection.

Plate 288
Hand blown glass, cobalt blue, collar button finial, circular base with bulbous body, possibly American, c. 1900, $180.00 – 200.00. Smith collection.

Plate 289
Hand blown green glass well with reticulated sterling silver casing, Georgian manner, c. late nineteenth century, $150.00 – 180.00. Smith collection.

Plate 290
American pattern glass, electric blue, 1,000 eye design, loose matching cover, c. 1890, $200.00 – 240.00. Smith collection.

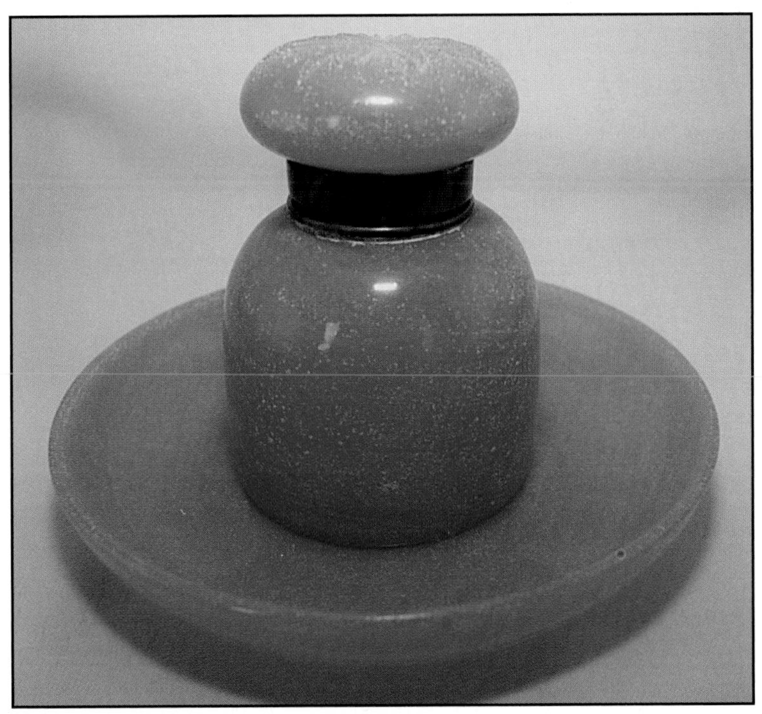

Plate 291
Opaline glass, saucer base, hinged brass collar with mushroom-shaped top, swirl motif on top of lid, glass insert, c. late nineteenth century, $230.00 – 250.00. Smith collection.

Plate 292
Art glass, purple iridescent threading, hand blown, Loetz type, hammered copper hinged circular top, concave sides, Art Nouveau glass insert, 4" square x 3" high, c. 1900, $250.00 – 300.00.

Plate 293
Pressed glass base, stepped, triple frontal pen rest with central recessed receptacle, stamp receptacle in center between wells, two glass wells with Sengbusch self-closing pen receivers, Art Deco, 8½" x 5¾" x 3½" high, c. 1920, $50.00 – 80.00.

Plate 294
Glass, blown in mold, cobalt blue, fluted, cushion-shaped, etched on bottom "H F Y 1887," American, 3" diameter x 1¾" high, $140.00 – 180.00.

Plate 295
Pressed glass in prism design, self-closing center, stamped on cover "EMERY DAVIS NEW YORK, PAT MARCH 19. OCT. 22, 1889," 3" high, $50.00 – 75.00.

Plate 296
Art glass, Loetz type, iridescent green, blue, and gold, water-lily pierced casing, hinged bronze collar and cover, Art Nouveau, cover marked "O.E.P. 10385 D.R.G.M. 100130," 3¼" square x 2¼" high, c. 1910, $350.00 – 380.00.

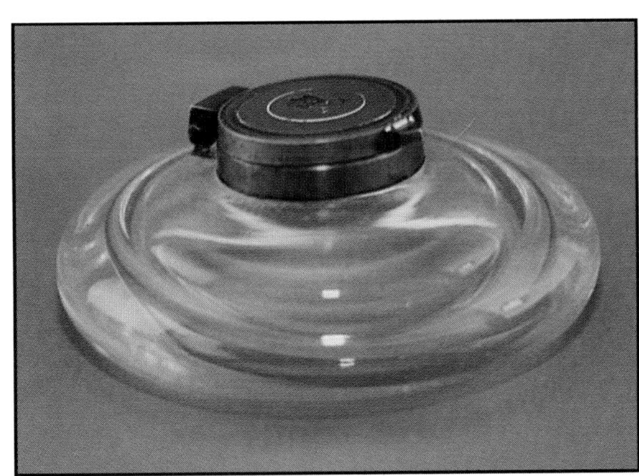

Plate 297
Lead crystal, hand blown ship's well, brass hinged collar and lead assembly, 3" diameter x 1½" high, c. mid-nineteenth century, $80.00 – 90.00.

Plate 298
Black opaque glass, circular base, left has a mottled green plastic receiver and right has a red plastic receiver, Art Deco, American, impressed on base "SWIV-O-DEX, ZEPHYR" on left, "SWIV-O-DEX, PROPERTY OF US NAVY," 3⅜" x 3¼", c. 1930, $85.00 each. Rodkey collection.

Plate 299
Black opaque base with pressed glass well, left has black pen receiver and right has mottled red, Art Deco, impressed on base "SWIV-O-DEX," American, $4\frac{1}{4}$" x $3\frac{1}{4}$", c. 1930, $85.00 each. Rodkey collection.

Plate 300
Crystal, blown in mold, iridescent, Art Nouveau design, lobed body, bronze hinged mounts, high relief foliate design on bronze cover, glass insert, $4\frac{1}{2}$" diameter x $3\frac{1}{2}$" high, c. 1900, $85.00 – 95.00.

Plate 301
Cut glass pineapple with gold leaves, wells are cut, faceted lids, gilt brass collars, frontal pen rest, deep amethyst base, French, c. 1900, $300.00 – 400.00. Wherry collection.

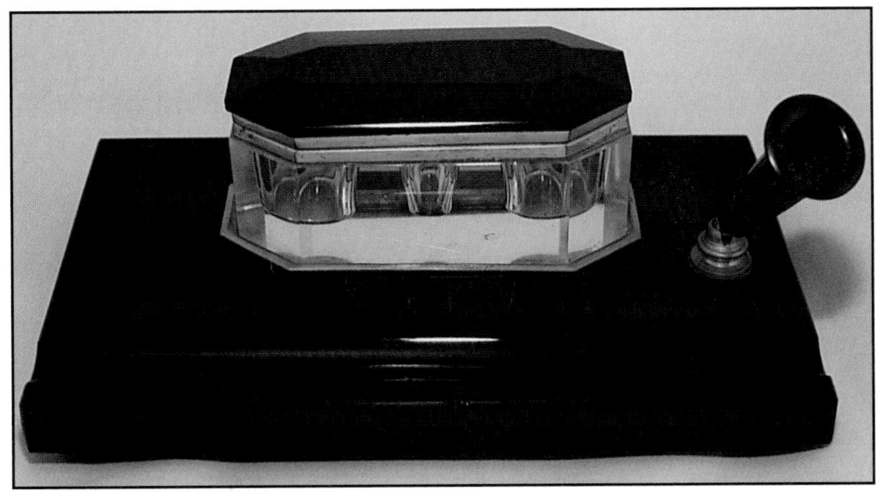

Plate 302
Hand cut, faceted lid and base, amethyst glass, ink well body is casket-shaped holding three wells, gilt brass mounts, pen rest is attached to brass swivel, Art Deco style, French, 8" x 4¾" x 2½", c. 1920 – 1930, $300.00 – 350.00. Wherry collection.

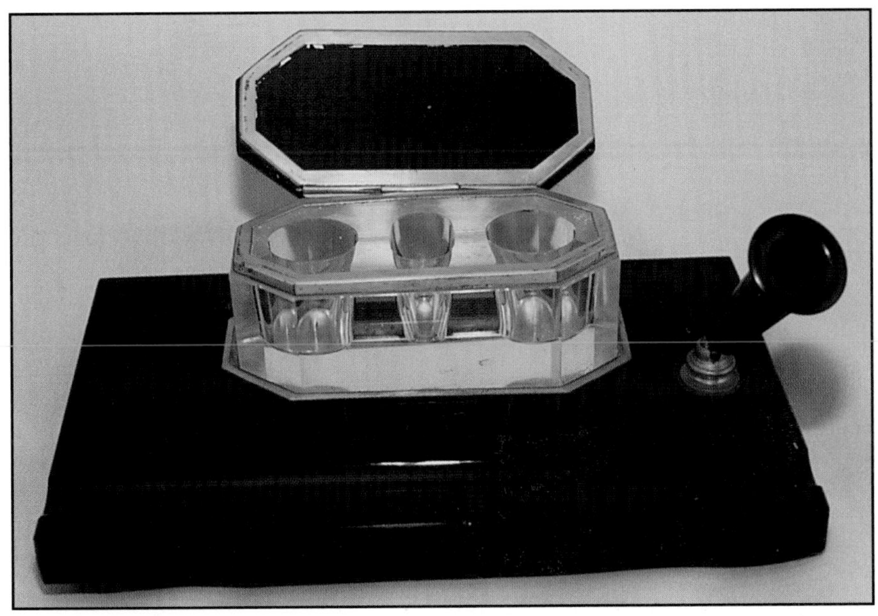

Plate 303
Same as Plate 302.

Copper, Brass & Related Materials

Plate 304
Flat glass base with pen channel, polished brass cylindrical container with hinged brass dome cover and brass insert, 3½" x 3¾" x 2⅝" high, c. early twentieth century, $70.00 – 80.00. Hummer collection.

Plate 305
Brass with attached concave well container, hinged matching cover with finial, Renaissance style, egg and dart motif on rim, Greek motif around flange, 4⅝" diameter, c. late nineteenth century, $120.00 – 130.00. Hummer collection.

Plate 306
Black painted wood oval base, brass-plated well, teacher and student portrayed by monkeys (lampoon on teaching), gilt finish, glass insert, 8" x 6¼" x 5⅛" high, c. late nineteenth century, $350.00 – 400.00. Hummer collection.

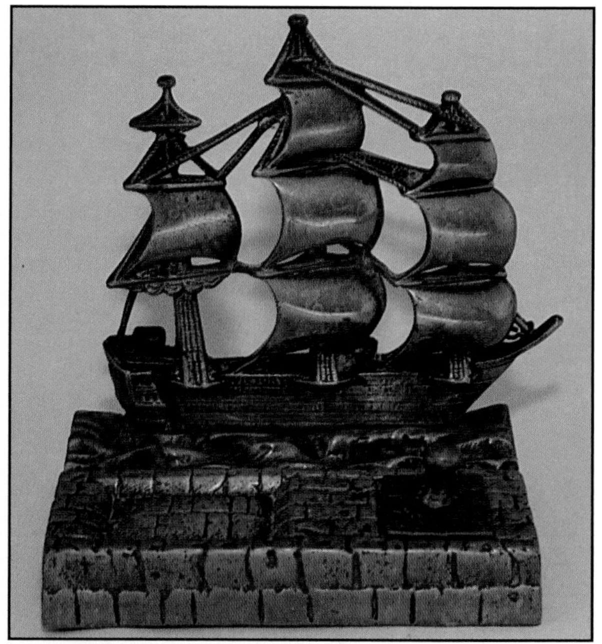

Plate 307
Cast brass with dull finish, three masted dimensional galleon, lid for well is a mooring post, loose square brass cover with finial, "VICTORY" on ship's hull, brass insert, 5½" x 3⅜" x 5¾" high, c. 1920, $180.00 – 200.00. Hummer collection.

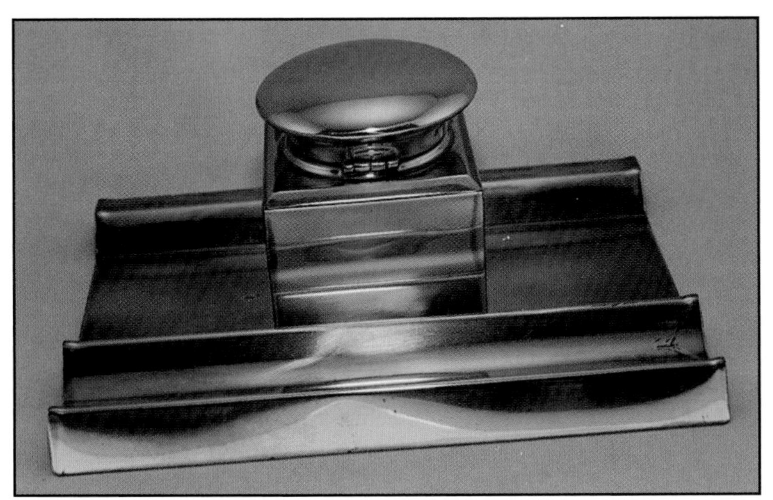

Plate 308
Polished brass with pen channel in rear, brass attached well container with round hinged cover, glass insert, Art Deco influence, 7⅛" x 5½" x 5" high, c. early twentieth century, $120.00. Hummer collection.

Plate 309
Gilt finish over sterling silver with low relief, neo-Japanese floral motif, hinged matching cover, glass insert, marked "STERLING" on back of cover, 2⅞" square x 2⅝" high, c. early twentieth century, $350.00 – 375.00. Hummer collection.

Plate 310
Polished brass with square hinged brass flat cover, Art Deco influence, marked "K. & CO." in oval insignia, glass insert, 3$\frac{1}{16}$" square x 2¼" high, c. early twentieth century, $65.00 – 70.00. Hummer collection.

Plate 311
Silver finish over copper with girl in relief on all four sides, hinged silver finish cover with berry design in relief, porcelain insert, Art Nouveau, 2⅞" x 2½" x 2¾" high, c. 1900 – 1910, $175.00 – 185.00. Hummer collection.

Plate 312
Silver finish stamped brass with pen channel, bell flowers in relief, hinged matching cover, classical style, marked "K & CO.," glass insert, 3¼" x 4¾" x 2⅜" high, c. early twentieth century, $75.00 – 80.00. Hummer collection

Plate 313
Cast brass, one-piece with two wells, side hinged covers, Italian Renaissance style, fonts surrounded by acanthus leaves, bracket feet, porcelain inserts are marked "SANDFORD FINE BONE CHINA — MADE IN ENGLAND," 9⅝" x 6" x 3¼" high, c. 1900, $200.00 – 300.00. Hummer collection.

Plate 314
Polished brass base with walnut wood inlay recesses, attached brass wells with hinged flat covers, milk glass inserts, French feet, marked on bottom "PAT'D DEC 15.08" plus etched in script "7237-7W-FRTU," 9" x 4½" high, c. 1915 $185.00 – 200.00. Hummer collection.

Plate 315
Polished brass base with hammered design, miniature fireplace, attached back plate with finials, attached wire type pen rack, Baccarat type swirl glass well with brass hinged matching cover, 6" x 3¾" x 4½" high, c. 1900, $150.00 – 175.00. Hummer collection.

Plate 316
Polished brass, bulbous body, lid is Rococo with scrolls, ball finial, ballister turned, milk glass insert, 2½" diameter x 2¾" high, c. 1900, $100.00 – 120.00. Hummer collection.

Plate 317
Cast brass with design in relief, classical influence, bracket feet, hinged brass matching cover trimmed with acanthus leaves, white pottery insert, marked on base "PEBRASE ENGLAND," 4½" x 3⅝" high, c. 1890 – 1900, $80.00 – 90.00. Hummer collection.

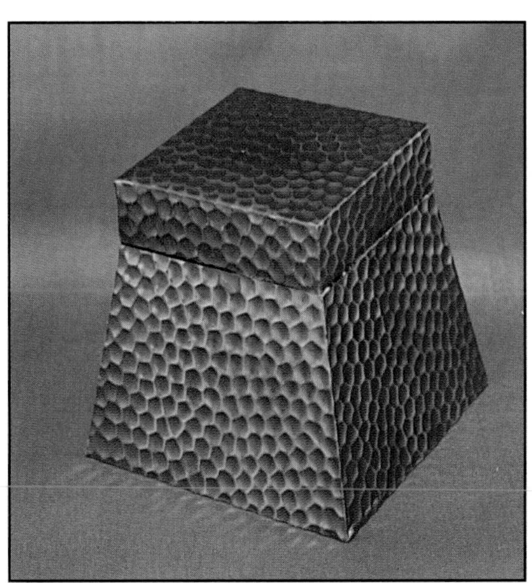

Plate 318
Hammered brass with hinged matching cover, Arts and Crafts movement, marked "FARBERWARE, BROOKLYN N.Y.," glass insert, 2½" square base x 2½" high, c. 1915 – 1920, $125.00 – 140.00. Hummer collection.

Plate 319
Brass with hinged brass cover, Italian Renaissance style, lid is trimmed with acanthus leaves and fruit finial, 2½" diameter x 2½" high, c. 1900, $85.00 – 95.00. Hummer collection.

Plate 320
Polished brass with concave body, hinged brass cover, glass insert, 5" diameter x 2½" high, c. early twentieth century, $60.00 – 70.00. Hummer collection.

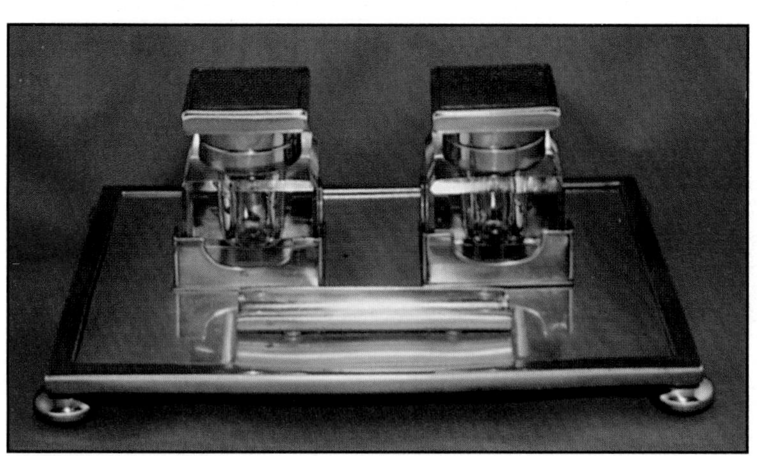

Plate 321
Polished brass plated standish with bun feet, attached pen channel and well holders, cut glass wells are square with hinged brass covers, modern movement, marked "GERMANY" on right well holder, 7⅜" x 5" deep, c. early twentieth century, $170.00 – 180.00. Hummer collection.

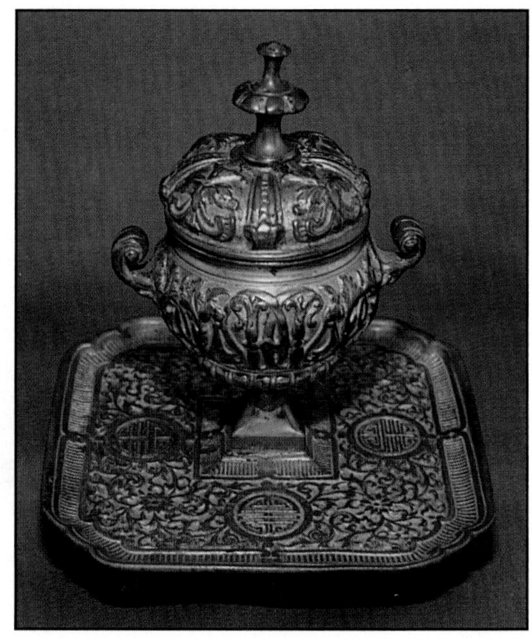

Plate 322
Cast brass, four-footed with pedestal urn attached to base, tray has Chinese good luck symbols, well is Renaissance influence, Italian urn with scroll handles and low relief floral motif, hinged brass cover with finial, round glass insert, with attached brass open type cover, marked "JW-72" plus "J.G." on base, 4½" square x 5" high, c. 1890, $125.00 – 150.00. Hummer collection.

Plate 323
Stamped brass with gilt finish, Rococo style, Baccarat type swirl well, loose cover with design in relief, possibly French, 5" x 3¾", c. 1900, $80.00 – 90.00. Hummer collection.

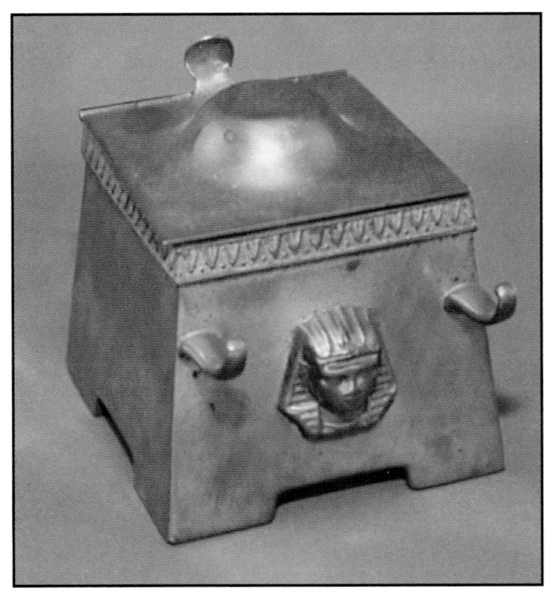

Plate 324
Bronze, shape is Egyptian gateway, relief pharaoh's head, attached pen rest, hinged flip cover, neo-Egyptian, 2¾" x 3" high, c. 1920, $80.00 – 90.00.

Plate 325
Cast brass, four-footed, surrounded by pen channels, acanthus leaves in relief motif, feet are three-toed lion's feet, Italian Renaissance influence, hinged round brass cover with finial, green glass insert, marked on base "XVO," 5¾" x 7" x 4" high, c. 1890, $125.00. Hummer collection.

Plate 326
Copper-plated cast brass with baseball-shaped well container attached to stepped base, hinged matching cover, porcelain insert, marked "PATD SEPT 2ND 1913," 4¼" square base x 3¼" high, $90.00 – 110.00. Hummer collection.

Plate 327
Brass-plated metal base with pen channel and well holder, Baccarat swirl type font with 24-point star pattern on base, fleur-de-lis (a lily or iris of France) and fruit motif, loose round brass-plated cover, marked on base "9239," 6½" x 4", c. 1900 – 1905, $100.00 – 130.00. Hummer collection.

Plate 328
Cast brass with recessed shell-shaped nib holder in center, brass side-hinged well covers with finials, rear pen rack with cherub face in high relief, lion's head in high relief in front of nib holder, French Baroque style, glass inserts, scroll feet. 12¼" x 8", c. 1890 – 1900, $300.00 – 350.00. Hummer collection.

Plate 329
Polished brass-plated metal tray with lift handles, cut glass well with recessed base, hinged brass cover, marked on cover "DRGM–468180–DEP10385," 8¼" x 4⅛" x 2¼" high, c. 1910 – 1915, $80.00 – 90.00. Hummer collection.

Plate 330
Polished brass with hinged cover, glass insert, Art Deco influence, marked "JB1202," 4" x 2⅞" x 2" high, matching rocker blotter, marked "JB1203," matching calendar holder, marked "JB1206," c. 1920 – 1930, $120.00 – 125.00. Hummer collection.

Plate 331
Polished brass base with foliate design in high relief, Italian Renaissance style, attached round concave wells, hinged covers with finials, this could have had removable inserts and there are indications there was a back plate attached, 7⅜" x 4" x 3¼" high, c. 1890, $160.00. Hummer collection.

Plate 332
Silver-finish bronze, classical influence, garland across front of well, silver finish hinged cover, glass insert, marked "REAL BRONZE 7455," 8¾" x 7", c. 1915, $140.00 – 150.00. Hummer collection.

Plate 333
Brass pen tray with bun feet, cameo and scroll work in low relief, Renaissance style, marked "WALKER & HALL SHEFFIELD" plus "W & H" insignia, 9½" x 3½", c. 1900, $40.00 – 60.00. Hummer collection.

Plate 334
Polished brass with pen channel and lift handles, pierced berry and foliage motif, Art Nouveau, brass attached well container and hinged cover with finial, glass insert, possibly French, 7¾" x 7" x 3¾" high, c. 1900 – 1910, $230.00 – 250.00. Hummer collection

Plate 335
Solid bronze grouse sitting on branch, dark bronze finish with remnants of silver finish decoration, tail is a letter holder, hinged grouse head cover, glass insert, 7¼" x 7½" x 6½" high, c. 1890 – 1900, $170.00 – 220.00. Hummer collection.

Plate 336
Polished solid brass base with three attached cobalt and opaque stones, spherical well with pendant ring channels and ruby paste on cover, brass flange attached to glass insert, marked on interior brass flange "ASSER & SHERWIN, 81 STRAND & 69 OXFORD ST, LONDON," 6" diameter x 3¾" high, c. 1890 – 1900, $185.00 – 195.00. Hummer collection.

Plate 337
Cast brass polished tray with cherub symbolic of the arts, well container and double pen rack are attached, Baroque style, hinged brass crown-shaped cover with finial, porcelain insert, 7" x 8" x 4" high, c. 1880 – 1890, $200.00 – 250.00. Hummer collection.

Plate 338
Polished brass with pen channel, hinged brass cover, glass insert, Art Deco influence, 3¾" x 3¼" x 2⅛" high, c. 1900 – 1910, $65.00 – 85.00. Hummer collection.

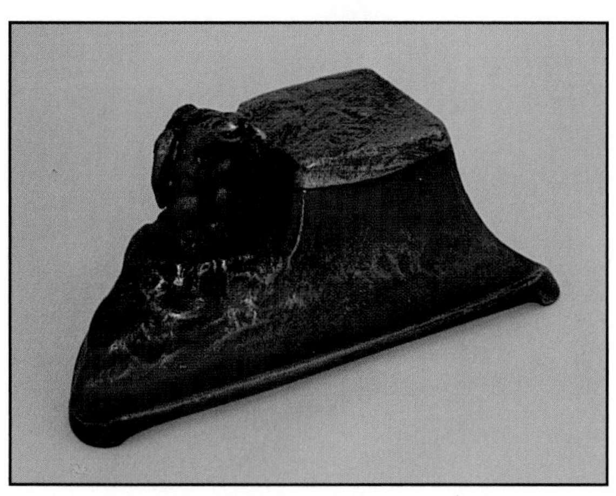

Plate 339
Bronze with pen channel and figural bald eagle, hinged cover and glass insert, rock pedestal, marked "AUSTRIA," 4½" x 2⅞" x 2¼" high, c. 1900 – 1910, $150.00 – 175.00. Hummer collection.

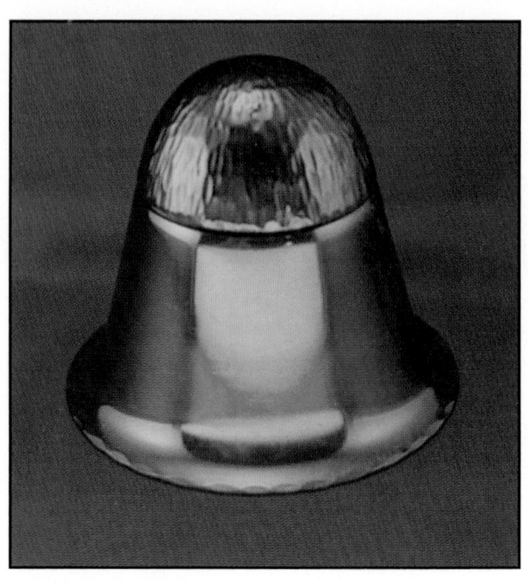

Plate 340
Polished brass, hand-crafted with flared base, hinged brass dome cover, Arts and Crafts movement, marked on base "HANDMADE" inside a hammer and anvil insignia surrounded by "CRAFTSMAN STUDIOS AT LAGUNA BEACH, CALIF. 626.," glass insert, 3½" diameter x 2⅞" high, c. 1900 – 1910, $80.00 – 95.00. Hummer collection.

Plate 341
Bottom of Plate 340.

Plate 342
Cast brass, four-footed, pen channels front and back, design in relief and hinged matching cover with finial, Renaissance style, glass insert, marked "HD44," 5⅜" x 5⅜", c. 1900 – 1910, $85.00 – 95.00. Hummer collection.

Plate 343
Polished brass with lift handles and hinged brass cover, stylized foliage on either end, Art Nouveau, two top threaded glass inserts, marked "GRIF" in script plus "REAL-BRONZE-AUSTRIA-DEPOSE," 9¾" x 6", c. 1900 – 1910, $250.00 – 275.00. Hummer collection.

Plate 344
Solid brass with round footed base, European design, relief flowers and leaves, form of base is lotus blossom, hinged dome-shaped matching cover with butterfly finial, glass insert, 5¾" diameter x 4" high, c. 1890 – 1900, $190.00 – 240.00. Hummer collection.

Plate 345
Dull brass Prussian helmet, loose cover with finial, World War I period, 2½" diameter x 2½" high, c. 1914 – 1918, $150.00. Hummer collection.

Plate 346
Brass with Greek key design, textured surface, Arts and Crafts movement, hinged matching cover, glass insert, marked "SILVER CREST DECORATED BRONZE–SHA CO" plus "2227," 3⅛" diameter x 2⅝" high, c. 1905 – 1910, $125.00. Hummer collection.

Plate 347
Brass well container with loose cover and finial, attached are black Scottish Terriers, iron bottom, glass insert, 4" wide x 1⅞" high, c. 1915 – 1920, $120.00. Hummer collection.

Plate 348
Brass with sunflower base, hinged brass cover with beetle finial, porcelain insert, marked "MADE IN BELGIUM," 7½" wide x 2" high, c. 1880 – 1890, $130.00 – 150.00. Hummer collection.

Plate 349
Hand-hammered copper, round concave shape, hinged matching cover with finial, riveted base, glass insert, marked "ALS-IK-KAN" with insignia plus "ARTS AND CRAFTS MOVEMENT. CA. 1910 GUSTAV STICKLEY," 5½" base, c. 1910, $400.00 – 600.00. Hummer collection.

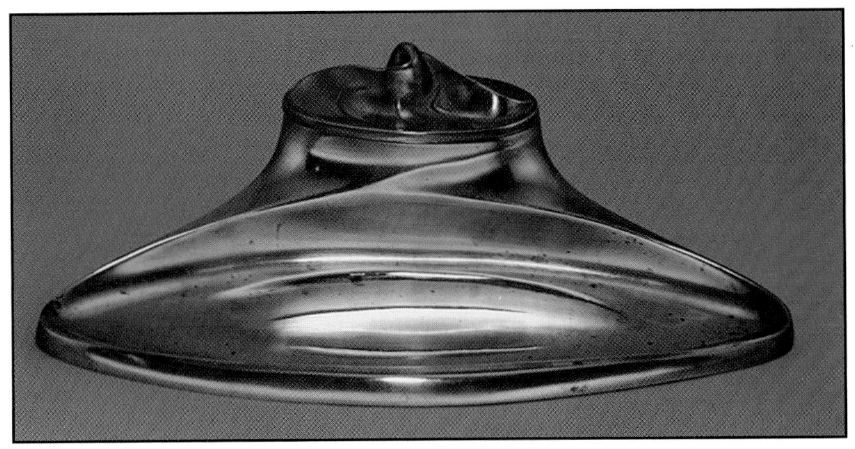

Plate 350
Polished solid brass with pen tray and hinged cover, Art Nouveau, milk glass insert, marked "BRADLEY & HUBBARD MFG CO.," 8⅝" x 4¾", c. 1910 – 1915, $150.00 – 175.00. Hummer collection.

Plate 351
Brass with four ball feet and attached well holder, hinged brass flat cover, glass insert, marked "BRADLEY & HUBBARD MFG. CO," 6" x 3½" x 2½" high, c. early 1900s, $175.00 – 200.00. Hummer collection.

Plate 352
Polished copper tray with bead trimmed flange, pressed glass wells with lattice bases, brass chains attaching designed covers to tray, marked "K & CO" plus "COLD ROLLED HARD COPPER," 7¾" x 4½", c. late nineteenth century, $130.00 – 150.00. Hummer collection.

Plate 353

Copper finish brass, hinged matching cover with silver overlay design, glass insert with attached copper finish cover and flip-type cap, Art Nouveau movement, marked "STERLING ON BRONZE PAT AUG 27.12" plus "AMHS" and "1149," 6¾" diameter x 2⅝" high, $200.00 – 300.00. Hummer collection.

Plate 354

Cast brass with pen tray, quill dish and well recessed, relief scrolls and foliates, scalloped shell recess, Baccarat swirl type glass wells with rayed bases, loose brass designed covers with finials, marked on base of glass wells "VM" plus marked on base "VM" plus "7–9," 11½" x 6½", c. 1890, $175.00. Hummer collection.

Plate 355

Gilt finish brass, empire style pedestals, hinged matching covers with flame finials, possibly French, belonged on a stand, 5½" high, c. 1830 – 1840, $250.00 – 350.00 each. Hummer collection.

Plate 356
Patinated brass well with pen channel, hinged matching cover, George III Adam style, milk glass insert, 3³⁄₁₆" square, marked "JB–1605," matching letter holder, 4¾" wide x 4½" high, marked "JB–1606," matching stamp box with hinged cover, 3½" wide x 1½" high, matching rocker blotter, 4½" x 2⅜", marked "JB–1608," matching letter opener, 8¾" long, c. 1910 – 1915, $350.00 – 400.00 for set. Hummer collection.

Plate 357
Patinated brass, relief flower border, fluting on exterior of font, hinged matching cover, bracket feet, porcelain insert, 7⅛" x 4¾", c. 1900 – 1915, $100.00 – 120.00. Hummer collection.

Plate 358
Cast brass with elaborate Italian Renaissance design, three-footed, hinged brass covers with finials, gold rimmed porcelain inserts, marked "PEC-973," 7⅞" x 8¼", c. 1890, $200.00 – 250.00. Hummer collection.

Plate 359
Bronze, rooster-shaped with red fabric comb, red and black glass eyes, attached pen rack, hinged head cover, glass insert, 4⅛" diameter base x 3¾" high, c. 1890, $175.00 – 200.00. Hummer collection.

Plate 360
Polished brass with hinged brass cover and ball finial, circular concave contour, marked "BRADLEY & HUBBARD MFG CO," 4⅜" diameter x 2⅞" high, c. 1915 – 1920, $150.00. Hummer collection.

Plate 361
Polished brass saucer with attached cup, hinged brass cover with finial, novelty well (possibly English), brass insert, 5" diameter x 2⅝" high, c. 1900 – 1910, $150.00 – 175.00. Hummer collection.

Plate 362
Patinated bronze with pen channel and book designed well holder, hinged matching cover, mint green glass insert, Art Deco influence, marked "K & O CO MADE IN USA" plus marked on books "SUCCESS" plus "ONONIN" plus "CHINA," matching rocket blotter, 8⅝" x 3⅞" x 2½" high, c. 1915 – 1920, $150.00 – 175.00. Hummer collection.

Plate 363
Brass, four-footed with Greek border (bound laurel leaves), attached concave well holder with loose cover and tall finial, bracket feet, glass insert, 2⅜" square x 5⅛" high, c. 1905 – 1910, $90.00. Hummer collection.

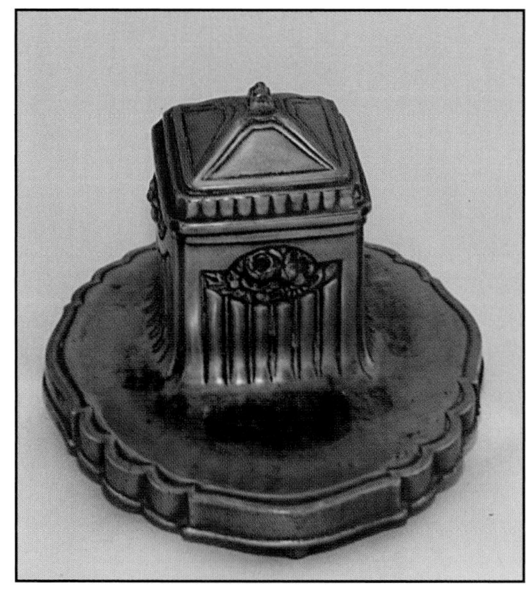

Plate 364
Brass with copper finish, four-footed, Adam in design, architectural, lobed base, hinged matching cover with finial, cobalt blue insert, marked "JB–3097," 5" x 5½" x 3⅝" high, c. 1920, $100.00 – 150.00. Hummer collection.

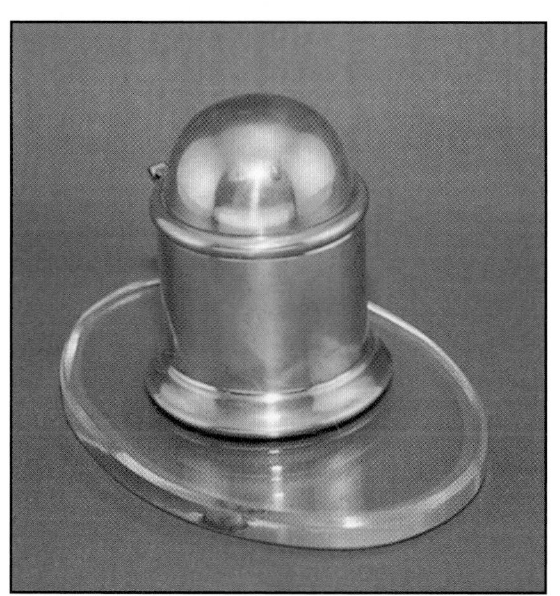

Plate 365
Brass rolled well with dome lid, oval tablet base, Art Deco influence, brass insert, 2⅝" base, 1⅝" diameter well, c. early twentieth century, $70.00 – 85.00. Thorp collection.

Plate 366
Stamped brass tray with gadroon and shell design, opaque glass wells with loose brass covers, 8" long x 6" deep, c. 1890, $175.00. Hummer collection.

Plate 367
Brass chair with paste gemstones, pen rack and well holder, hand-painted white decoration, pressed glass swirl well with brass hinged matching cover, French, 3" wide x 5" high, c. 1890, $250.00 – 275.00. Hummer collection.

Plate 368
Cast brass with four-pen rack, square pressed glass well with dome-shaped glass stopper with air traps, cameo on front in relief wearing laurel garland in hair, classical style, 6½" x 5½" x 4¾" high, c. late nineteenth century, $185.00 – 200.00. Hummer collection.

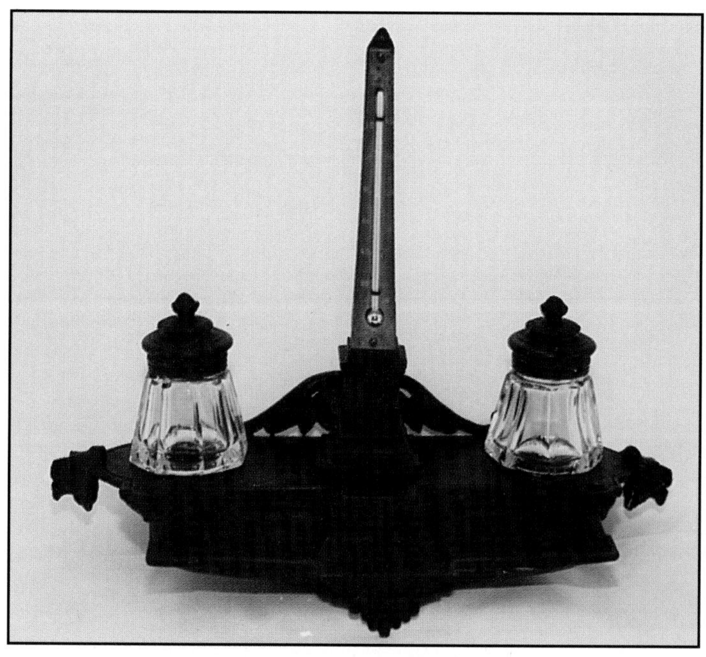

Plate 369
Black painted brass with pen channel, figural lion heads at each end and lion head design in relief in pen channel, clear cut tapered eight-sided inset type wells with hinged black metal covers with finials, Arabic symbols on three sides of monument, obelisk working thermometer on brass back plate, marked on thermometer "FR," 10½" c 6¾" x 8" high, c. 1880 – 1890, $150.00 – 190.00. Hummer collection.

Plate 370
Bronze, dished oval base, hinged matching cover with flame finial, bracket feet, Arts and Crafts movement, markings on front and opposing feet "FRT–J.B.," rear "3223," American, c. 1910 – 1915, $125.00. Thorp collection.

Plate 371
Brass square well with concave sides, has incised floral and phoenix bird decoration, hinged lid with enameled decoration, Chinese, 3" square sloping to 2¾" square, c. 1920, $195.00 – 225.00. Thorp collection.

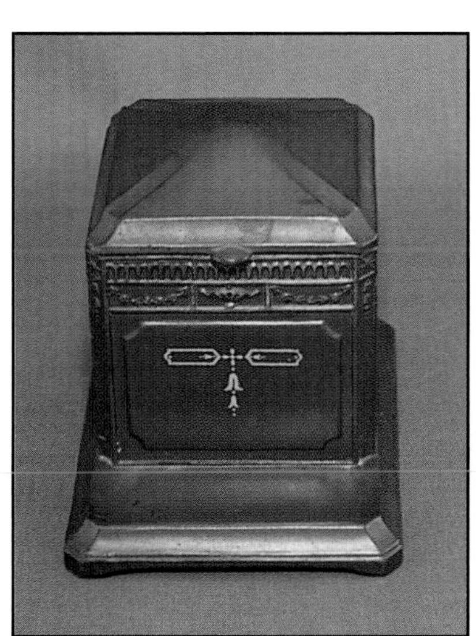

Plate 372
Heavy cast bronze, Federal style, urn with classical garlands below two panels with bell flowers, hinged matching lid and glass insert, marked "BENEDICT-ADAM-VERD," c. 1915 – 1920, $85.00 – 125.00. Thorp collection.

Plate 373
Bronze base with scroll feet and relief decoration, onyx insert with bronze mounts holds crystal well with hinged bronze mount and faceted lid, possibly French, c. 1890 – 1900, $200.00 – 300.00. Thorp collection.

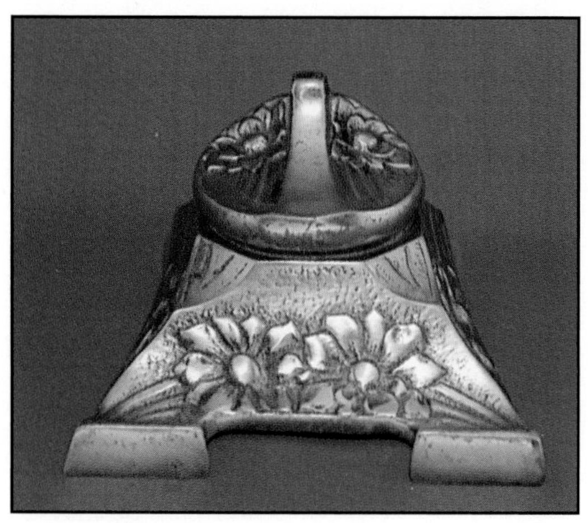

Plate 374
Heavy brass, square in contour with bracket feet, Art Nouveau influence with relief flowers, hinged matching cover, American, c. 1900, $85.00 – 95.00. Thorp collection.

Plate 375
Brass with original glass insert, European, 4" x 2½", c. 1910, $80.00 – 90.00. Thorp collection.

Plate 376
Brass, square contour, surmounted by horseshoe with calendar, stamped "EQUAL TO CUSTOM MADE," base stamped "DAVID MARKS & SONS OF N.Y.," patinated finish, glass insert, 4¾" square x 4¼" high, c. 1900 – 1910, $150.00 – 175.00. Wherry collection.

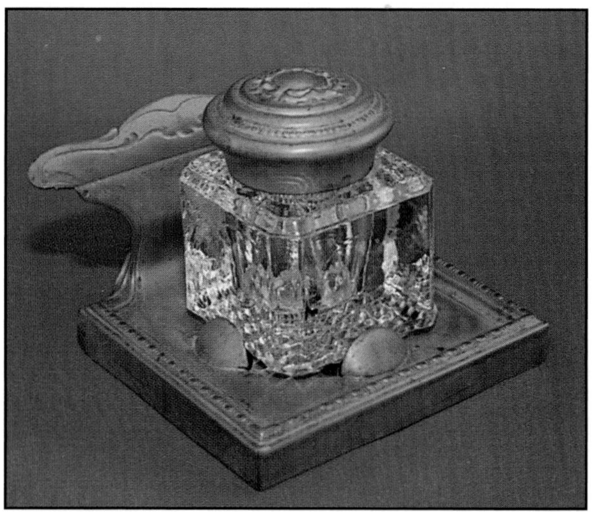

Plate 377
Bronze square base with relief bead trim, pressed glass well with waffle bottom, domed lid with relief decoration, c. early twentieth century, $85.00 – 95.00. Thorp collection.

Plate 378
Cast brass inkwell in tray, neo-Japanese with dragonfly, birds, and flowers, bracket feet and handles, turned finial with relief flower lid, 9½" x 6¼" x 3⅞", c. 1890, $175.00 – 200.00. Wherry collection.

Plate 379
Cast brass, pierced Moorish design, central well with hinged cover, pottery insert, 8" round x 4¾" high, c. 1890 – 1900, $125.00. Wherry collection.

Plate 380
Brass, boat-shaped with pierced floral pattern, George III style, central cut glass well with loose cover, 10½" x 4¾" x 2½", c. 1900 – 1910, $125.00 – 150.00. Wherry collection.

Plate 381
Cast brass base and hinged lid, hand-blown and cut glass well with recessed frontal area with two pen rests, 6¾" x 5" x 3½", c. 1910, $150.00 – 180.00. Wherry collection.

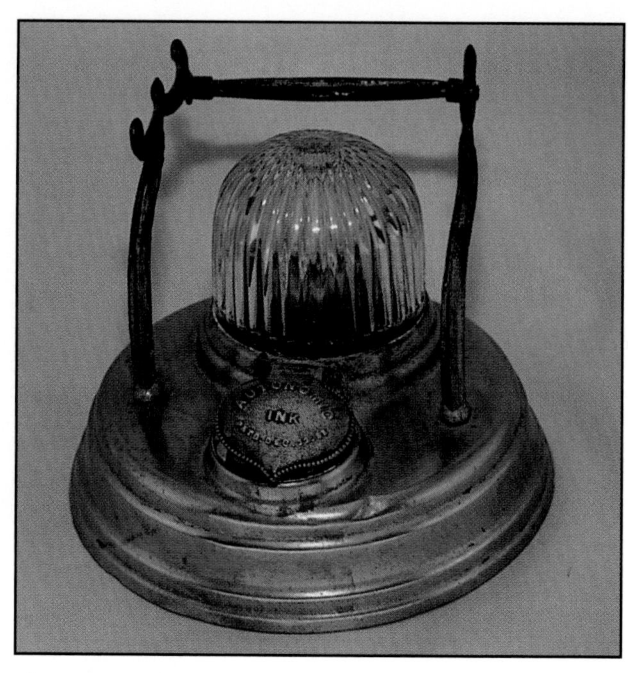

Plate 382
Stamped brass, pot metal pen rest, reeded dome-shaped reservoir, gravity feed, lettering on hinged pen receiver "AUTONOMIC PATD. DEC 11, 91," 5¼" diameter x 4" high, c. 135.00 – 160.00. Wherry collection.

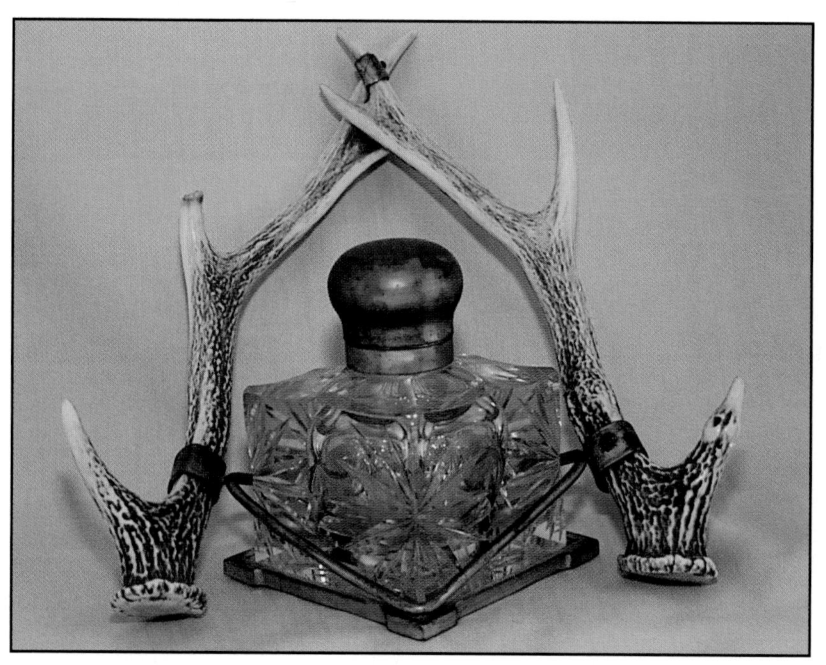

Plate 383
Brass base with projecting corners with flanking deer antler pen rest, pressed glass well in sunburst design with brass hinged cover, 4" square x 5" high, c. 1900 – 1915, $125.00 – 140.00. Wherry collection.

Plate 384
Brass, chair form, shell art, scroll work on back and arms, hand engraved decoration in foliate form, made in Holland, scroll feet, hinged lid, 3¼" x 5" high, c. 1850 – 1860, $200.00 – 300.00. Wherry collection.

Plate 385
Rolled and stamped brass, bell-shaped, American, porcelain insert, 4" x 3½", c. early twentieth century, $70.00 – 80.00. Wherry collection.

Plate 386
Brass, baronial style heraldic coat of arms in relief on cylindrical form, leather textured surface in old red, hinged dome-shaped matching cover, Tiffany, c. 1900 – 1920, $300.00 – 400.00. Wherry collection.

Plate 387
Rolled and stamped brass, simulated hammered surface, Arts and Crafts movement, hinged cover with ball finial, milk glass insert, c. 1900 – 1910, $70.00 – 80.00. Wherry collection.

Plate 388
French enameled brass with blue and green decoration, pedestal well, hinged brass matching cover, base has acanthus leaf trim, glass insert, 2¾" diameter base x 3" high, c. 1875 – 1900, $185.00. Hummer collection.

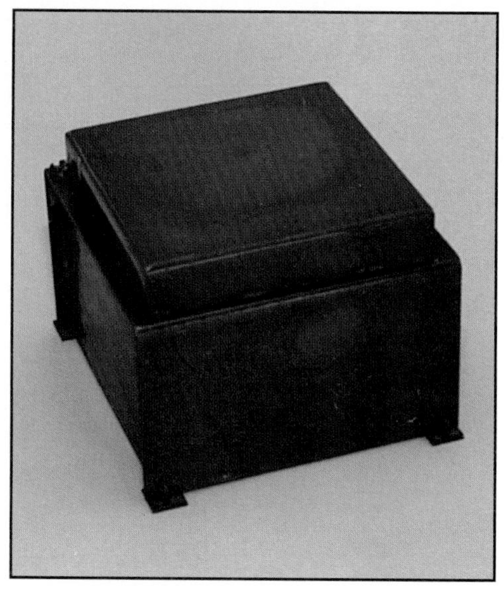

Plate 389
Patinated copper, four-footed with matching cover, Arts and Crafts movement, marked "K CO" in oval insignia, 2¾" square x 2⅛" high, c. 1900 – 1915, $90.00 – 100.00. Hummer collection.

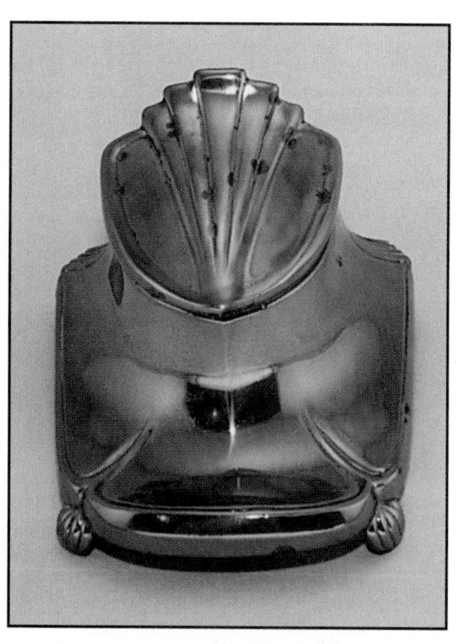

Plate 390
Polished brass metal with hinged cover, four-footed, milk glass insert, 3⅛" x 3⅝" x 2½" high, c. 1905 – 1910, $75.00 – 85.00. Hummer collection.

Plate 391
Polished brass metal with hinged cover and finial, four-footed, scroll feet, glass insert, 2¾" x 3¼" x 2⅜" high, c. 1890, $75.00 – 85.00. Hummer collection.

Plate 392
Sheet brass, cylindrical frontal pen rest, rectangular contour, loose square lid, possibly American, 3⅛" x 4¾" x 2⅛", c. early twentieth century, $80.00 – 95.00. Rodkey collection.

Plate 393
Stamped brass, circular with concave sides, decorative bands, hinged dome top, glass insert, 2¾" diameter x 2" high, c. 1910, $90.00 – 100.00. Rodkey collection.

Plate 394
Brass square base with silver overlay trim on front, pressed glass well with swivel Bakelite lid, Art Deco influence, silver crest on bottom, "PAT'D 1916" stamped on base, 4⅝" square x 2⅜" high, $150.00 – 175.00. Rodkey collection.

Plate 395
Brass cylindrical well with hinged brass domed top, jade green pressed glass base with frontal pen rest, Art Deco influence, 3½" x 3¾" x 2¼", c. early twentieth century, $150.00. Rodkey collection.

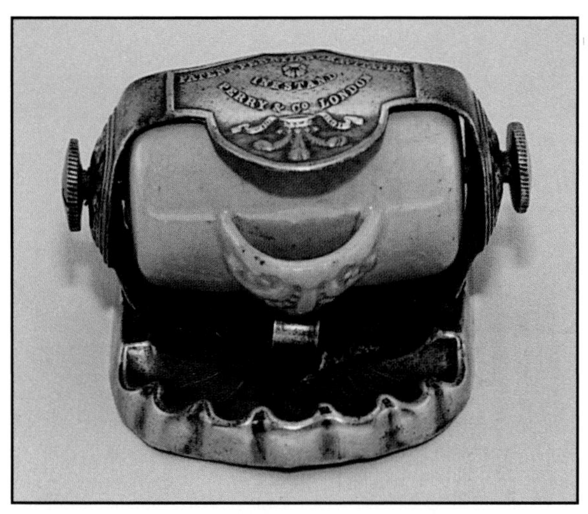

Plate 396
Cast brass, fluted concave body, ceramic reservoir with Prince of Wales (three ostrich plumes) on cover, stamped "PERRY & CO GRAVITATING INKSTAND, PAT'D," 3" x 2½" x 2", c. 1870 – 1880, $200.00 – 300.00. Rodkey collection.

Plate 397
Brass, cylindrical well on stepped base, frontal pen rest, receding top, glass insert, 3¾" x 4¼" x 2¾" high, c. early twentieth century, $120.00 – 130.00. Rodkey collection.

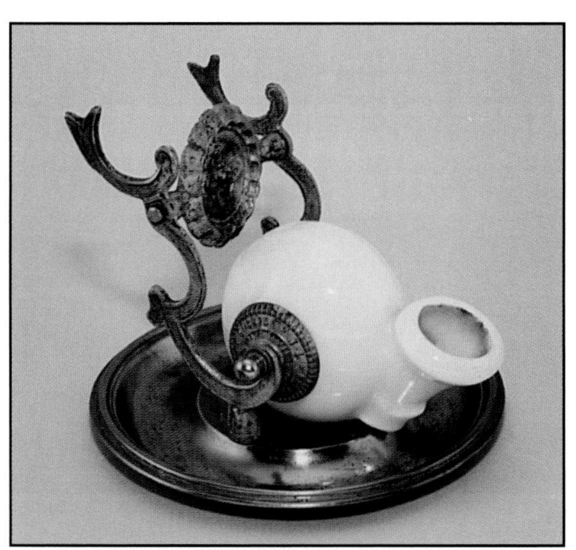

Plate 398
Stamped brass base with cast brass pen rest and holder, Paris white porcelain snail well, Renaissance influence, stamped "J.L. BASCULE," 4¼" diameter x 3⅜" high, c. 1890 – 1900, $250.00 – 300.00. Rodkey collection.

Plate 399
Patinated bronze, bell-shaped with hard rubber insert, receding cover, English, 4⅜" x 3⅝" high, c. early twentieth century, $120.00 – 150.00. Rodkey collection.

Plate 400
Patinated cast brass, ovoid in contour, relief bell flowers with gilt embellishment, hinged lid with finial, bun-shaped feet, Adam style, blown glass funnel insert with cork stopper in bottom, c. 1910 – 1915, $150.00 – 175.00. Rodkey collection.

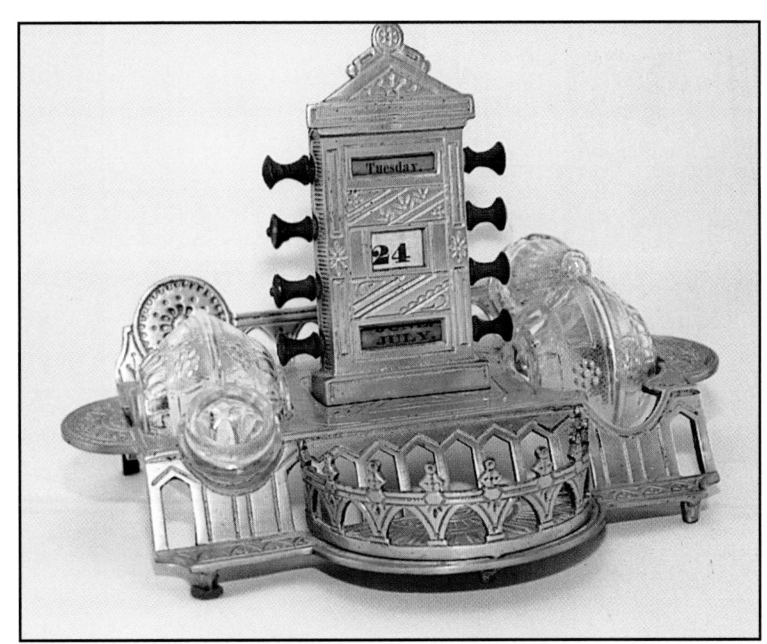

Plate 401
Cast brass, Gothic style with classical influence, complete desk calendar on ancient Greek tombstone form, two pressed glass snail reservoirs, semicircular pen rest, $8\frac{3}{4}$" x $6\frac{1}{4}$" x $5\frac{3}{4}$" high, c. 1890, $350.00 – 400.00. Rodkey collection.

Plate 402
Brass with copper accents, rectangular contour with rolled scrolled motif, matching letter opener and rocker blotter, amber glass insert, Art Deco influence, stamped "S.K. Company (MFG.)," $7\frac{3}{8}$" x $4\frac{3}{4}$" x $2\frac{1}{4}$" high, c. 1910 – 1915, $200.00 – 275.00. Rodkey collection.

Plate 403
Bronze rectangular base surmounted by two griffins supporting candle holders, central polished crystal well with domed lid, hinged brass collar, possibly French, 10¼" x 2⅞" x 4⅞" high, c. 1880, $200.00 – 300.00. Rodkey collection.

Plate 404
Brass, two half-spherical base, ball feet, pressed glass wells with cork closure, ribbed bodies, back is three crossed bayonets, possibly European, 5½" x 3" x 5¾" high, c. 1915, $200.00 – 300.00. Rodkey collection.

Plate 405
Brass rectangular base and frontal tray, ball feet, 2" cut glass well with beveled corners, loose brass lid, Art Deco influence, 7¾" x 4½" x 3" high, c. 1920 – 1925, $100.00 – 130.00. Rodkey collection.

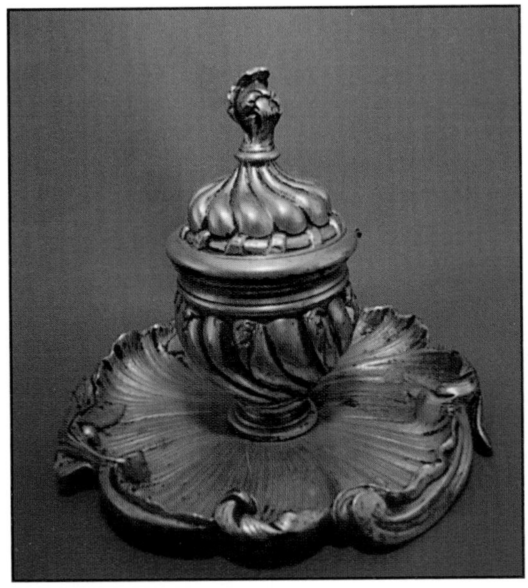

Plate 406
Cast brass, saucer base with attached lobed body and cover with flame finial, high relief laurel and roses, impressed on base "P.E. GUERIN #615," 5" diameter x 4" high, c. 1890, $125.00 – 135.00.

Plate 407
Stamped brass base, classical style, pressed glass well with stamped collar, shell motif and hinged brass lid, marked on base "W.SCH. & CO PAT JULY 1899 HOBOKEN, N.J.," 4" x 5¼" x 3½", $100.00 – 120.00.

Plate 408
Hammered copper with patinated finish, cylindrical contour, indented bands pattern, domed lid with egg shape finial, marked with Roycroft insignia, 2½" diameter x 2¼" high, c. 1910, $175.00 – 200.00.

Plate 409
Rolled brass, cast iron weighted base, urn-shaped, loose cover with ball finial, 2½" x 3", c. 1900, $80.00.

Plate 410
Cast white metal with antique bronze finish, Rococo form with relief flowers, hinged lid, matching stamp box and desk blotter, c. 1890, $100.00 – 120.00.

Plate 411
Cast bronze, champleve, Persian style, pen rest holding matching pen, turned feet, cast bronze hinged lid with pinecone finial, glass insert, c. 1870 – 1880, $160.00 – 175.00.

Plate 412
Stamped brass base, pressed glass well with waffle design, stamped relief rosette on cap, neo-Oriental design, 5¼" x 3⅜", c. 1890 – 1900, $60.00 – 75.00.

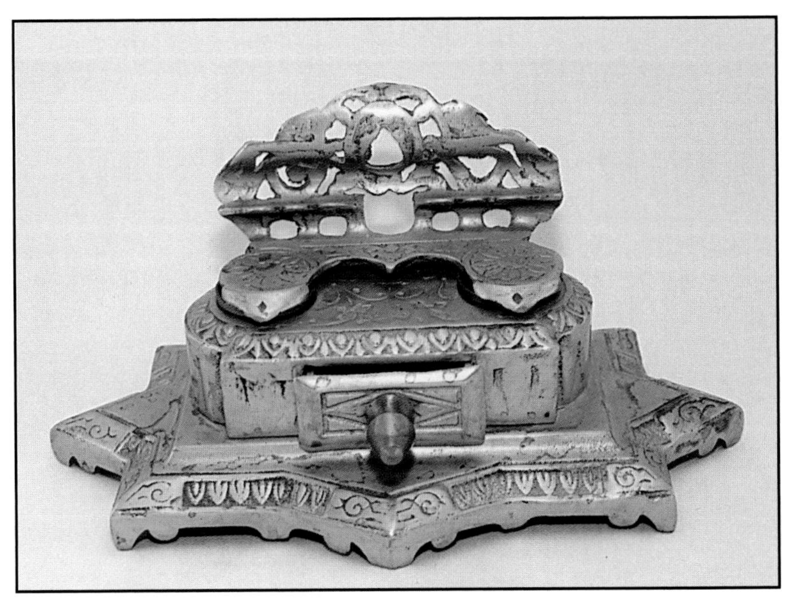

Plate 413
Cast brass, relief decoration, Gothic style, bracket feet, rectangular drawer above platform, double pen rest above covers (open work), brass inserts, American, 10" x 5⅝" x 5" high, c. 1880 – 1890, $200.00 – 240.00. Rodkey collection.

Plate 414
Patinated brass covered pot metal, lobed platform with human mask feet, front of base is a leopard with extended paws, concave receptacle, back surmounted by a terrier dog with a ball, irregular shaped lids, glass inserts, 9" x 5" x 2¾" high, c. 1885 – 1900, $175.00 – 200.00. Rodkey collection.

Plate 415
Brass, rectangular tray base, pressed glass well with hinged brass cover, rear pen rest, Art Nouveau influence, possibly American, 8⅜" x 5⅞" x 2½" high, c. 1900 – 1910, $120.00 – 150.00. Rodkey collection.

Plate 416
Rolled brass, bell-shaped, hinged top, glass insert, possibly American, 2½" x 2⅜", c. 1910 – 1920, $50.00 – 60.00. Rodkey collection.

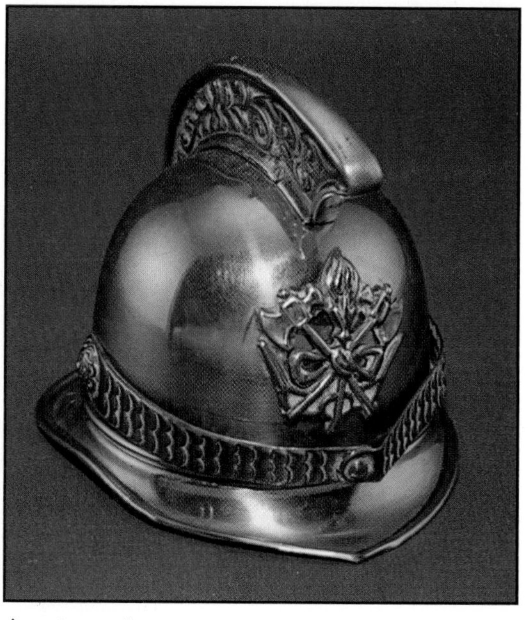

Plate 417
Brass dragoon's helmet, applied silver decorations, military insignia above visor (bound weapons), top of helmet is hinged, glass insert, possibly French, 2½" x 3½" x 2¾", c. 1880 – 1890, $200.00 – 250.00. Rodkey collection.

Plate 418
Brass, oval contour, cream can style with hinged lid, side brackets with bale handle, English, 2" x 1½" x 2¼" high, c. 1890, $185.00 – 195.00. Rodkey collection.

Plate 419
Brass pail-shaped well, bale handle, loose lid with ball finial, porcelain insert, possibly English, c. 1880, $175.00 – 190.00. Rodkey collection.

Plate 420

Brass low circular well with stone fragment trim, brass pen with stone fragments and heart-shaped finial, India, 2" x 1½", c. 1900 – 1910, $85.00 – 100.00. Rodkey collection.

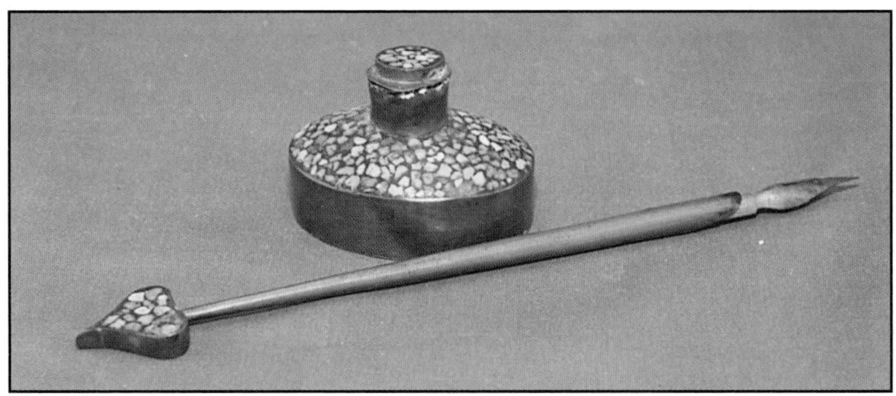

Plate 421

Sheet brass rectangular base with frontal pen rest, bun feet, and paling gallery, cylindrical well with recessed lid, 4¾" x 5¾" x 3½", c. early twentieth century, $160.00 – 175.00. Rodkey collection.

Plate 422

Bronze, coffer-shaped well, low relief decoration in Classical style, bracket feet, hinged lid, glass well inside with two-piece funnel top, 4" x 3" x 2½", c. early twentieth century, $150.00 – 175.00. Rodkey collection.

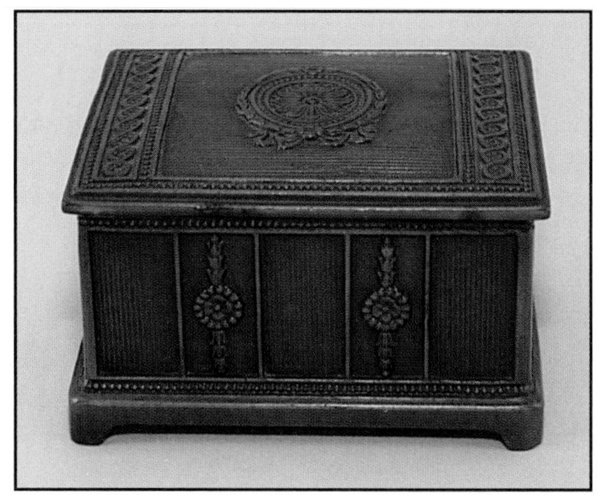

Plate 423
Desk set, brass, Arts and Crafts influence, hand polished crystal well, marked "Bradley and Hubbard," c. 1910 – 1920, $200.00 – 300.00. Wherry collection.

Plate 424
Cast brass desk set, calendar, blotter, well with pen tray, relief floral decoration, pressed glass insert, Art Nouveau influence, American, c. 1910, $185.00 – 200.00. Wherry collection.

Plate 425
Cast brass alligator form, two porcelain inserts, American, 10" x 3½" x 2½", c. 1900 – 1910, $200.00 – 300.00. Wherry collection.

Plate 426
Opaque glass wells and central medallion, hand-painted floral decoration, gilt brass mounts, brass wirework frame, bird and flower motif, marked "G.D. PARIS, DEPOSE," ladies' inkwell, French, missing central dish, 8" x 7½", c. 1870 – 1880, $300.00. Wherry collection.

Plate 427
Stamped brass, Rococo style, pressed glass well with waffle bottom, brass cover with chain attached to base, 5" x 3½" x 2¼" high, c. 1900, $65.00 – 70.00. East Bloomfield collection.

Plate 428
Copper plated brass with black enamel trim, hinged matching cover, impressed on front "H.W.S.," American, 2⅞" square x 2⅝" high, c. 1910 – 1920, $85.00 – 95.00. Hummer collection.

Plate 429
Cast brass, square base with bracket feet, pressed glass font with ball tipped brass bracket and Bakelite top, lyre-shaped, 2½" base x 3¾" high, c. 1900 – 1910, $75.00 – 100.00. Rodkey collection.

Plate 430
Brass rectangular, concave pen rest in front, bracket feet, hand chased floral design, hinged lid, India, 3½" x 3" x 1⅜", c. 1900, $65.00 – 75.00. Rodkey collection.

Plate 431
Cast brass, base is heavy cast relief chestnut leaf, well is chestnut with another chestnut resting on base, pottery insert, 5½" x 2⅜", c. early twentieth century, $150.00 – 175.00. Rodkey collection.

Plate 432
Cast brass base, leaf, stamped brass spherical well with hinged lid, glass insert with brass collar, 4¾" x 5⅜" x 2⅜", c. early twentieth century, $125.00 – 150.00. Rodkey collection.

 **Plate 433**
Vienna bronze, segmented platform with turned feet, surmounted by game table and two cast enameled frogs, hinged table-top lifts to reveal two wells, c. 1900 – 1910, $250.00 – 300.00. Smith collection.

Plate 434
Bronze, American bison heads on corners, paw feet, pressed glass well with waffle bottom, European, c. late nineteenth century, $150.00. Smith collection.

Plate 435
Cast bronze, Renaissance style, owl's head lid, four owls surmounting legs, Baccarat swirl type pressed glass wells, 6" x 3½" high base, 2" square well, c. late nineteenth century, $140.00 – 150.00. Smith collection.

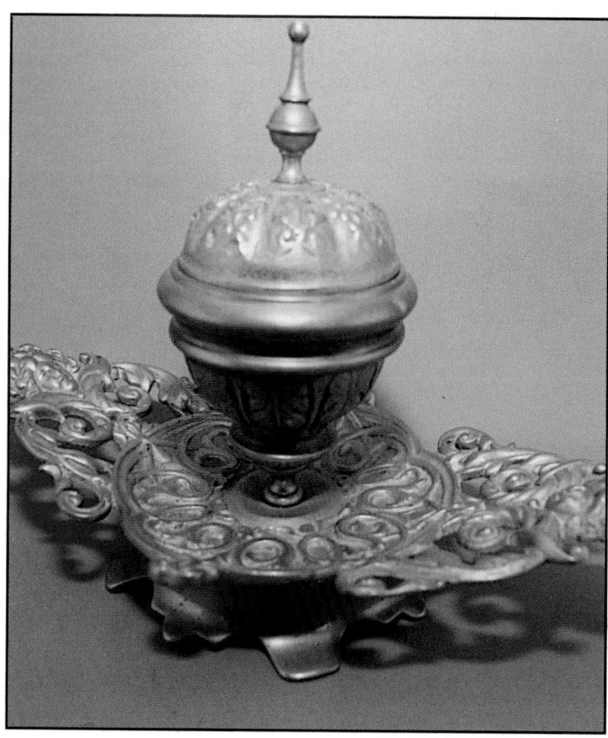

Plate 436
Bronze, Italian style, female masks on base, pad feet, Moorish domed cover with turned finial, glass insert, c. 1890 – 1900, $100.00 – 125.00. Smith collection.

Plate 437
Cast bronze, stepped base with frontal pen channel, surmounted by bust of Napoleon, porcelain insert, hinged bronze cover, marked "SOUVENIR OF PARIS," 5¼" x 3" x 4½" high, c. early twentieth century, $120.00 – 150.00.

Plate 438
Bronze chariot drawn by pair of American bison, driver of chariot is a griffin, green patination, pressed glass well, loose cover with scroll motif, pen rest on back of chariot, 1⅞" square well, c. late nineteenth century, $250.00 – 300.00. Smith collection.

Plate 439
Sterling silver, lid is tortoise shell, 3¼" x 2", c. 1900, $300.00 – 350.00. Wherry collection.

Plate 440
Sterling silver, concave pyramidal form, European, hinged sterling lid, glass insert, frontal pen rest, 4" square x 2" high, c. 1890 – 1910, $350.00 – 400.00. Wherry collection.

Plate 441
Cast bronze base, Baccarat swirl type design well, Italian Renaissance manner, sterling lid, 4½" x 5½" x 3", c. 1890 – 1900, $85.00 – 95.00.

Plate 442
Rock crystal well with elaborate sterling silver overlay, hand chased decoration, diamond faceted hinged lid, 3⅝" round x 3" high, c. 1905, $500.00 – 600.00. Wherry collection.

Plate 443
Hand chased silver-plated standish, two cut glass wells with silver-plated lids, silver-plated statue of buffalo with ram's horns and buffalo tail, ball feet, marked "JON DIXON & SONS," Sheffield, 8¼" x 6¾" x 3¼", c. 1860 – 1870, $500.00 – 550.00. Wherry collection.

Plate 444
Sterling silver boat-shaped base, bound fillet design, ball feet, staghorn well, domed hinged lid, 9½" x 3½" x 3", c. 1900, $350.00 – 400.00. Wherry collection.

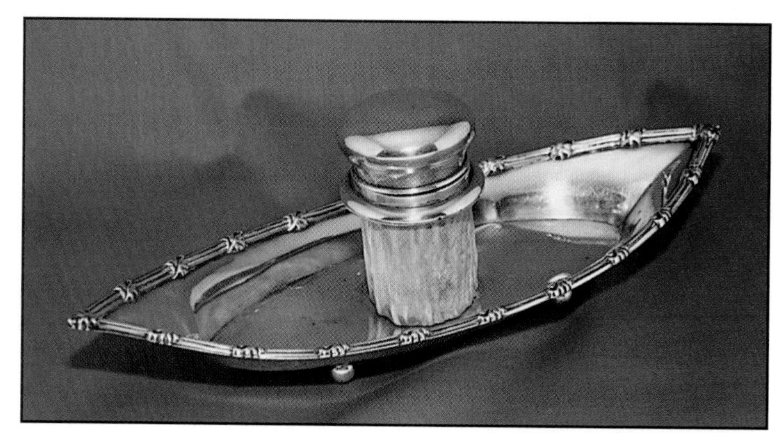

Plate 445
Silver-plated base with repoussé floral motif, hinged ball-shaped cover, swirled lobed design, 5⅜" round x 4¼" high, c. 1890 – 1900, $200.00 – 275.00. Wherry collection.

Plate 446
Silver-plated standish, Rococo revival with scroll feet, flowers, two cut glass wells, Victorian period, sealing taper stick, 10¾" x 7" x 4¾", $350.00 – 375.00. Wherry collection.

Plate 447
Sterling silver boat-shaped standish with scrolled feet, bead mounts, two cut glass wells, sawtooth design, hinged lids with urn-shaped finials, 9¼" x 6½" x 3¼", England, c. 1900, $450.00 – 550.00. Wherry collection.

Plate 448
Silver-plated standish, elaborate Rococo mounts, scroll feet, two cut glass wells with hinged mushroom tops, central reservoir, 10½" x 7¾" x 4", c. 1890, $300.00 – 325.00. Wherry collection.

Plate 449
Silver-plated standish, four-footed tray with attached well holders, ball and claw feet, shell and gadroon mounts, George II style, cut glass diamond design wells with hinged covers, marked in script on base "28–GH 1–M," possibly English, 13" x 9½", c. 1890, $275.00 – 325.00. Hummer collection.

Plate 450
Silver-plated, one-piece with pen tray and cylindrical well, hinged silver cover with pomegranate on top, glass insert, marked "CM" plus "DA," anchor within a shield plus "22," 10¾" x 5¼" x 2¾" high, c. 1900 – 1910, $175.00 – 225.00. Hummer collection.

Plate 451
Silver four-footed tray with pen channel and recess for well, double pad feet, designed border, Chippendale type, clear cut glass well, hinged silver cover, etched on base "1024B," impressed hallmarks on front left corner of tray, 6¾" x 4¾" base, c. 1890, $500.00 – 600.00. Hummer collection.

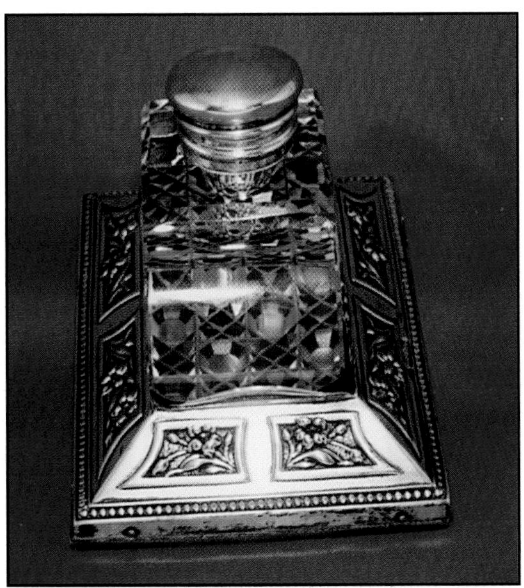

Plate 452
Silver frame with well holder and design in relief, mounted on black painted wood base, clear cut glass well with cane pattern base and channel, hinged silver cover and glass insert, base has repoussé floral pattern, marked on collar "J & RG" plus hallmarks, 3½" x 4⅞" base, c. 1890, $300.00 – 375.00. Hummer collection.

Plate 453
Sterling silver, cylindrical with monogram in script on lid "KWH, XMAS 96," 1⅝" x 1¾" high, c. 1896, $300.00 – 400.00. Rodkey collection.

Plate 454
Silver-plated, wide base, circular contour, ship type, porcelain insert, 2⅝" diameter x 1½" high, c. 1900 – 1910, $125.00 – 150.00. Rodkey collection.

Plate 455
Sterling silver with hinged matching lid, blown glass insert, repoussé in a plume design, bulbous contour, c. 1890, $200.00 – 250.00. Thorp collection.

Plate 456

Silver-plated Brittania metal, pressed glass umbrella shape, nine-sided inset well, Rococo design, lid missing, marked "WILCOX SILVER PLATE CO MERIDEN CONN–QUADRUPLE SILVER–2849," 8¾" wide, c. 1890 – 1900, $65.00 as is. Hummer collection.

Plate 457

Silver-plated with well holder and containers for stamps and calendar, base has butler finish, supports are classical lyres, Rococo revival, pressed glass well with chain attached to loose silver cover, American, incised in script on base "HOWE," 5¾" x 3⅞" base, c. 1890, $250.00 – 300.00. Hummer collection.

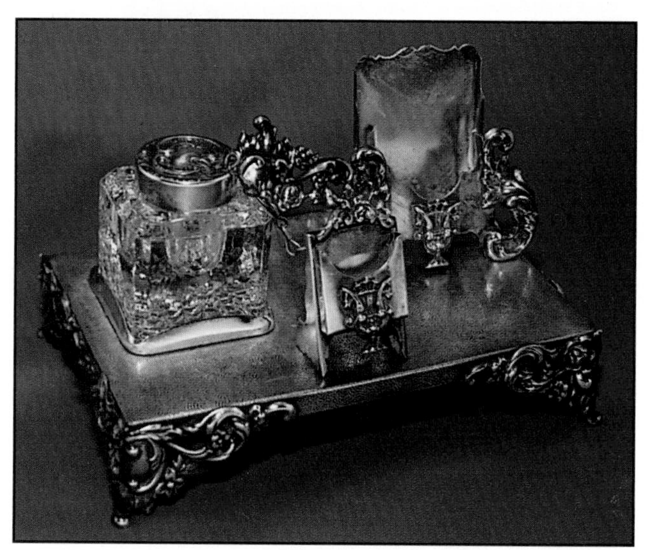

Plate 458

Silver-plated six-footed with designed border, pen rack, quill container, scroll feet, Rococo mounts, loose Baccarat swirl type wells with hinged silver dome-shaped covers, marked "POOLE SILVER CO, TAUNTON MASS–QUADRUPLE PLATE" plus "1455," 7½" x 4½" tray, c. 1900, $130.00 – 150.00. Hummer collection.

Plate 459
Silver-plated on white metal with small quill holder, double Baccarat swirl type wells with hinged and silver-plated crown covers with finials, floral design, marked "DERBY SILVER CO. QUADRUPLE PLATE–1754" on base, 7½" x 4½" x 2¾" high, c. 1900, $175.00 – 190.00. Hummer collection.

Plate 460
Metal horse hoof with silver-plated rim, hinged silver-plated flat cover with stylized hair, silver-plated mounts, cut glass insert with silver-plated cover, possibly English, 4¾" x 6½" x 3⅜" high, c. 1880 – 1890, $185.00 – 230.00. Hummer collection.

Plate 461
Silver-plated, revolving dome, Empire style, three lion's paw feet, possibly English, 3¼" diameter x 3" high, c. early twentieth century, $180.00 – 200.00. Rodkey collection.

Plate 462
Silver-plated white metal, designed with attached emblem, hinged matching cover, glass insert, souvenir type, "CAPITOL WASHINGTON" on emblem, 3¹⁄₁₆" x 3½" x 2¼" high, c. 1915, $85.00 – 95.00. Hummer collection.

Plate 463
Silver-plated white metal, boat-shaped, cut glass well with elaborate Rococo mounts, hinged domed lid with relief flowers, double pen rest, ladies' inkwell, American, marked "E.J. WEBSTER & SON," 4½" x 3" x 2¾", c. 1890 – 1900, $125.00. Rodkey collection.

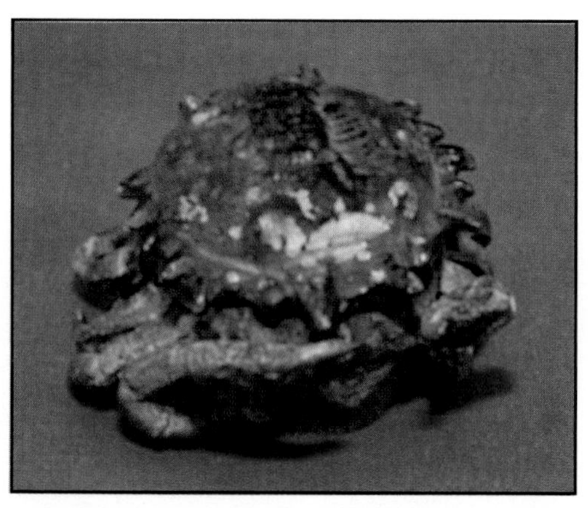

Plate 464
Cast white metal crab (original finish distressed), pottery insert, 2⅝" x 1⅝", c. 1890, $75.00 – 85.00. Rodkey collection.

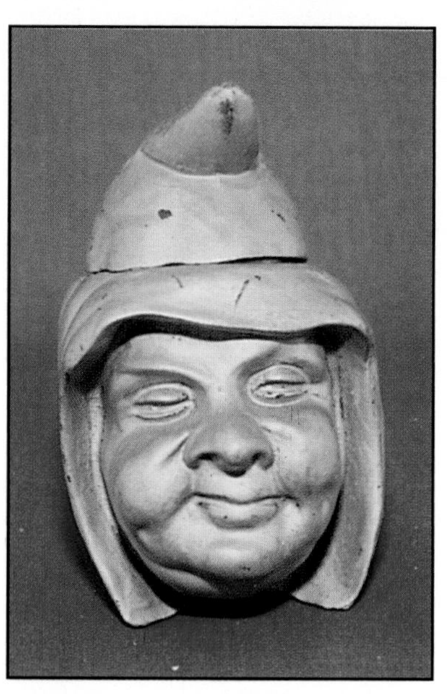

Plate 465
Cast metal with silver finish, comic monk's head with cowl, peak of cowl is hinged lid, glass insert, c. 1900, $175.00 – 200.00. Rodkey collection.

Plate 466
Sheet brass with incised lines, inverted cone shape with hinged dome cover, American, 4½" x 3½" high, c. 1900, $65.00 – 80.00.

Plate 467
Sheet brass with steel weighted bottom, pyramidal, hinged flip top, Art Deco influence, opaque glass insert, American, 4¼" square x 2½" high, c. early twentieth century, $65.00 – 75.00.

Plate 468
Stamped sheet brass tray with attached griffin-shaped urn pen wipe, pressed glass wells with pegged bottom, eight-sided, stamped brass ball finial, loose cover, Italian Renaissance style, 8" x 3", c. early twentieth century, $100.00 – 140.00.

Cast Iron & Other Metals

Plate 469
Cast iron with gilt finish, Baccarat swirl type pressed glass well, loose cover with fruit motif in relief and ball finial, Rococo influence, possibly French, c. late nineteenth century, $90.00 – 110.00. Smith collection.

Plate 470
Cast iron, Gothic style, swivel opaque glass well with attached font, recessed pen tray and pen rest back, funnel feeder to reservoir font, c. late nineteenth century, $250.00 – 300.00. Smith collection.

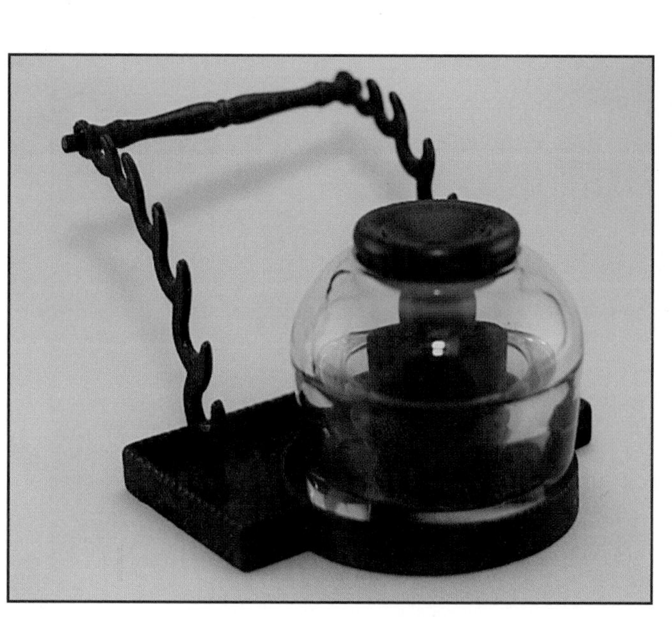

Plate 471
Cast iron base, black finish with multiple pen rest, round pressed glass well with self-closing Bakelite top, Sengbusch, stamped "MADE IN USA, MILWAUKEE, WIS, PAT'D 1907," $100.00 – 120.00.

Plate 472
Cast iron rectangular form, two shield-shaped lids with low relief decoration in Gothic style, double pen rest in front, when pens are removed, tops open, American, stamped "SPECIAL NOVELTY IRONWORKS – CHICAGO, PAT'D OCT. 28, 84," 5½" x 4" x 2⅜" high, $200.00 – 225.00. Rodkey collection.

Plate 473
Cast iron rectangular cabinet form, triple frontal pen rest, two hinged doors with attached wells, one milk glass and one pressed glass, recessed top with brush pen wipe, American, 5" x 4½" x 3" high, c. 1880 – 1890, $300.00 – 350.00. Rodkey collection.

Plate 474
Picture of Plate 473 open.

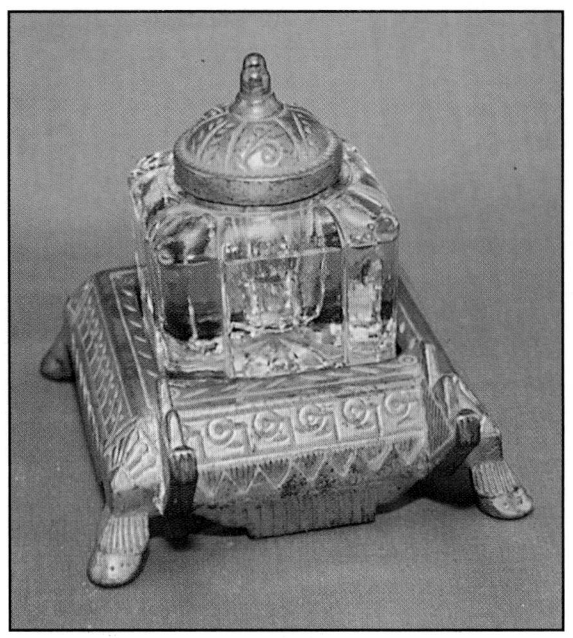

Plate 475
Copper-plated cast iron, hoof feet, Medieval style, double pen rest, pressed glass well with loose cover, stamped "PAT'D DEC 11, 1877, P.S. AND W CO.," 3⅞" square x 3½" high, $80.00 – 90.00. Rodkey collection.

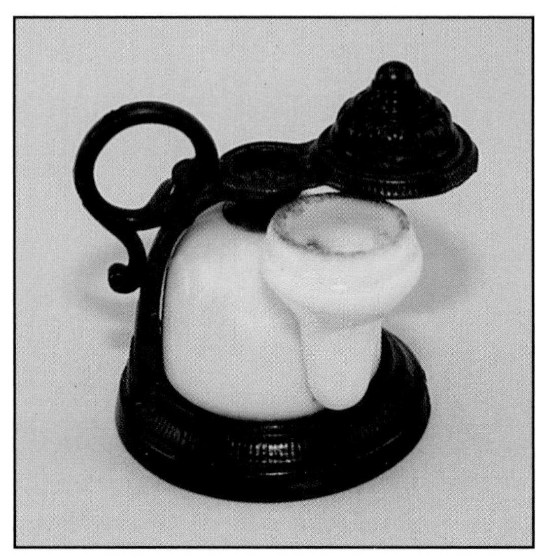

Plate 476
Cast iron cylindrical relief base, gravity feed side swivel milk glass well, dome lid, ring handle, English, 3" diameter x 3⅜" high, c. 1880 – 1890, $300.00 – 350.00, rare. Rodkey collection.

Plate 477
Cast iron frame, Renaissance style with pair of pressed glass snail wells, three pen rests, brass screw finials on revolving apparatus, "USE CONGRESS RECORD INK" imprinted on base, 7¾" x 5¼" x 4¼", c. 1880 – 1890, $200.00 – 250.00. Rodkey collection

Plate 478
Cast iron domed base, black, cushion-shaped reeded body, hard rubber reservoir with metal cover, trumpet-shaped quill pen receiver, stamped "THE CENTURY INKSTAND CO. CANTON, OHIO, PATENT 11233 & 11234, c. 1825," $350.00 – 400.00, scarce. Rodkey collection.

Plate 479
Cast iron circular base with gilt bronze finish, three milk glass swivel snail wells surrounded by open scroll platform, flower finial, American, marked "PAT'D MAY 14, 1878," 6⅞" diameter x 6" high, $350.00 – 400.00, scarce. Rodkey collection.

Plate 480
Cast iron base, hard rubber tops with attached steel quills, clover leaf design for desk or architect's table, c. 1900, $40.00 – 50.00.

Plate 481
Cast iron, patinated finish, Greek inspired relief trim, pressed glass wells with loose covers, recess between wells, 10¾" x 7" x 4½", c. 1890, $125.00 – 150.00. Wherry collection.

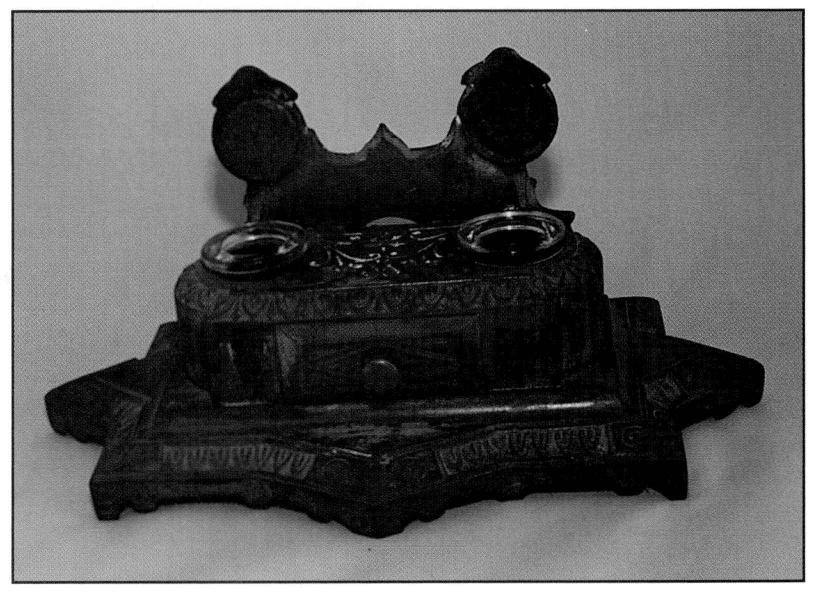

Plate 482
Cast iron with bronze finish, Gothic style, pressed glass wells, flip-top lids, marked Bradley and Hubbard, American, c. 1880, $300.00 – 400.00. Wherry collection.

Plate 483
Cast iron, silver finish, scroll feet, cylindrical retractable cover, triple pen rest at top, Renaissance influence, two pressed glass wells, 4½" x 3⅝" x 5⅛", c. 1880 – 1890, $200.00 – 240.00. Rodkey collection.

Plate 484
Brass plated cast iron, rectangular, low relief decoration, Renaissance style, hinged lids, lobed pressed glass wells, triple pen rest with blotter slot, pierced scrolled support, 8½" x 4¾" x 5¼" high, c. 1880 – 1890, $200.00 – 250.00. Rodkey collection.

Plate 485
Cast iron electro-bronze-plated, right: double model, left: single model. Pressed glass fonts with lobed corners, triple pen rest and blotter slots at rear, hinged lids, open-work sunburst motif in supports, American, c. 1880 – 1890, left: $150.00, right: $200.00 – 250.00. Rodkey collection.

Plate 486
Cast iron nickel-plated with blue glaze, pressed glass snail-shaped reservoir, crenelated top, Gothic style, rounded pen holder, in 1893 McClurg catalog, 2⅝" x 4¼" x 4¼", c. 1880 – 1890, $250.00 – 300.00. Rodkey collection.

Plate 487
Cast iron with incised decoration, Gothic style, triple pen rest, crenelated Gothic gallery, pressed glass well, sponge receptacle and brush cleaner, 8⅛" x 5⅛" x 4½" high, c. 1885, $170.00 – 190.00. Rodkey collection.

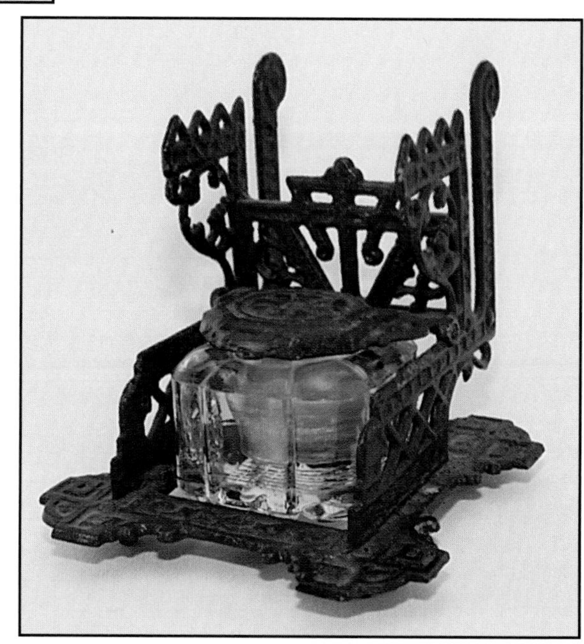

Plate 488
Cast iron irregular shaped base, pressed glass well, lobed contour, hinged lid, triple pen rest above, "TATUM'S BLOTTER INKSTAND," American, 5¼" x 5¼" x 5⅜" high, c. 1880 – 1890, $140.00 – 190.00. Rodkey collection.

Plate 489
Bronzed cast iron base and triple pen rest, cast iron collar with hinged lid on pressed glass well, c. 1880 – 1890, $80.00 – 125.00. Rodkey collection.

Plate 490
Cast iron with distressed bronze finish, Renaissance style, matching hinged lid and glass insert, 3" wide x 3⅞" x 2½", c. 1915 – 1920, $85.00 – 100.00. Thorp collection.

Plate 491
Cast iron with bronze finish, circular saucer-shaped base with a dag design, well has some Renaissance influence, domed hinged top, relief design of leaves on base, c. 1890 – 1900, $85.00 – 125.00. Thorp collection.

Plate 492
Cast iron with brass plating, two milk glass inserts, Gothic influence, pierced paling design on pen rest, roll top desk design, marked Bradley and Hubbard, 5¾" x 4¾" x 3¼", c. 1870 – 1880, $250.00 – 300.00. Wherry collection.

Plate 493
Open picture of Plate 492.

Plate 494
Copper-plated iron with relief classical lyre, Art Nouveau form, neo-Japanese floral trim, attached cylindrical wells with hinged covers, marked "GESHUTZT," 6½" x 4½", c. 1910 – 1915, $150.00 – 175.00. Hummer collection.

Plate 495
Cast brass painted black, with pen rack, ceramic snail type wells, 8" x 5⅜" x 4⅜" high, c. 1880, $200.00 – 285.00. Hummer collection.

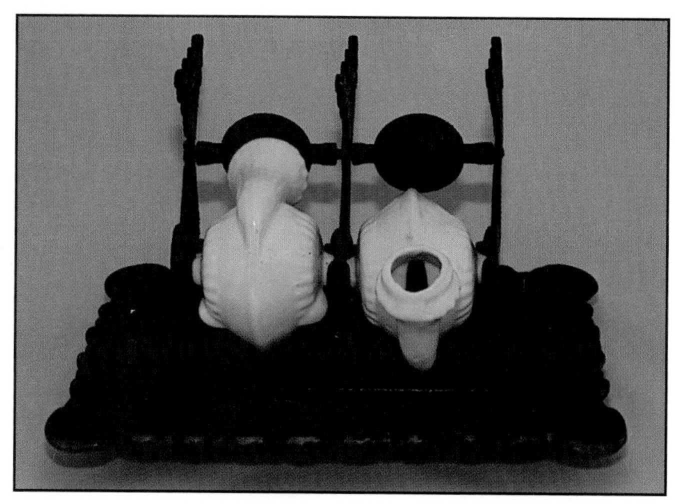

Plate 496
Cast iron with patinated bronze finish, Italian Renaissance style, scroll feet, bead trimmed flange, relief cherubs on side of well, stationary handles on either side, flower bud finial, originally owned by founding president of Colby College, 9" square x 5½" high, c. 1880 – 1890, $160.00 – 220.00. Wherry collection.

Plate 497
Cast iron, copper finish, pierced Rococo design, pressed glass wells with ribbing and horizontal concave channels, loose glass covers, marked "3118–NB" and "IW," 9⅞" x 9⅞", c. 1890 – 1900, $250.00. Hummer collection.

Plate 498
Cast iron lion design, enameled in brown and black, hinged cover, milk glass insert, lion's body forms tray, 10½" x 8½", c. 1890 – 1900, $200.00. Hummer collection.

Plate 499
Cast iron with distressed finish, low relief decoration, Renaissance style, pen channel, hexagon cut glass tapered inset wells with loose covers, marked "DEP. – B.H.S." surrounding eagle insignia, American, 7⅞" x 5⅜", c. 1885 – 1890, $150.00 – 160.00. Hummer collection.

Plate 500
Cast iron with pen channel, six-sided, Italianate della Robbia design in relief, polychrome, fruit and leaves, pressed glass well with loose cover and finial, 5¼" hexagon, c. 1910 – 1920, $125.00 – 150.00. Hummer collection.

Plate 501
Cast iron hotel type, bronze finish, Medieval style, covered recess, cut glass wells with loose conical iron covers with finials, 8" x 6¼" x 5½" high, c. 1890, $150.00 – 200.00. Hummer collection.

Plate 502
Cast iron hotel type, painted black with attached pen rack, stamp box in base with loose cover and finial, pressed glass well, loose cover with finial, 7½" x 5¼" x 3⅞" high, c. 1880 – 1890, $125.00 – 150.00. Hummer collection.

Plate 503
Cast iron, black finish with remnants of green and tan decoration, bulldog and terrier sitting at mailbox, hinged cast iron cover, glass insert, marked "PULL DOWN – LETTERS – U.S. MAIL" on cover plus "4610" marked on base, 5⅝" square, c. 1900, $160.00 – 210.00. Hummer collection.

Plate 504
Cast iron hotel type, dark brown finish, neo-Japanese, attached back plate has crane design in relief and triple pen rack, wells have lobed corners, base has nib tray with loose cover with finial, 2" square pressed glass wells each marked "P.S. & W. CO. PAT DEC. 11, 77," loose cast iron covers with finials, American, 6⅛" x 5" x 5" high, $120.00 – 140.00. Hummer collection.

Plate 505
Cast iron, dark bronze finish, octagonal base with attached pen rack, pressed glass swirl well with loose matching cover, marked on base "BRADLEY & HUBBARD MFG CO.," surrounding an insignia plus "6033–PAT APLD FOR," 4⅞" x 5" high, c. 1890, $95.00 – 120.00. Hummer collection.

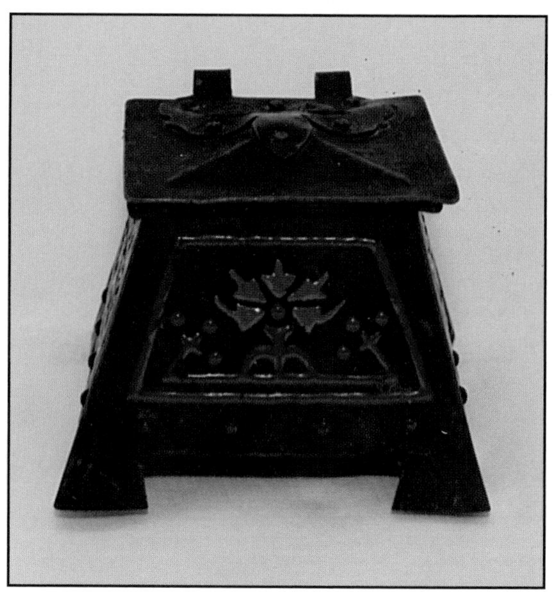

Plate 506
Black painted, hand-crafted copper with riveted base and extended feet, relief enamel design decoration (Japanese form), hinged lid has riveted applied design, marked "The Arts & Crafts Shop" within insignia, 4$\frac{3}{16}$" wide x 3⅛" high, c. 1910, $225.00 – 250.00. Hummer collection.

Plate 507
Cast iron, trifid feet, Greek key and egg in low relief, glass swirl well with 24-point star pattern base, loose square cut glass pyramidal cover, marked "1888" on frame, 3⅜" square, $80.00 – 90.00. Hummer collection.

Plate 508
Cast iron, black, Tatum's revolving snail reservoir, Rococo revival, 3" x 3½" x 3¾", c. 1890, $150.00. Rodkey collection.

Plate 509
Cast iron, Persian style base with pen rack, square pressed glass well with lobed corners, round loose cast iron cover, marked "PRR" on top in relief, 4½" square base, c. late nineteenth century, $85.00 – 90.00. Hummer collection.

Plate 510
Cast iron, polychrome decoration, dish below well is camel-shaped tray, well is pressed glass, waffle bottom with loose cast metal lid, 7" x 5½" x 2½", c. 1920, $185.00 – 200.00. Rodkey collection.

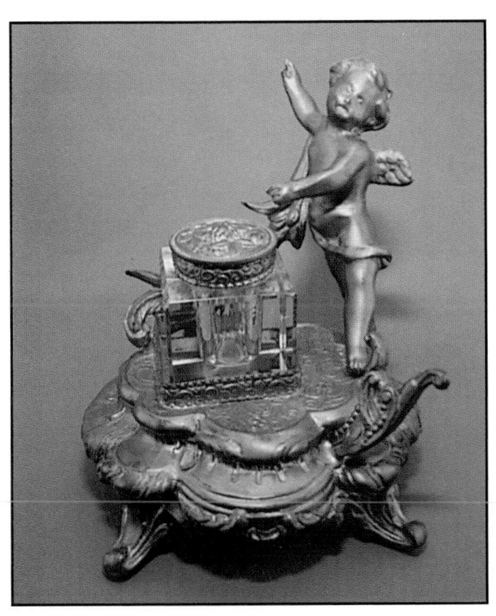

Plate 511
Cast white metal, gilt bronze finish, scroll feet and cherub, Rococo revival, hand cut and hand polished ink bottle, individual cover with rose design, 4¾" x 4¾", c. 1890 – 1900, $190.00 – 200.00.

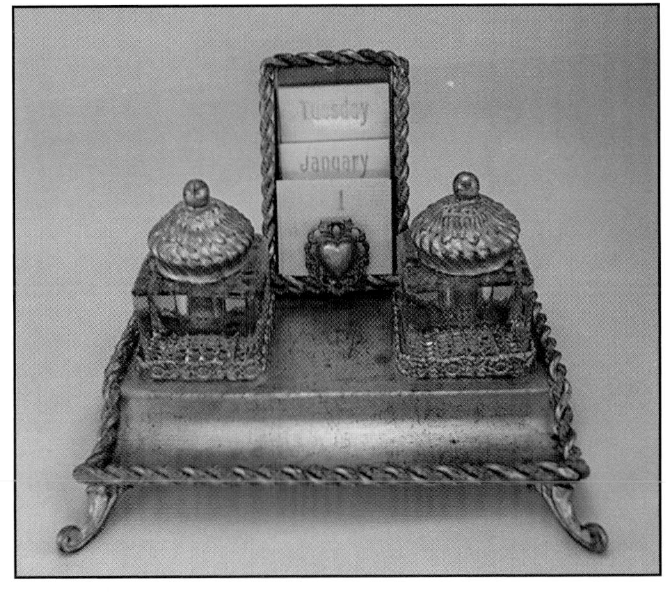

Plate 512
Gilt finish white metal, scroll feet, two pressed glass wells with waffle bottoms, heart with scroll motif in front of calendar, holder in center with celluloid dates, individual lobed domed covers, marked on base "ROYAL M MFG CO," 6½" x 4½" x 4", c. 1880, $150.00 – 175.00.

Plate 513
Tin coal scuttles or hods, decorative hinges in Gothic manner, twisted carrying handle, left is ink well, right has ball feet and is a match holder with striker on front, English, $1\frac{3}{4}$" x $3\frac{1}{2}$" x 3" high, c. late nineteenth century, $150.00 – 175.00 each. Rodkey collection.

Plate 514
Pot metal, silver finish, pen rest across front, projecting stamp box with Arc d' Triomphe on interior of lid, hinged Eiffel Tower cover, Art Deco influence, souvenir, c. 1920, $75.00 – 85.00. Rodkey collection.

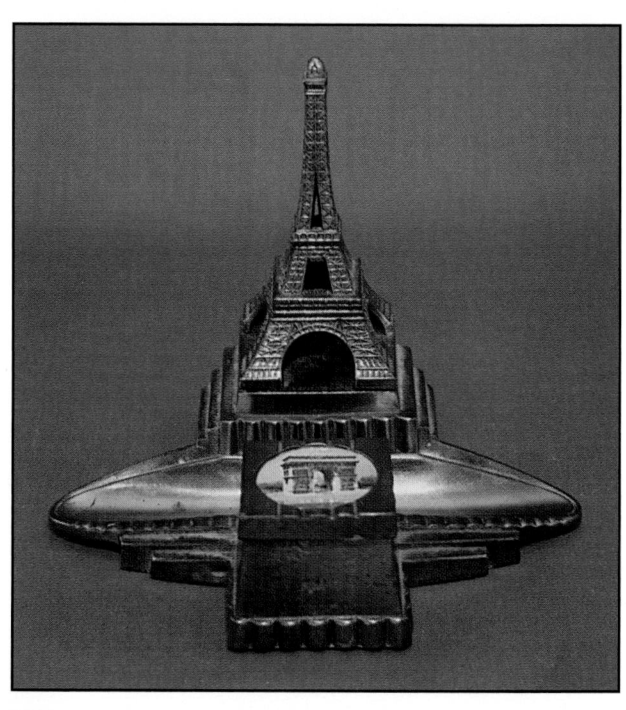

Plate 515
Cast aluminum crab, hand chased decoration, scrolls and flowers, glass insert, $5\frac{1}{2}$" x $5\frac{1}{2}$" x $1\frac{1}{4}$", c. 1900, $200.00 – 225.00. Rodkey collection.

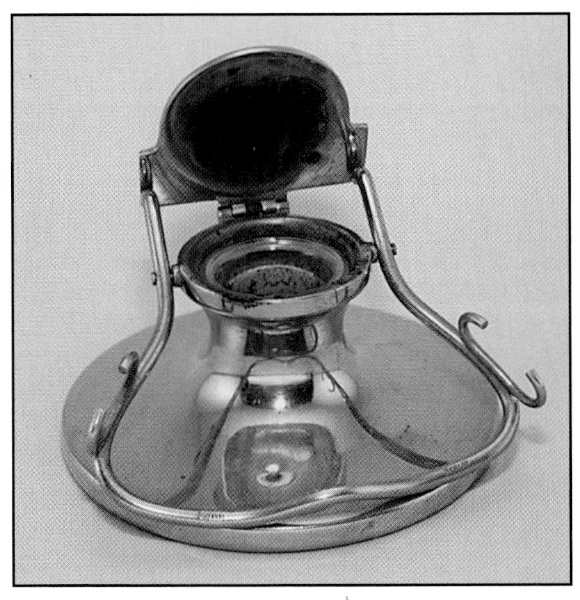

Plate 516
Nickel-plated circular well with concave sides up to flat hinged lid, undulating base with pen rest, pen rest controls movement of the lid, glass insert, 4" diameter x 2" high, c. early twentieth century, $175.00 – 190.00. Rodkey collection.

Plate 517
Same as Plate 516.

Plate 518
Cast white metal, oak tree branch surmounted by two owls with glass eyes, large owl is well, glass insert, 3¾" x 2¼" x 3" high, c. 1900, $150.00 – 175.00. Rodkey collection.

Plate 519
Pewter novelty well, six-sided in shape of weight, black glass insert, 2⅞" x 1⅝", c. mid-nineteenth century, $150.00 – 175.00. Rodkey collection.

Plate 520
Bronze plated pot metal, Art Nouveau contours with floral trim, concave tray across front, calendar frame at rear, green glass insert, 6½" x 5½" x 3" high, c. 1900 – 1910, $200.00 – 250.00. Rodkey collection.

Plate 521
Metal cylindrical wells with flared bases, typical ship's design (for stability), c. early twentieth century, $110.00 – 150.00 each. Rodkey collection.

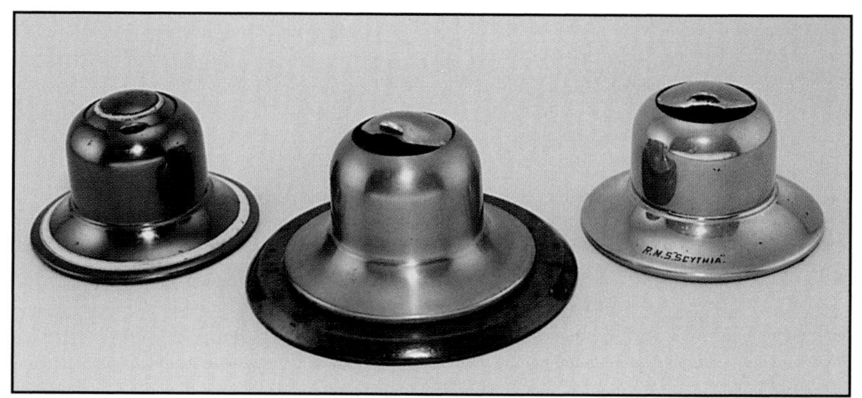

Plate 522
Nickel-plated cylindrical domed top, saucer base with three projecting finials, hard rubber insert, lid recedes, ship's well, 4" x 2½", c. early twentieth century, $160.00. Rodkey collection.

Plate 523
Tin base, patinated bronze finish with floral embellishment, two receptacles with chained lids, one has applied butterfly, Japan, copper inserts, 6½" x 3" x 3" high, c. late nineteenth century, $200.00 – 300.00. Rodkey collection

Plate 524
Brass plated pot metal, rectangular form with pad feet, low relief flowers, souvenir of Washington, D.C., applied plaque with the Capitol Building on it, stag's head antlers form triple pen rest, hinged lid, glass insert, Renaissance style American, 6⅝" x 3¾" x 4½" high, c. 1900, $150.00 – 175.00. Rodkey collection.

Plate 525
Cast pot metal with patinated finish, irregular shaped base, cylindrical well with St. George's head surmounted by dragon, scroll feet, swivel lid marked "ST. LOUIS OCT. 4, 1898," 5½" x 3¾" x 2½" high, $175.00 – 200.00. Rodkey collection.

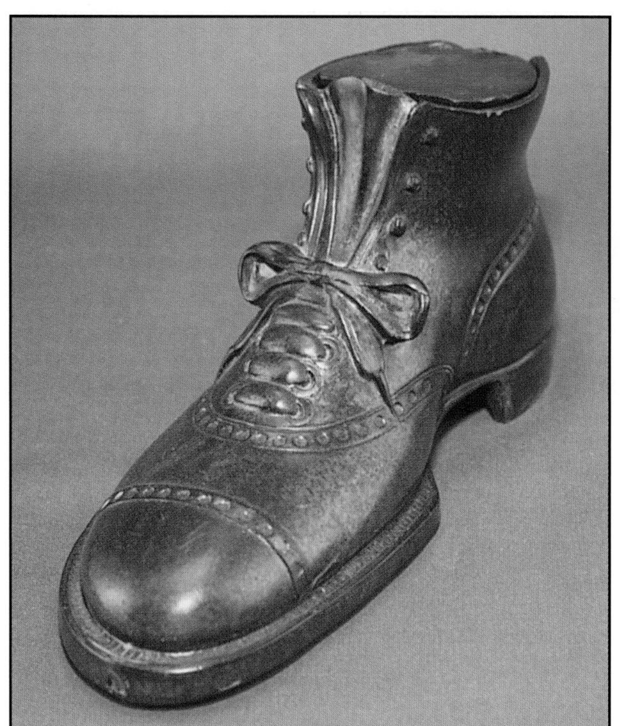

Plate 526
Bronze finish pot metal gentleman's shoe, laced, high-top, hinged flat lid, 6⅝" x 2½" x 3¼" high, c. 1900 – 1910, $160.00 – 200.00. Rodkey collection.

Plate 527
White metal high-top shoe, silver finish, pull tab on back of shoe is lid handle, porcelain insert, 2" x 5½" x 2¾", c. 1890 – 1900, $200.00. Rodkey collection.

Plate 528
Left: cast pot metal, polychrome finish, Indian chief with feather bonnet, stamped "Germany," c. 1900 – 1910, $200.00.
Right: pot metal Indian chief with feather bonnet, applied badge polychrome enamel, Carlsbad Caverns souvenir, glass insert, 3½" x 4", c. 1900 – 1910, $200.00 – 225.00. Rodkey collection.

Plate 529
Pot metal dragoon's helmet, silver-plated, crest is dragon, top of helmet is hinged lid, porcelain insert, European, c. 1880 – 1890, $200.00 – 250.00. Rodkey collection.

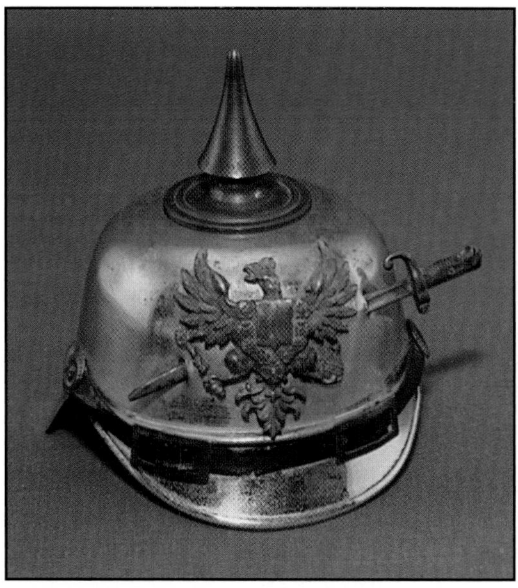

Plate 530
Tin World War I German helmet impaled by English sword, German eagle in relief above visor, top of helmet is loose lid, souvenir, marked ENGLISH VICTORY, glass insert, brass accessories, c. early twentieth century, $325.00 – 375.00. Rodkey collection.

Plate 531
Bronze finish pot metal doghouse with English bulldog projecting from front, porcelain insert, American, 2 x 2⅛" x 2⅜", c. 1910, $125.00 – 150.00. Rodkey collection.

Plate 532
Shield-shaped wooden base with applied metal shield, pot metal partial suit of armor with helm, face guard swivels to expose bearded male, head tilts back to expose well, Medieval style, marked "BRENETE SDGG," French, c. 1890, $225.00 – 275.00. Rodkey collection.

Plate 533

Bronze pot metal, back pen rest projecting Arc d' Triomphe, La Sacre Coeur, hinged Eiffel Tower cover, Art Deco influence, souvenir, 5⅝" x 3¾" x 4⅜", c. 1920, $120.00 – 140.00. Rodkey collection.

Plate 534

Pot metal, La Sacre Coeur, cover of well has sepia tone picture of Eiffel Tower, Paris souvenir, bottom stamped "DEPOSE 201," pot metal insert, 5¼" x 4¼" x 5¼", c. 1920, $110.00 – 120.00. Rodkey collection.

Plate 535

Pot metal, rectangular platform with projecting pen rest across front, eight-sided wells with photographic tops under glass, souvenir, Le Sacre Coeur in center, Art Deco influence, pot metal inserts, 8¼" x 3¾" x 5⅛", c. 1920, $110.00 – 120.00. Rodkey collection.

Plate 536
Bronze finish pot metal fire hydrant, marked "FIRE ASSOCIATION OF PHILADELPHIA, 1817 – 1917," souvenir, glass insert, 4¼" x 3¼", $150.00 – 175.00. Rodkey collection.

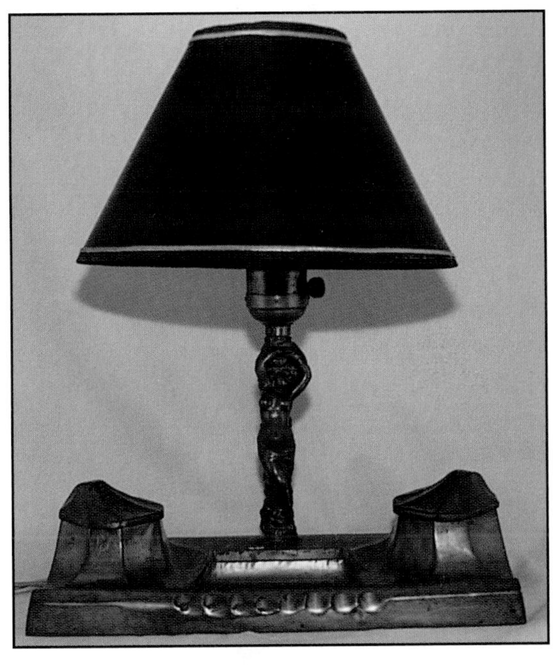

Plate 537
Cast white metal, antique bronze finish, nude woman forms lamp base, Art Deco influence, c. 1920, $200.00 – 300.00. Wherry collection.

Plate 538
Plaster of Paris barrel-shaped well with clover-shaped glass finial stopper, glass bottle insert, 2⅛" x 2¾" high, c. 1890, $60.00 – 65.00. Rodkey collection.

Plate 539
Wooden grip miniature pistol with metal mounts, ink bottle in cylinder holder, pen is butt ring, pencil in barrel, 5" long, c. 1890 – 1900, $185.00 – 250.00. Rodkey collection.

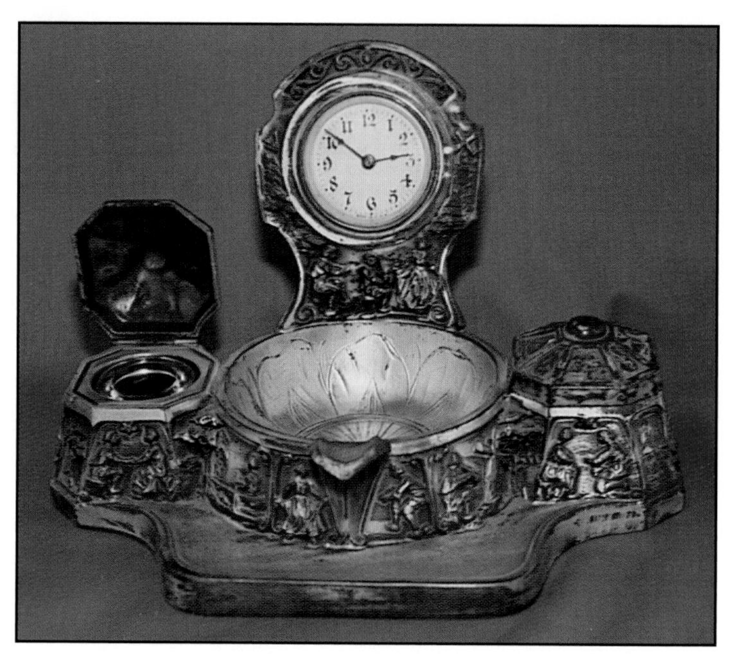

Plate 540
Silver-plated cast spelter, relief ladies and gentlemen in period costume, recessed ashtray flanked by hinged wells, surmounted by a clock, pressed glass wells, American, 9⅜" x 6¼" x 6", c. 1920, $225.00 – 275.00. Wherry collection.

Plate 541
White metal with gilt finish, Rococo style with cherub, pressed glass well, loose cover with bead trim finial, 1¾" square x 2½" high, c. 1890 – 1900, $130.00 – 150.00. Wherry collection.

Plate 542
Pot metal with dark patinated finish, thermometer has "FAHRENHEIT, BUFFALO, N.Y., H.D. & CO" in center, hinged lid, glass insert, 6" x 3¾", c. 1880 – 1890, $150.00 – 175.00. Wherry collection.

Plate 543
Pressed red flash glass wells, silver-plated base is Empire style, foliate feet surmounted by acanthus leaves, urn-shaped sponge holder in center, 9" x 4" x 4", c. 1900, $200.00 – 275.00. Wherry collection.

Plate 544
Cast pot metal, deliberately distressed alligator finish, ocher color enamel finish, pressed glass swirl wells, missing covers, cherub in center playing lyre, relief flowers that decorate stand have touches of color, 6½" x 2½" x 5¾", c. 1900, $95.00 – 120.00 as is. Wherry collection.

Plate 545

Cast white metal, antique bronze finish, subject is neo-Chinese, gentleman with peaked hat, hat is lid, stamped "650TH CONSECUTIVE PERFORMANCE HOYT'S THEATRE, TRIP TO MADISON SQ. THEATRE CHINATOWN AUG 7, 1893," green glass insert, $5\frac{3}{4}$" x 3", \$250.00 – 300.00. Wherry collection.

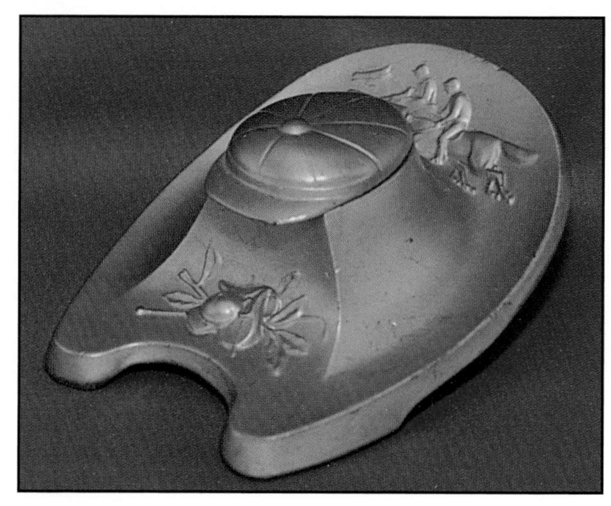

Plate 546

Metal with distressed gilt finish, relief polo players and polo emblem, hinged polo cap cover and porcelain insert, marked "DEPOSE-278," $3\frac{7}{8}$" x $5\frac{1}{4}$" x $1\frac{3}{8}$" high, \$150.00 – 175.00. Hummer collection.

Plate 547

Cast white metal with polychrome decoration, tree stump with stag, Germany, $3\frac{3}{4}$" x $2\frac{1}{4}$" x 3", c. 1900, \$150.00 – 175.00. Wherry collection.

Plate 548
Pewter saucer base, amber colored swirl glass well threaded into base, French, 5" diameter x 1½" high, c. 1890, $150.00 – 175.00. Wherry collection.

Plate 549
Silver-plated pot metal, Renaissance style, central motif is flaming torch in relief surrounded by basket of flowers and a cascade of fabric, Depose, French, 8" x 6¼" x 2¾", c. 1910 – 1920, $90.00 – 100.00. Wherry collection.

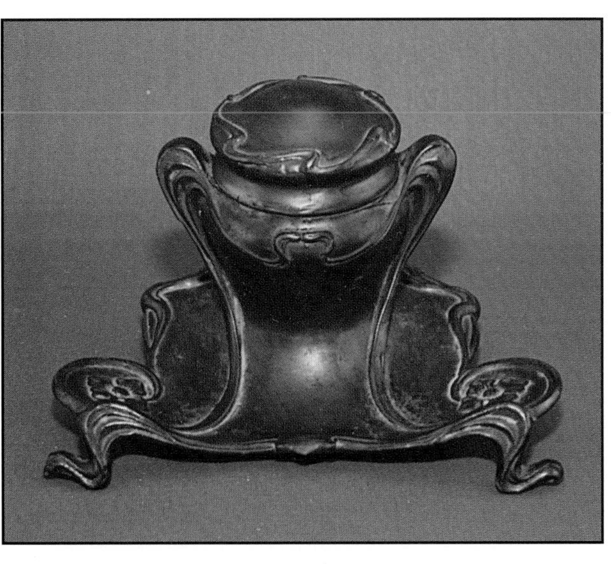

Plate 550
Cast white metal with patinated bronze finish, Art Nouveau, relief decoration with floral trim, hinged matching lid, footed base with pen rest, milk glass insert, c. 1900 – 1910, $120.00 – 150.00. Thorp collection.

Plate 551
Cast white metal of short-haired dachshund with bow tied around his neck, polychrome enamel finish, hinged head, milk glass insert, c. 1890 – 1900, $125.00 – 150.00. Thorp collection.

Plate 552
Cast metal with patinated bronze finish, hinged matching lid and glass insert, lid is marked "SEAL OF THE NATIONAL COMMERCIAL BANK OF ALBANY, N.Y.," center of lid depicts Columbus and his men on board a ship with a banner under the crest with the words "FORTITER FIDELITER FELICITER A.D.," dated 1825, $165.00 – 175.00. Thorp collection.

Plate 553
Silver-plated cast metal flower form saucer base, pressed glass well with waffle bottom, domed lid with relief scrolls, c. 1890 – 1900, $75.00 – 85.00. Thorp collection.

Plate 554
White metal with pen tray, well holder and attached Eiffel Tower, Art Deco, souvenir type, hinged metal cover and insert, marked on base "MADE IN FRANCE 279–PC" plus cover with picture "PARIS L'ARC DE TRIOMPHE," $4\frac{7}{8}$" x $4\frac{1}{8}$" x 4" high, c. 1900, $80.00 – 90.00. Hummer collection.

Plate 555
Pewter, drip pan and double pen rest, Bakelite Sengbusch self-closing insert, marked on bottom "PROPERTY OF THE WALDORF ASTORIA 4, INSICO PEWTER," 6¾" diameter, c. early twentieth century, $200.00 – 250.00. Thorp collection.

Plate 556
Pot metal, originally silver-plated, now gilded, pressed glass well with waffle bottom, pyramidal pressed glass lid, Rococo style, 6" x 4" x 3", c. 1890 – 1900, $60.00.

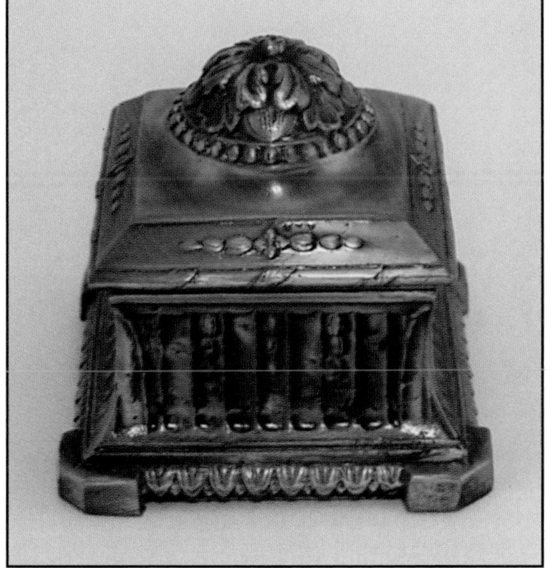

Plate 557
Cast metal, classical Renaissance style with acanthus leaves, hinged matching cover with glass insert, 3¹⁄₁₆" square x 2¾" high, c. 1905, $75.00 – 95.00. Hummer collection.

Plate 558
Gold finish metal with well holder, Art Nouveau, high relief floral motif, pressed glass well, flower topped lid, 4" x 3⅝" x 2" high, c. 1900, $60.00 – 80.00. Hummer collection.

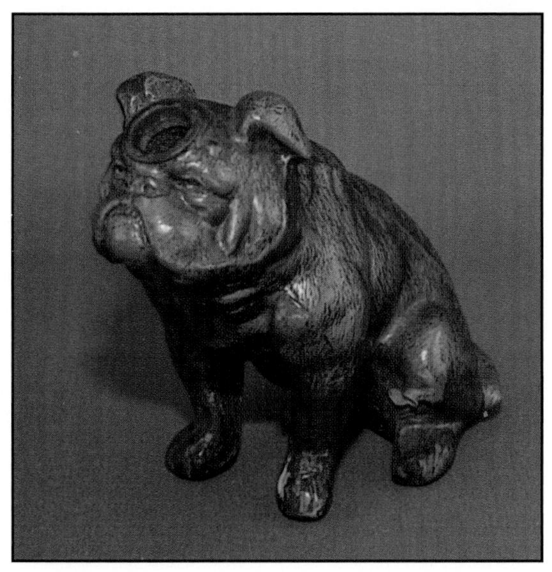

Plate 559
White metal with bronze finish, English bulldog pen holder, marked on bottom "PATENTED A.M.W., NEWARK, N.J.," 3⅛" high, c. 1905, $100.00 – 135.00. Thorp collection.

Plate 560
Cast white metal with gilt finish, oval in contour with scroll feet, pierced scroll decoration on the lower portion, relief dragon decoration on hinged cover, Japanese export, two milk glass inserts, c. early twentieth century, $100.00 – 135.00. Thorp collection.

Plate 561
Gilt finish metal tray, swirl well with hinged cover, attached pen rack, Rococo style, 6½" x 4⅜" x 2⅛" high, c. 1890 – 1900, $100.00 – 125.00. Hummer collection.

Plate 562
Brass-plated pot metal, square in contour with frontal pen rest and hinged lid, George III style, oval medallions on sides, milk glass insert, marked "J.B. 1605," 3⅛" square x 2½", c. 1910, $95.00 – 120.00. Rodkey collection.

Plate 563
White metal, horse head-shaped, equestrian well, enameled finish in natural colors, porcelain insert, American, 2" x 2⅞" x 3⅛" high, c. 1890 – 1900, $200.00 – 300.00. Hummer collection.

Plate 564
Gold-tone pot metal, square contour, architectural bank building "CITY NATIONAL BANK, DALLAS, TEXAS. SURPLUS AND PROFITS 4 MILLION 3 HUNDRED THOUSAND DOLLARS," souvenir, 3¼" square x 2½" high, c. early twentieth century, $80.00 – 100.00. Rodkey collection.

Plate 565
Metal well holder with pen rack, relief flower form lid, pressed glass well with lattice base, remnants of gilt, 3⅛" high, c. 1890, $60.00 – 70.00. Hummer collection.

Plate 566
Nickel-plated cylindrical well attached to oval early fiber type material base, hinged dome-shaped matching cover, brass insert, 3⅞" x 2¾" base x 2⅝" high, c. early twentieth century, $85.00. Hummer collection.

Plate 567
Gilt finish metal holding pressed glass well with lattice base, filigree of scroll and flower forms, square faceted stopper cover with applied cork, marked on top "PAT APLD FOR," 1¹³⁄₁₆" square base x 2¾" high, c. 1905, $85.00 – 95.00. Hummer collection.

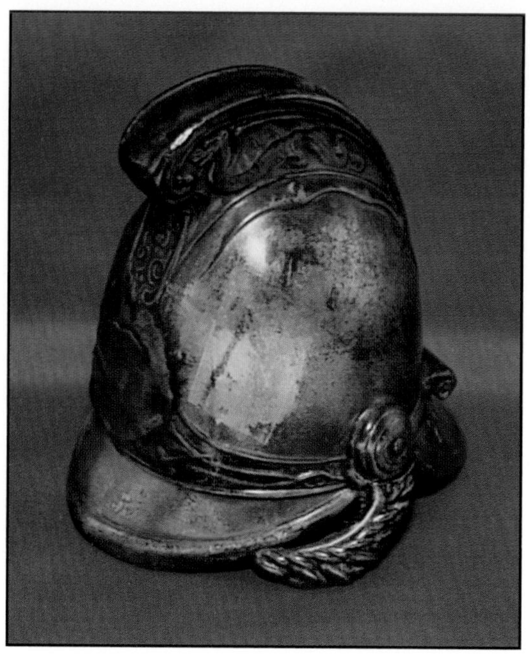

Plate 568
Silver finish metal, dragoon's helmet with Roman influence, porcelain insert, 3½" x 3⅝" x 3¾" high, c. 1880, $185.00 – 195.00. Hummer collection.

Plate 569
Bronze finish metal, swirl style, red felt base, hinged matching cover with finial, cobalt blue insert, 3⅜" diameter base x 3" high, c. early twentieth century, $90.00 – 100.00. Hummer collection.

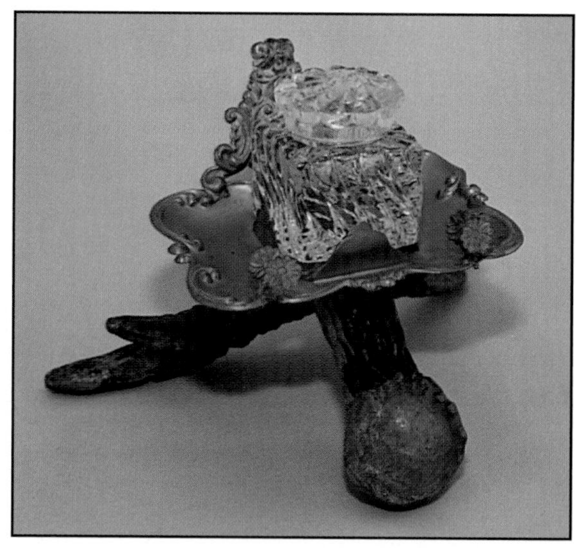

Plate 570
Brass coated tray with pen rack, Rococo embellishment, tray and well swivel on faux staghorn, swirl well with matching cover, 3⅞" wide tray, c. 1890, $110.00 – 130.00. Hummer collection.

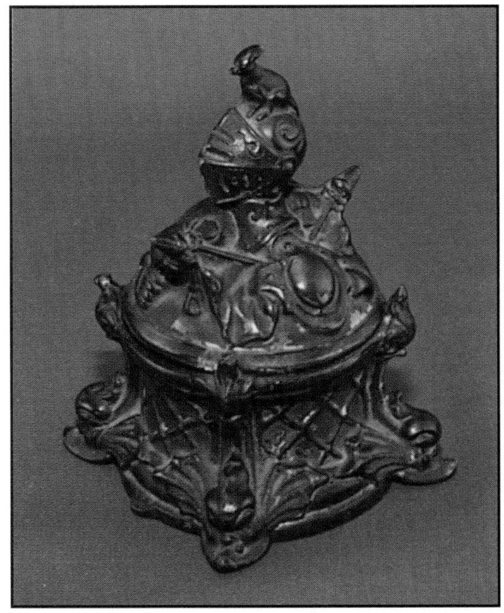

Plate 571
Cast white metal, elaborate Baroque design, dolphin-shaped corners, lid surmounted by armor and helmet with animal finial, c. 1900 – 1910, $85.00 – 125.00. Rodkey collection.

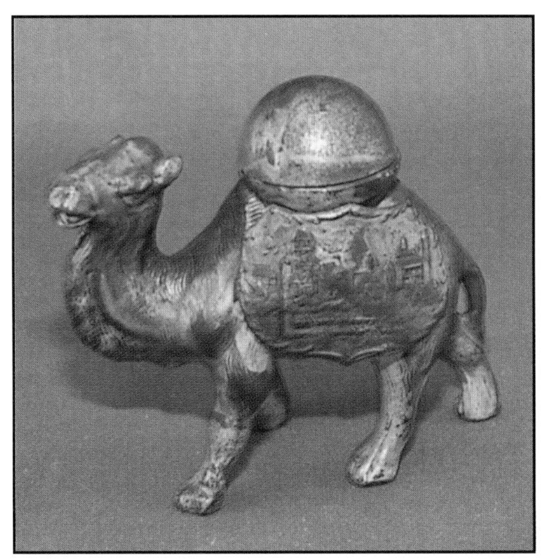

Plate 572
Cast white metal, gilt surface, camel-shaped, stamped metal dome lid, souvenir of "THE BELGIAN VILLAGE, CHICAGO WORLD'S FAIR," made in Japan, 3" high, c. 1893, $100.00 – 120.00. Rodkey collection.

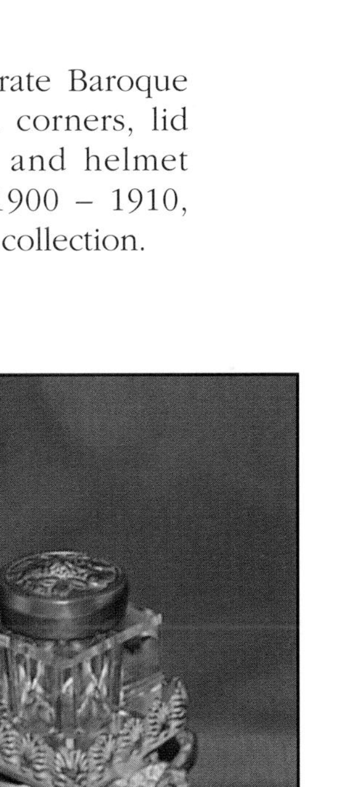

Plate 573
Gold finish metal with figural cupid, pen rack and well holder, Rococo style, foliate feet, Greek anthemion gallery, clear cut glass well with loose brass cover, $5\frac{5}{8}$" x 3" x $4\frac{3}{8}$" high, c. 1890 – 1900, $150.00 – 175.00. Hummer collection.

Plate 574
Gilt finish metal, four-footed with figural American bison heads and well holder, paw feet, pressed glass well with waffle bottom, loose metal cover with American bison in relief, $3\frac{1}{2}$" x $2\frac{5}{8}$", c. 1900, $150.00 – 175.00. Hummer collection.

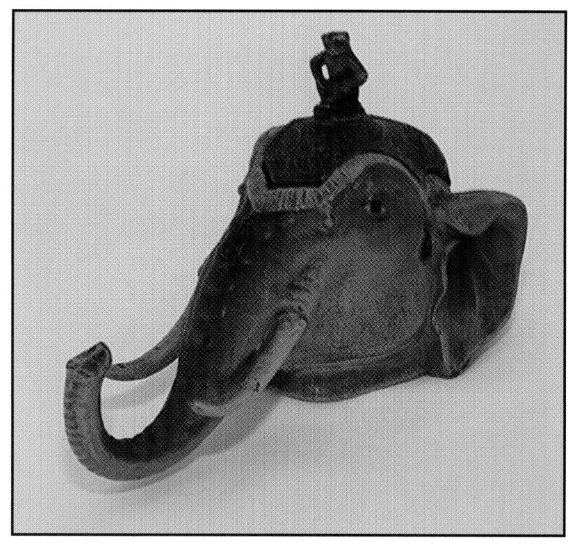

Plate 575
White metal circus elephant head with tusks serving as pen rack, enameled gray, tan and brown, hinged metal cover with figural monkey, glass insert, $3\frac{1}{8}$" x 6" x 4" high, c. 1900, $300.00 – 400.00. Hummer collection.

Plate 576
Polished pewter with flared base, three quill holes and hinged matching cover with finial, pewter insert, marked "WILLIAMSBURG STEIFF PEWTER – C.W.78.3," plus "WILLIAMSBURG RESTORATION–C.W.," $4\frac{3}{4}$" diameter base x $2\frac{1}{2}$" high, c. 1930 – 1940, $150.00 – 175.00. Hummer collection.

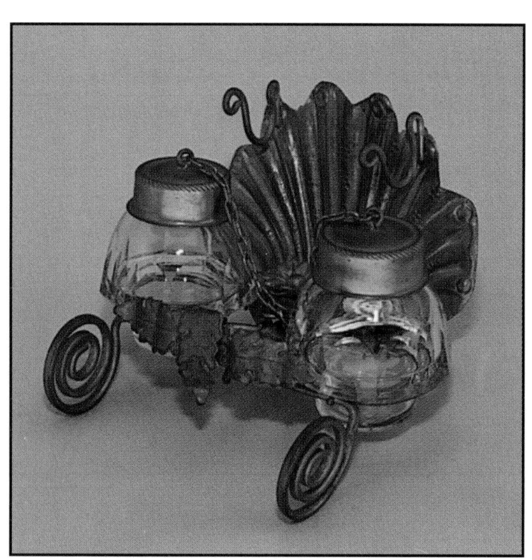

Plate 577
Gold finish metal with pen rack and well holder, cut glass wells, loose matching covers with connecting chains, wire spirals as feet, back support is scallop shell, possibly French, $3\frac{5}{16}$" x $4\frac{1}{2}$" x $2\frac{7}{8}$" high, c. 1890 – 1900, $150.00. Hummer collection.

Plate 578
Brass finish with design in relief, hinged brass matching cover, opalescent glass insert, front of well says "1862–1912 –H.H. GEILFUSS & SON, PHILIP J. GEILFUSS, PHILADELPHIA, PA, COMMEMORATIVE," Rococo embellishment, American, $125.00. Hummer collection.

Plate 579

Gold finish metal with Capitol Building pen rack and well holders, loose brass covers, foliate feet, Rococo influence, wells have galleries around them that are Greek anthemions, wells are crystal with beveled edges, 6⅝" x 4" x 4" high, c. 1890 – 1900, $200.00 – 225.00. Hummer collection.

Plate 580

Cast white metal with polychrome enamel finish, man pulling rickshaw holding pressed glass eight-sided inset well, hinged silver finish metal collar, crown glass cover, neo-Japanese, 5" wide, c. 1885 – 1890, $185.00 – 200.00. Hummer collection.

Plate 581

Dull copper finish, pad feet, Arts and Crafts movement, stylized Celtic decoration, glass insert, marked on base "B & H" in insignia plus "3183," American, 10½" x 7", c. 1905 – 1910, $175.00. Hummer collection.

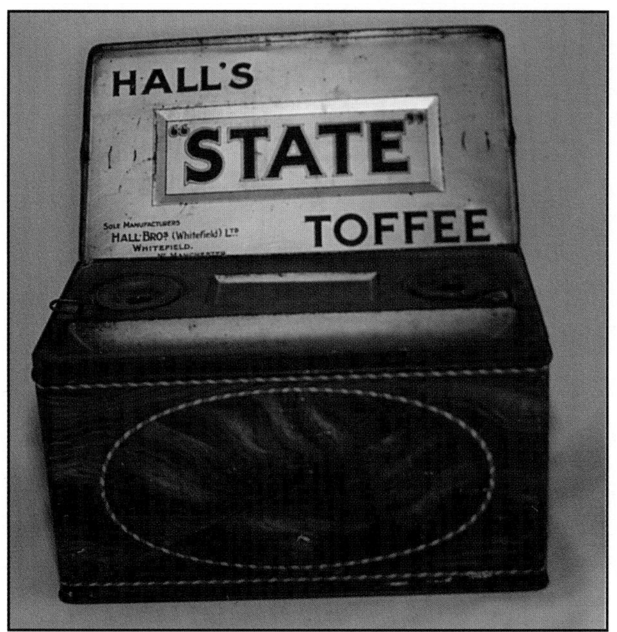

Plate 582
Lithographed tin box with wood grain, Hall's State Toffee, Manchester, brown pottery inserts, English, c. 1900 – 1910, $200.00 – 300.00. Wherry collection.

Plate 583
Metal figural animals, left: pug dog with swirl metal lid on ribbed glass well, middle: kitten attached to tree trunk, polychrome enamel, hinged metal cover, right: gray European hare with ribbed glass well and swirl metal cover, c. 1890 – 1900, $150.00 – 200.00 each. Hummer collection.

Plate 584
Gold finish white metal with figural cupid, hand-polished crystal well with loose cover, Rococo influence, pen rack, 4¾" wide x 5½" high, c. 1900, $185.00 – 200.00. Hummer collection.

Plate 585
Brass-plated tray with floral design, opaque glass well with hinged brass cover and design in relief, Art Nouveau, gilt finish, 6" x 4⅛", c. 1900 – 1910, $90.00 – 110.00. Hummer collection.

Plate 586
Nickel-plated metal base, frontal pen rest, hinged domed covers with flower and foliate design, egg-shaped finials, Renaissance style, possibly German, 6¾" x 5⅜" x 2¼", c. 1890 – 1900, $150.00 – 175.00. Rodkey collection.

Plate 587
Brass-plated pot metal, gilt embellishment, casket-shaped, chrysanthemum trimmed apron, scroll feet, lid in high relief tropical foliage, two milk glass wells and pen wipe holder, frontal pen rest, Japanese, c. 1900 – 1910, $150.00 – 175.00. Rodkey collection.

Plate 588
Same as Plate 587.

Wood, Stone, Plastic & Miscellaneous

Plate 589
Soapstone, open type with three quill holes, hand carved figural and trees, possibly European, 2¾" x 1¾" x 1⅜", c. 1900, $60.00 – 100.00. Hummer collection.

Plate 590
Alabaster mottled in brown and tan, brass hinged matching cover, 2¹³⁄₁₆" diameter x 2½" high, c. 1890 – 1900, $125.00 – 150.00. Hummer collection.

Plate 591
Wood, hand-carved, antelope under fir tree, well container holding glass bottle, pen channel, marked "APPENZELL," souvenir, Germany, cover missing, 4½" x 2⅝" x 6" high, c. 1890 – 1910, $150.00 – 190.00. Hummer collection.

Plate 592
Marble, dark, apple-shaped, light veined with loose lid, ball finial, 2⅝" x 3", c. early twentieth century, $150.00 – 175.00. Rodkey collection.

Plate 593
Dark mottled stone bottom, quartz cover, silver hinged collar, 2⅜" x 1½" x 2⅛" high, c. 1900, $80.00 – 100.00. Hummer collection.

Plate 594
Jade, inkpot, green translucent serpentine, hand carved, Chinese, Ching Dynasty, 1⅝" diameter x ¾" high, c. 1860, $400.00 – 500.00. Hummer collection.

Plate 595
Bakelite, cylindrical, black with flat slip-in cover that screws onto glass insert, has loose marble stopper, marked on base "SQUIRES INKWELL CO–PITTSBURGH, PA, USA," 2$\frac{7}{16}$" diameter x 2" high, c. 1900, $75.00 – 100.00. Hummer collection.

Plate 596
Black and green marble base, pen cleaner brush, French Empire style, gilt bronze, 3" square base, c. 1900, $60.00 – 65.00. Hummer collection.

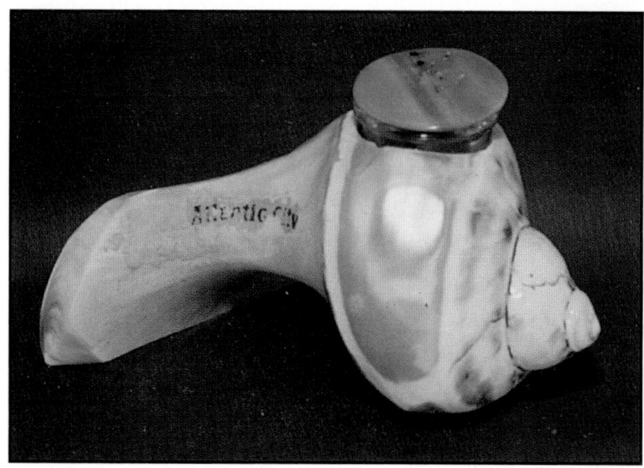

Plate 597
Seashell with brass hinged shell cover, Turk's head shell, glass insert marked "RPN CO," shell marked "SOUVENIR OF ATLANTIC CITY," 4¾" wide, c. 1900, $35.00 – 45.00. Hummer collection.

Plate 598
Light gray and tan marble base with pen channel, attached cylindrical wells with brass-hinged matching cover, four brass feet, glass inserts, separate rocker blotter and nib holder, 16¾" x 9½", c. 1900, $200.00 – 250.00. Hummer collection.

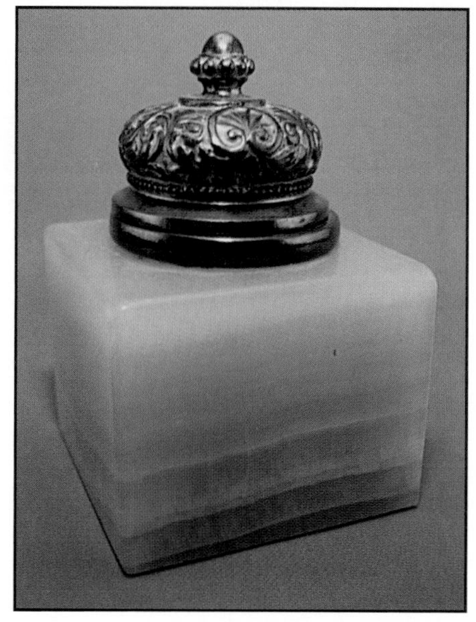

Plate 599
Onyx with bronze mounts, Greek motif, hinged bronze collar and cover with bead trim finial, 2½" square x 3½" high, c. 1890 – 1900, $80.00 – 90.00.

Plate 600
Dark brown hard fiber tray with attached pen holders and four brass feet, cut glass inset well with block and triangle faceted panels, loose polished brass cover, glass insert, 6⅞" x 4⅝" x 4½" high, c. 1900 – 1910, $85.00 – 90.00. Hummer collection.

Plate 601
Dark brown composition base with pen channel and felt bottom, black amethyst glass wells with loose flanged dome-shaped cover and Bakelite screw-on stopper, loose black amethyst pen dip, paper label on base "SENGBUSCH," 8⅞" x 6¾" base, c. early twentieth century, $95.00 – 120.00. Hummer collection.

Plate 602
Green, black, and white eight-sided marble base with pen channel, attached are two metal birds (possibly finches) and well container with hinged cover, distressed silver finish, Adam style, glass insert, 9" x 7" x 4" high, c. 1900, $185.00 – 195.00. Hummer collection.

Plate 603
Composition with three-tier pen ledge, brown with matching loose covers, glass flanged inserts, base marked "FRANK A. WEEKS MFG CO, NEW YORK U.S.A. PARAGON NO. 410," covers marked "PARAGON 1256," inserts marked "PARAGON," 5" x 4¾" x 3" high, c. 1900 – 1910, $50.00 – 60.00. Hummer collection.

Plate 604
Alabaster with palmette feet, pen tray and well recesses, hand-painted floral decoration with blue trim, pressed glass inset umbrella wells, loose alabaster covers, lattice work and flowers, Italian, 4¼" x 2⅝", c. 1860 – 1870, $150.00 – 175.00. Hummer collection.

Plate 605
Mottled onyx, base has pen channel and four brass ball feet, attached matching well and brass hinged cover, two-piece glass insert, marked "MADE IN GERMANY," 10½" x 6⅝", c. 1905 – 1910, $100.00 – 120.00. Hummer collection.

Plate 606
Soapstone, single dip hole, early American, 2¼" x 1½", c. 1850, $90.00 – 125.00. Thorp collection.

Plate 607
Alabaster, vase-shaped, bulbous, 2¼" high x 3¼" diameter, c. early twentieth century, $60.00 – 70.00. Thorp collection.

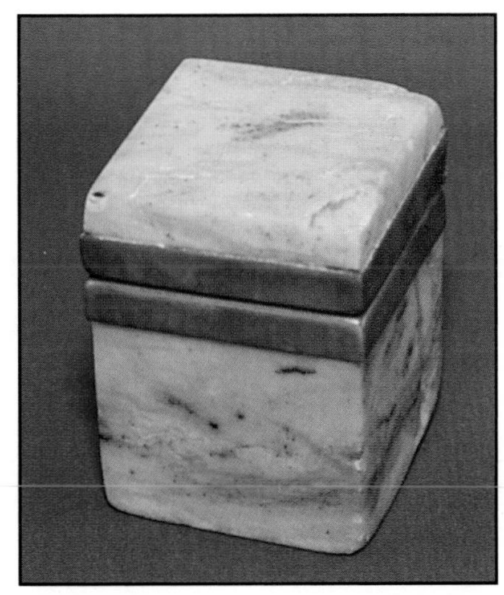

Plate 608
Marble cube with brass mounts, hinged lid, white marble veined in gray and ocher, 2⅛" high x 1⅝" wide, c. 1890 – 1900, $125.00. Thorp collection.

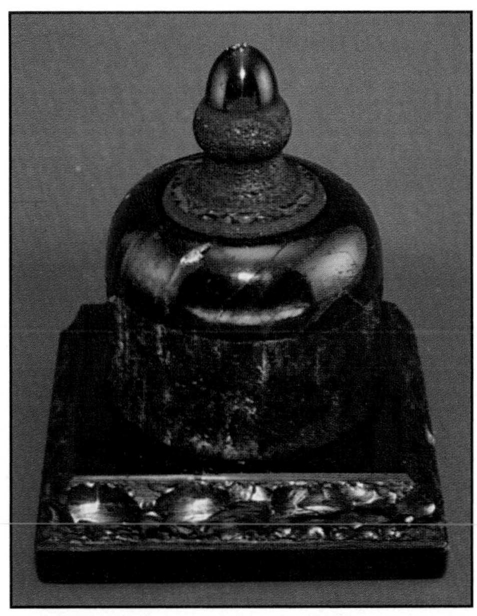

Plate 609
Square based, carved anthracite with domed lid and acorn finial, American, c. early twentieth century, $100.00 – 120.00. Thorp collection.

Plate 610
Circular marble base, polished crystal well with brass mounts, lid is onyx, standing on base is cast metal Arab trader holding an elephant tusk, c. 1920, $150.00 – 175.00. Thorp collection.

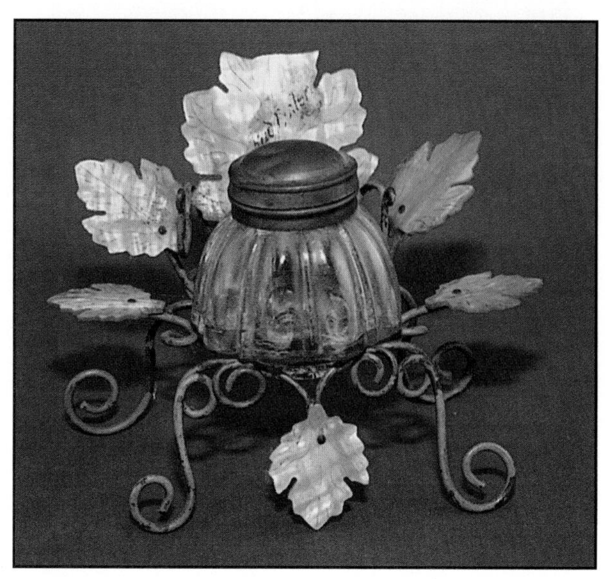

Plate 611
Enameled brass scrolled wire with mother-of-pearl leaves, pressed glass lobed well with hinged brass domed lid, souvenir, pen rest, c. 1870 – 1880, $150.00 – 175.00. Thorp collection.

Plate 612
Square, tapered, covered with geological specimens that are numbered, stones including agates, etc., brass hinged collar with faceted crystal top, c. 1890 – 1900, $150.00 – 175.00. Thorp collection.

Plate 613
Enameled brass and scrolled wire with mother-of-pearl leaves, pressed glass lobed well with hinged brass domed lid, has two attached shell dishes, souvenir, c. 1870 – 1880, $150.00 – 175.00. Thorp collection.

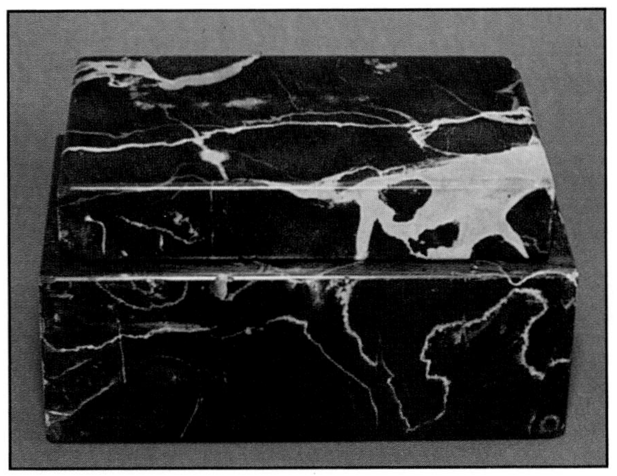

Plate 614
Light ocher veined deep gray marble, rectangular double inkwell, Art Deco influence, c. early twentieth century, $150.00 – 175.00. Thorp collection.

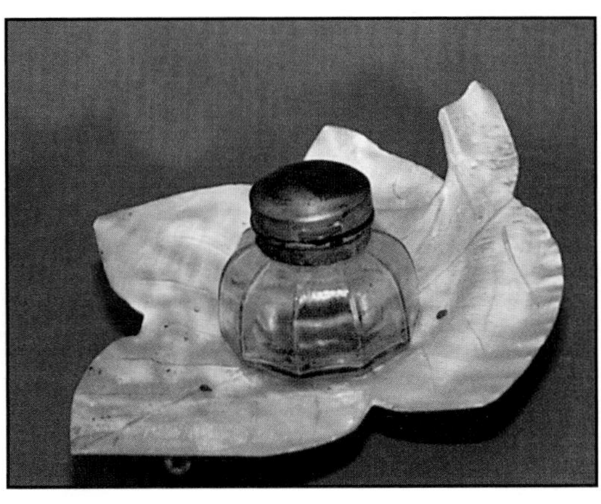

Plate 615
Mother-of-pearl maple leaf with incised veining, brass ball feet, fluted pressed glass well with hinged cover, 5" x 4" x 2", c. 1900, $75.00 – 85.00. Wherry collection.

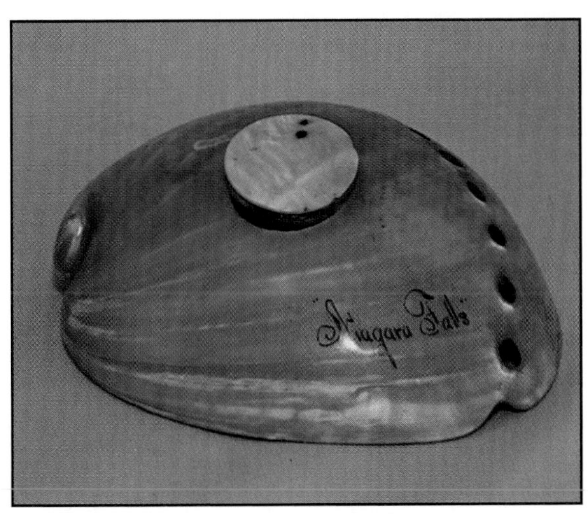

Plate 616
Abalone shell, lid on well is mother-of-pearl, souvenir of Niagara Falls, hinged lid, 5" x 4" x 1½", c. 1900 – 1910, $80.00 – 90.00. Wherry collection.

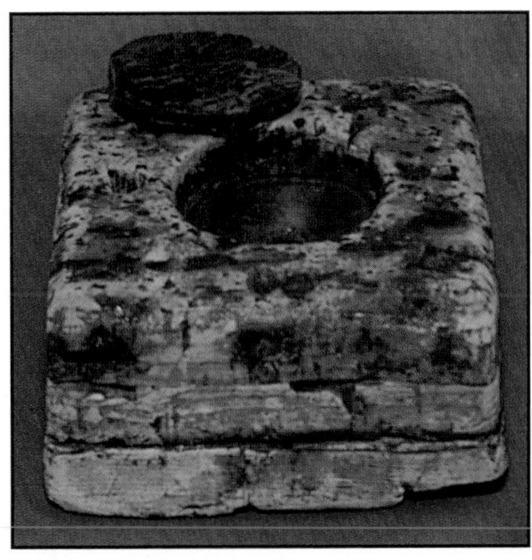

Plate 617
Cork, blown glass insert, loose lid is leather, possibly Spanish or Portuguese, 3" square x 1½" high, c. 1850 – 1870, $150.00. Wherry collection.

Plate 618
Bakelite base, recess containing boxed equipment and central pressed glass bottle with cork closure, frontal pen rest, Art Deco influence, c. 1920 – 1930, $150.00 – 175.00. Rodkey collection.

Plate 619
Bakelite base with glass wells and recessed receptacle and pen rest, Esterbrook model #427, Art Deco influence, 8¾" x 5⅞" x 2¼" high, c. 1930, $125.00 – 150.00. Rodkey collection.

Plate 620
Left: Bakelite, black with glass well, original dip pen and beaded chain, Esterbrook #407; right: Bakelite, brown with glass well, original pen with nib #9550, Esterbrook #407, 4" x 5½" x 2¼" high, c. 1930, $65.00 – 75.00 each. Rodkey collection.

Plate 621
Papier-mache over inlays of mother-of-pearl, translucent enamel hand painted, recessed pen tray, pressed glass well, Moorish spiral dome cover, English, c. mid nineteenth century, $350.00. Smith collection.

Plate 622
Ceramic circular base with tiered collar, upright plastic cylindrical reservoir with glass bottle insert, gravity feed to pen receiver, mottled red/purple with matching pen, Art Deco, American, 3⅞" x 4⅜", c. 1930 – 1940, $95.00. Rodkey collection.

Plate 623
Black ceramic circular base, upright plastic cylindrical reservoir with glass bottle insert, gravity feed to pen receiver with matching pen, Art Deco, "FOUNT-O-INK," American, c. 1930 – 1940, $85.00. Rodkey collection.

Plate 624
Plastic base with two upright wells, one green and one red, Art Deco, American, 7½" x 5¼" x 4¼", c. 1930, $100.00. Rodkey collection.

Plate 625
Plastic, Morriset Model B with Morriset 2½ oz. glass bottles, matching pens, Art Deco, American, 3⅛" x 3⅞" x 3⅜", c. 1930, $80.00 – 90.00 each. Rodkey collection.

Plate 626
Black plastic base with plastic cylindrical covers, glass bottle inserts, Sengbusch, Art Deco, American, 3½" x 3¼", c. 1930, $60.00 – 80.00 each. Rodkey collection.

Plate 627
Early Carter advertisement. Rodkey collection.

Plate 628
Hard plastic (Carter cubes), left: red; center: blue; and right: mottled brown, Art Deco, American, 4" x 5" x 3¾", c. 1930, $85.00 each, Rodkey collection.

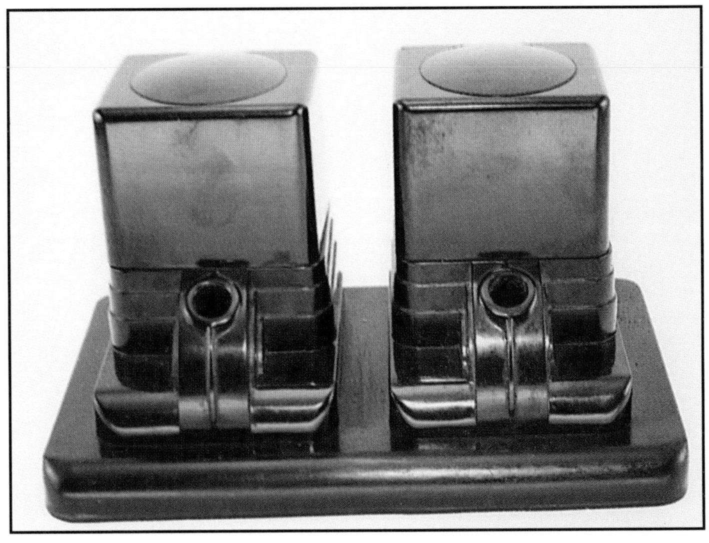

Plate 629
Black hard plastic base holding double Carter's cubes with bottles, Art Deco, American, 7" x 4¼" x 4", c. 1930, $95.00. Rodkey collection.

Plate 630
Plastic, black, cylindrical, Sheaffer's Rite-O-Way, glass bottle inside, 3¼" x 3⅜", c. early twentieth century, $50.00. Rodkey collection.

Plate 631
Burgundy plastic base and cylindrical cover, glass bottle insert, Sengbusch, Art Deco, American, 3½" x 3¼", c. 1930, $50.00 – 70.00. Rodkey collection.

Plate 632
Brown Bakelite, cash register form, Art Deco influence, American, c. 1930, $80.00 – 90.00. Rodkey collection.

Plate 633
Sealing wax red rubber, gutta-percha, hinged swivel cover, 2" x 1¼" high, c. late nineteenth century, $185.00 – 225.00. Rodkey collection.

Plate 634
Gold-tone pot metal base and covers, cube-shaped brown plastic wells with pen holders, two F-O-I pens with cherry amber handles, "Double Fount-O-Ink," American, 8⅝" x 3" x 3½", c. 1930, $100.00 – 150.00. Rodkey collection.

Plate 635
Two Fount-O-Ink desk sets, left is brown with gold-tone base, right is mottled green, both have matching pens, glass bottle liner, 5⅝" x 3" x 3¾", c. 1930, $50.00 – 75.00 each. Rodkey collection.

Plate 636
Plastic double wells on plastic base, cash register form with drawers, spill-proof screwtop covers, Art Deco influence, American, 7¾" x 5" x 3", c. 1930, $100.00 – 120.00. Rodkey collection.

Plate 637
Marbled brown Bakelite with double glass inserts, stepped base, central recess flanked by wells, sliding covers marked "FRANK A WEEKS MFG CO NEW YORK, U.S.A. PARAGON NO 510 PAT JUNE 3, 1913, 1411," $120.00 – 150.00. Thorp collection.

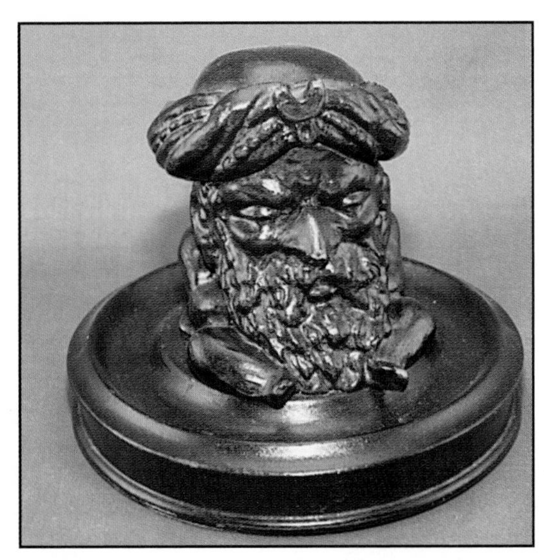

Plate 638
Composition, turned wood base, well is a Saracen, hinged head, porcelain insert, 3¾" diameter base, c. 1900, $125.00. Rodkey collection.

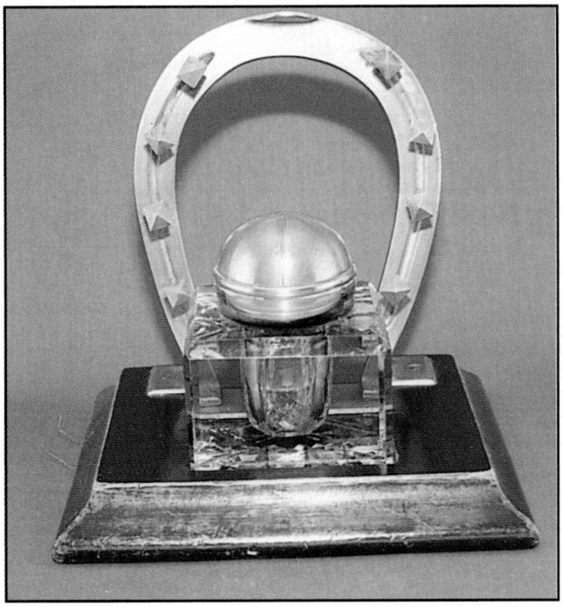

Plate 639
Enameled wood base with cut glass well and domed jockey cap cover, nickel-plated horseshoe back with nail head trim, 6" base, c. early twentieth century, $200.00 – 300.00. Rodkey collection.

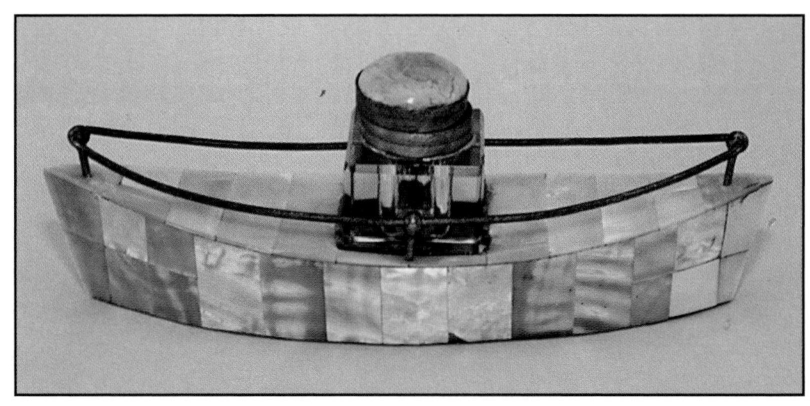

Plate 640
Mother-of-pearl boat, cut glass well with polished stone top and hinged collar, 6¼" x 1½" x 2⅜", c. early twentieth century, $150.00. Rodkey collection.

Plate 641
Cowry shell (South Pacific), souvenir of Galveston, Texas, attached swirl pen receptacle and attached chain from body of well to lid, milk glass insert, 3" x 2" x 1¾", c. early twentieth century, $35.00 – 45.00. Rodkey collection.

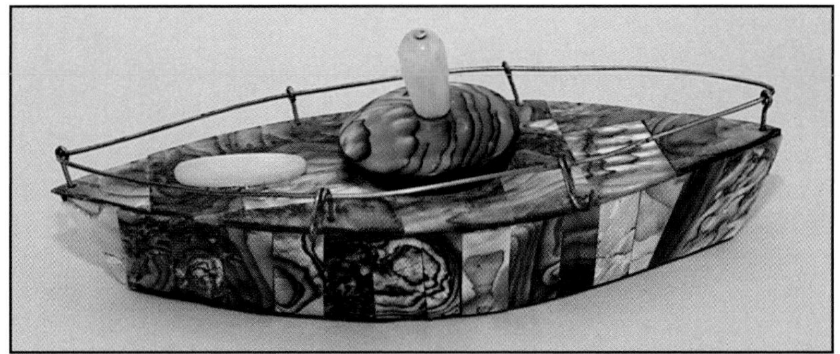

Plate 642
Boat overlaid with abalone shell, has brass wire gallery with abalone lid and mother-of-pearl smoke-stack, hinged cover, glass insert, 4⅝" x 1½" x 1⅞", c. early twentieth century, $150.00. Rodkey collection.

Plate 643
Wood base with pen channel, gilt applied, Rococo corners, Italian Renaissance lids, blue pressed glass cylindrical wells with vertical ribbing design, marked on brass covers "F. SOENNECKEN" plus marked on glass wells "Nr177–D.R.G.M" plus marked on glass covers "SOENNECKEN," 7" x 4½" base, c. 1890 – 1900, $200.00 – 300.00. Hummer collection.

Plate 644
Same as Plate 643.

Plate 645
Wood, hand-carved, boat-shaped with matching loose cover, lobed pressed glass font with vertical ribbing, Black Forest type, cover is overturned flower, "GENEVE" impressed on side, 7⅛" x 2½" x 3⅛", c. 1890 – 1900, $75.00 – 90.00 as is (stern damage). Hummer collection.

Plate 646
Dark brown hand-carved leaf-shaped, Black Forest type, brass hinged carved bird cover opens into nib compartment, bodies of wells are lobed, loose silver cover with woman's head in relief, covers marked "F. & B. STERLING PAT'D 1919," 10" x 6½" x 4½" high, $175.00 – 185.00. Hummer collection.

Plate 647
Wood log with two quill holes and holding glass bottle with Bakelite screw cap, marked on base: "H INKWELL" plus marked on front "PENNSYLVANIA GRAND CANYON" plus marked on bottle "FOR A HOLE 1½" IN.," souvenir type, 4" diameter, c. 1930, $40.00. Hummer collection.

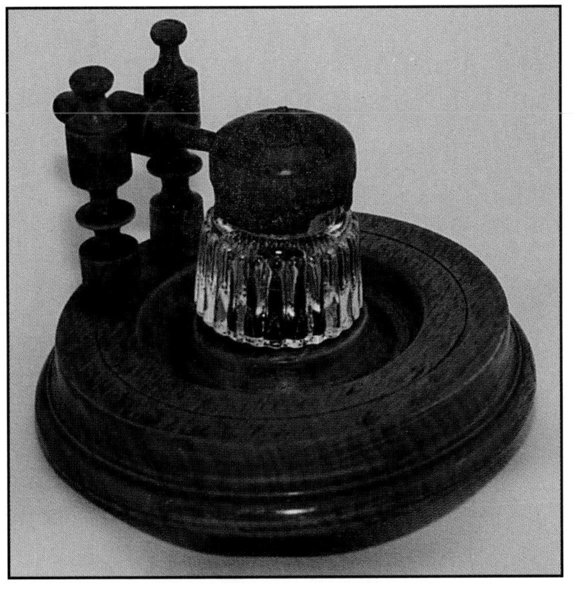

Plate 648
Treenware with hinged semi-automatic cover, pressed glass inset well with vertical ribbing, 5" diameter base, c. 1890 – 1900, $110.00 – 120.00. Hummer collection.

Plate 649
Wood, three compartments with hinged covers and pen channel, office commercial, porcelain inserts, marked on covers "COPYING RED BLACK," 9½" x 4⅞" x 2¾", c. 1940, $85.00 – 100.00. Hummer collection.

Plate 650
Wood with side pen racks and pressed glass cylindrical bottle, 9¼" x 4⅞", c. 1910 – 1915, $80.00 – 90.00. Hummer collection.

Plate 651
Carved wood tree stump surmounted by owl (emblem of wisdom) with glass eyes, German, Black Forest region, pen rest across front, 4½" x 3½" x 4½" high, c. 1890 – 1900, $175.00 – 200.00. Wherry collection.

Plate 652
Olivewood, carved wooden camel, brass hinged backpack, tinted in color, Jerusalem, 5¾" x 3½", c. 1930, $90.00 – 120.00. Wherry collection.

Plate 653
Wood, English style, front of drawer is burl walnut with porcelain knob, central carrying handle, Gothic lancet design, bun feet, front and back pen rest, recessed nib holder, pressed glass wells with hinged brass collars, 10½" x 6½" x 5½", c. 1870 – 1880, $200.00 – 300.00. Wherry collection.

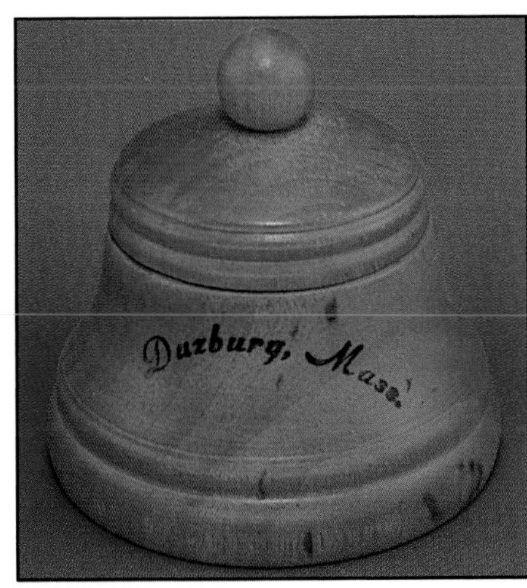

Plate 654
Maple treenware, bell-shaped well with ball finial, printed on well "DUZBURG, MASS.," c. early twentieth century, $70.00 – 80.00. East Bloomfield collection.

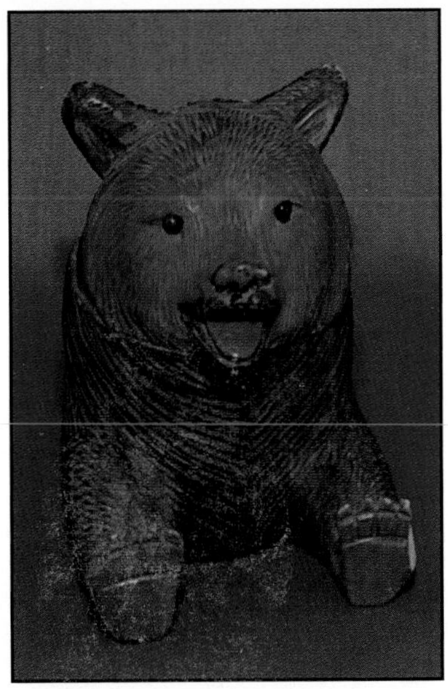

Plate 655
Carved wood bear, Germanic in origin, inset glass eyes, Black Forest region, slight damage on foot, 2¼" x 3" x 3" high, c. 1890 – 1900, $150.00 – 175.00. Wherry collection.

Plate 656
Wooden base with two lead bullets, World War I souvenir, says "WOMAN KILLED WAS JENNY, IN BAKING BREAD, A BEAUTIFUL LADY ENGAGED AT THE TIME. JOHN BURNE," made to hold small porcelain well, c. 1915, $70.00 – 85.00. Wherry collection.

Plate 657
Same as Plate 656.

Plate 658
Wood carved cat with glass eyes and paws resting on a trough, cat's head is lid, glass bottle insert, German (Black Forest), novelty, 6" x 3½" x 3½", c. 1890 – 1900, $175.00. East Bloomfield collection.

Plate 659
Standish, carved wood, French Provincial style, shallow carving and spindle trim, two Faience inserts with hand-painted lids, berry motif, c. early twentieth century, $180.00 – 200.00. Smith collection.

Plate 660
Treenware, distressed gilt bronze finish quill holder, marked "T.W.B.," American, $3\frac{1}{2}$" diameter x 2", c. 1840 – 1850, $175.00 – 190.00.

Plate 661
Cork with four quill holes and well hole, aqua blown well, marked on paper sticker in handwriting "From Artemas Gridley House, Southington, Conn.," $2\frac{15}{16}$" square x $1\frac{3}{8}$" high, c. 1850, $300.00. Hummer collection.

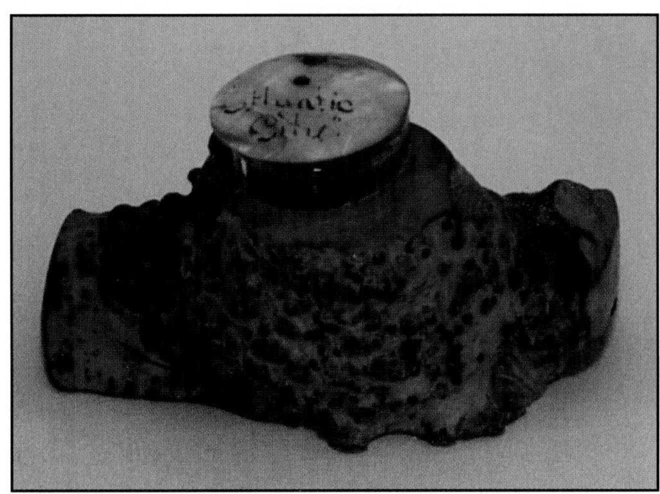

Plate 662
Made from a burl, lid is mother-of-pearl, glass insert, souvenir type, marked on cover "ATLANTIC CITY," $3\frac{3}{4}$" x $2\frac{1}{2}$", c. 1900, $50.00 – 60.00. Hummer collection.

Plate 663
Wood square base with rusticated feet, well is a Swiss chalet or log cabin, hinged roof lid, pressed glass well inside cabin, souvenir, 3" x $2\frac{5}{8}$" x $2\frac{3}{4}$" high, c. late nineteenth century, $150.00 – 175.00. Rodkey collection.

Plate 664
Same as Plate 663.

Travelers

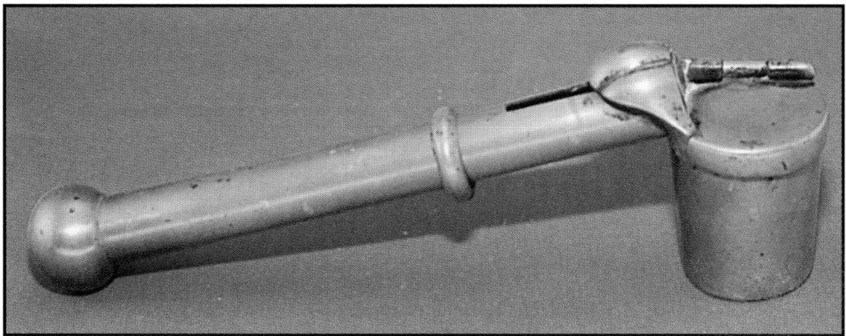

Plate 665
Cast brass portable scribe case and attached well, Eastern origin, hinged lid, 7½" long, c. 1790 – 1830, $200.00. Rodkey collection.

Plate 666
Brass scribe case with enameled decoration, feet are winged insects, pen case is surmounted by a dragon's head, Near Eastern, possibly Japanese, 9" long, c. 1790 – 1830, $400.00 – 500.00. Rodkey collection.

Plate 667
Chased brass portable scribe case with pen case and attached well, scallop shell hinged cover, near Eastern, 8¾" long, c. eighteenth century, $250.00 – 300.00. Wherry collection.

Plate 668
Islamic portable scribe pen case and well, pen case has incised running animal and well has shell-shaped cover, 8" long, c. nineteenth century, $200.00 – 250.00. Rodkey collection.

Plate 669
Brass portable scribe pen case and well, cast scallop shell hinged cover, Near Eastern, 9" long, c. eighteenth century, $300.00 – 400.00. Rodkey collection.

Plate 670
Islamic portable scribe pen case and well, chased brass (floral design), 7¼" long, c. 1790 – 1810, $300.00 – 400.00. Rodkey collection.

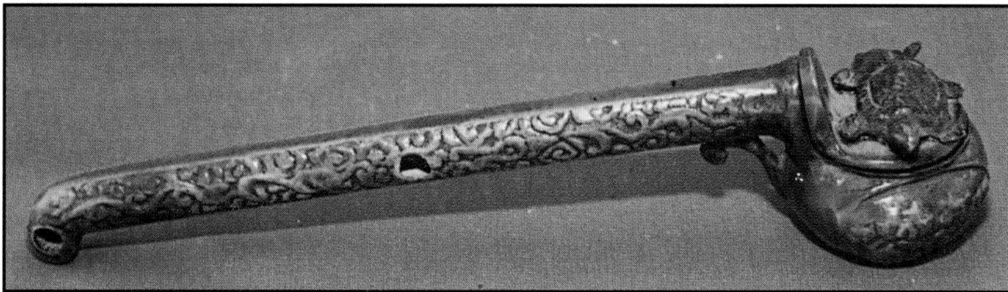

Plate 671
Brass portable scribe case and well, allover foliate design with turtle on cover, possibly Near Eastern, 7" long, c. nineteenth century, $250.00 – 300.00. Rodkey collection.

Plate 672
Heavy brass, silver-plated portable scribe case, Eastern origin, Islamic form, 10½" long, c. 1830 – 1840, $250.00 – 300.00. Rodkey collection.

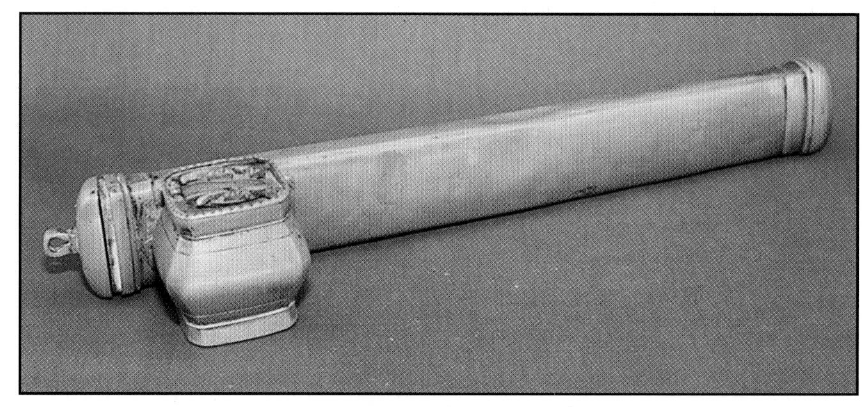

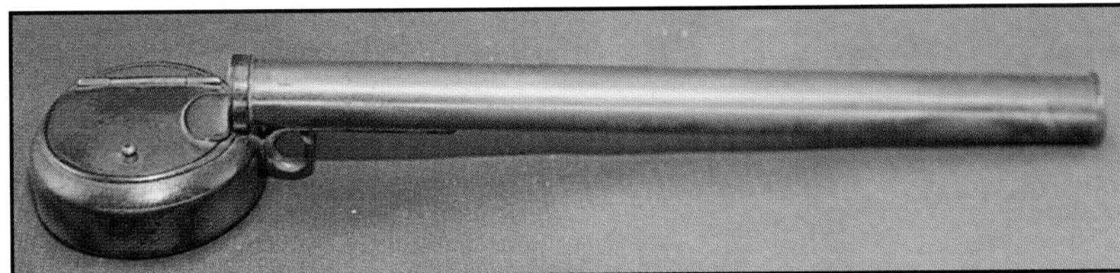

Plate 673
Brass portable scribe case and attached round inkpot, 8¼" long, c. nineteenth century, $125.00 – 150.00. Rodkey collection.

Plate 674
Green Morocco (leather), brass fittings, brass bale handles, second from left stamped "DEPOSE, PERRY AND CO.," c. 1890, $150.00 – 200.00 each. Rodkey collection.

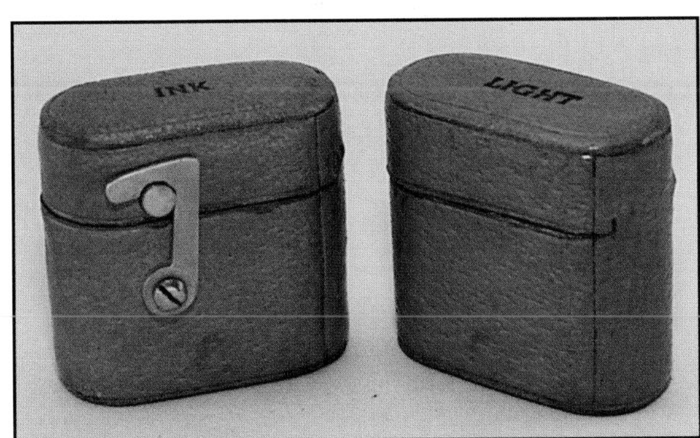

Plate 675
Left: brown leather covered well, oval in contour, "INK" printed on top, 2" x 1" x 1⅞"; right: brown leather covered, match holder case to match traveler well, "LIGHT" printed on top, 2" x 1" x 1⅞", c. 1915 – 1920, $70.00 – 90.00 each. Rodkey collection.

Plate 676
Cherry wood rectangular base with rounded corners, dog house with hinged lid, carved wood dog's head with glass eyes, roof has slight damage, glass insert, c. 1900 – 1910, $125.00 as is. Rodkey collection.

Plate 677
Brown Morocco cover, cylindrical well, brass body and interior fittings, retractable pen, "INK" in gold on lid, 2" x 2½", c. 1890, $100.00 – 125.00. Rodkey collection.

Plate 678
Finished wood with brass band, c. 1890 – 1900, $125.00. Rodkey collection.

Plate 679
Oval well with red Morocco cover and brass interior fittings, 1¾" x 1⅜" x 1¼", c. 1890, $100.00 – 125.00. Rodkey collection.

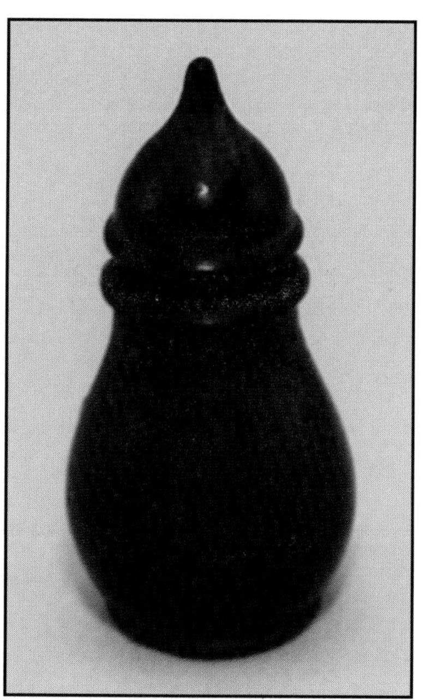

Plate 680
Bottle-shaped, dark finish, screw top, gutta-percha, c. 1850 – 1900, $150.00 – 175.00. Rodkey collection.

Plate 681
Brown Morocco cover, hexagonal, "INK" stamped in gold on lid, brass interior, 1¾" x 1½" high, c. 1850 – 1890, $125.00. Rodkey collection.

Plate 682
Brown cylindrical body, screw-top lid, gutta-percha, 2⅛" x 1⅞", c. 1885, $100.00 – 125.00. Rodkey collection.

Plate 683
Silver-plated cylindrical well with bead trimmed base, rope gadroon trimmed cover, double swivel snap closure, engraved bands on lid, 1¼" x 1⅜", c. 1850 – 1890, $185.00. Rodkey collection.

Plate 684
Black leather covered dice, brass interior, stamped in leather "AUSTRA & SCHUTZ," 1¾" x 1⅞", c. late nineteenth century, $125.00 – 175.00. Rodkey collection.

Plate 685
Sheet metal, dog's head is pot metal, riding helmet in green and blue, quirt with dog's head, 4¼" x 1¾" x 1½", c. 1910, $185.00. Wherry collection.

Plate 686
Same as Plate 685.

Plate 687
Sheet metal, French helmet known as an "Adrian," worn by French soldiers, called "Playloo," front piece has a flaming bomb, 3" x 3¼" x 1¾", $350.00, rare. Wherry collection.

Plate 688
Pressed glass, miniature, lid is medallion, classical in cameo, c. 1890 – 1900, $90.00. East Bloomfield collection.

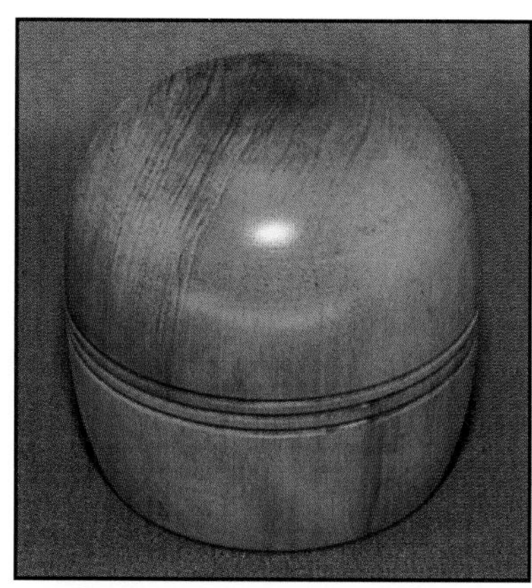

Plate 689
Maple wood, turned, removable screw lid, interior metal, 2" round x 2¼" high, c. 1910, $100.00 – 125.00. Wherry collection.

Plate 690
Same as Plate 689.

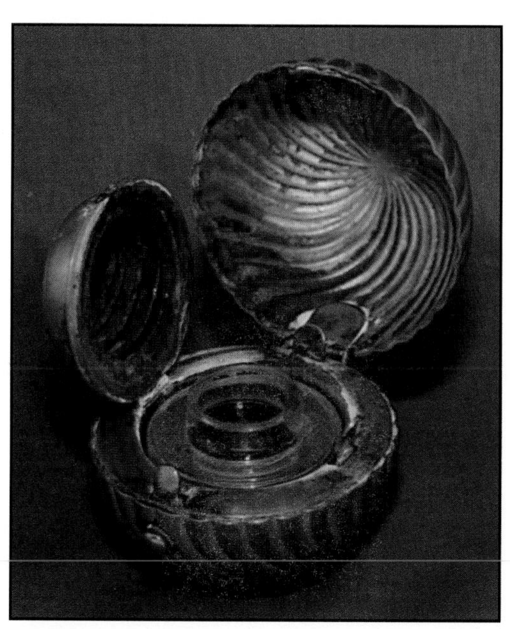

Plate 691
Spherical, brass twisted ribbed design, double hinged top, 2½" diameter x 2½" high, c. 1880, $100.00 – 125.00. Wherry collection.

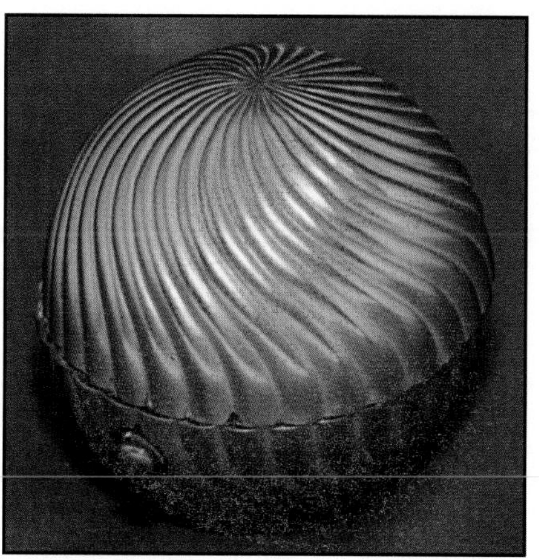

Plate 692
Same as Plate 691.

Plate 693
Nickel-plated brass, pocket type, spring-loaded cover with thumb release button and security catch, English, c. 1910, $70.00 – 100.00. Meyer collection.

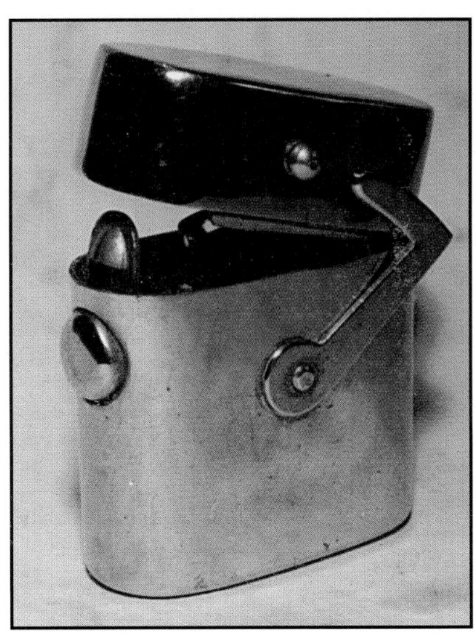

Plate 694
Nickel-plated brass, pocket type, spring-loaded cover with thumb release button and security catch, English, c. 1910, $70.00 – 100.00. Meyer collection.

Plate 695
Nickel-plated heavy cast iron, spring-loaded cover with thumb release button and security bar, security bar covers container entirely in closed state and functions as a stand in opened state, embossed lettering "PUSH" on top, embossed crown between lettering "RANSOME'S PATENT" and embossed lettering "DE LA RUE & CO.," on body, English, c. 1900, $100.00 – 140.00. Meyer collection.

Plate 696
Silver-plated brass, pocket type, spring-loaded with thumb release button and security catch, English, c. 1900 – 1910, $70.00 – 100.00. Meyer collection.

Plate 697
Brown leather cover on brass interior, rugby ball shape, two spring-loaded covers with thumb release button and security catch, English, c. 1900, $250.00 – 300.00. Meyer collection.

Plate 698
Black leather cover on brass and iron interior, oval contour, spring-loaded with thumb release button, heavy sterling silver top with hand-engraved floral design, embossed initials "MLM," hallmarked "STERLING," "BIRMINGHAM," and "1888," hand-blown and cut crystal insert with faceted body and two engraved opposing feathers, English, $500.00 – 600.00. Meyer collection.

Plate 699
Brown crocodile cover on sheet steel interior, spring-loaded cover with thumb release button, gold embossed lettering "INK," English, c. 1890, $150.00 – 200.00. Meyer collection.

Plate 700
Black leather cover on brass and iron interior, brass carrying handle, spring-loaded cover with thumb release button, gold embossed lettering "DE LA RUE & CO. LONDON," English, c. 1910, $100.00 – 150.00. Meyer collection.

Plate 701
Black leather cover on brass interior, oval contour, chased decoration, two spring-loaded covers with thumb release button and security catch, gold embossed lettering "INK," English, c. 1870, $80.00 – 120.00. Meyer collection.

Plate 702
Brown leather cover on brass interior, two spring-loaded covers with thumb release button and catch, gold embossed lettering "INK," possibly American, c. 1910, $90.00 – 110.00. Meyer collection.

Plate 703
Burgundy leather cover on nickel-plated brass interior, two spring-loaded covers with thumb release button and security catch, possibly French, c. 1900, $75.00 – 95.00. Meyer collection.

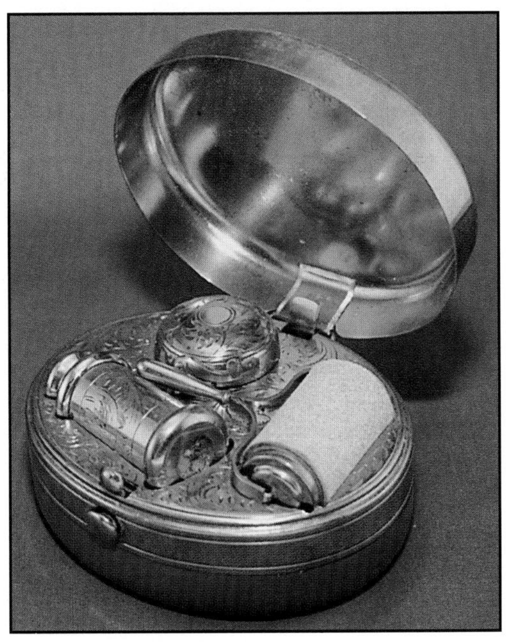

Plate 704
Low circular design, fitted interior with roller blotter, cylindrical container and well, chased decoration, gold plated interior, brown leather covered base, possibly French, c. 1890, $500.00 – 600.00. Rodkey collection.

Plate 705
Brown gutta-percha, cylindrical, mushroom-shaped screw lids, c. 1850 – 1900, $90.00 – 125.00 each. Rodkey collection.

Plate 706
Red leather cover on brass interior, chased decoration, two spring-loaded covers with thumb release button and security catch, inside embossed lettering "KPRI," gold embossed lettering "INK," English, c. 1900, $100.00 – 150.00. Meyer collection.

Plate 707
Green Morocco covered case with brass fitted interior, stamped "NOUVEL ENCRIER, BREVETTE S.G.D.G.," 1½" x 2⅛" x 1", c. 1890 – 1900, $150.00 – 175.00. Rodkey collection.

Plate 708
Brass, barrel-shaped, brass engraved bands, 1⅛" x 1⅝", c. late nineteenth century, $150.00 – 175.00. Rodkey collection.

Plate 709
Cylindrical, brass, leather covered, spring-loaded twist release covers, one is pounce pot, each lid with "A.K. PAT'D" inscribed, glass inserts, 1½" x 1⅜" high, c. 1890 – 1900, $250.00 pair. Rodkey collection.

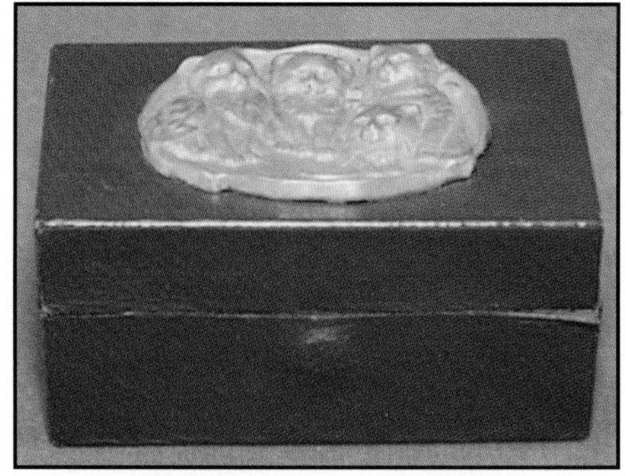

Plate 710
Rectangular with green leather covering, applied plaque on lid with four cats in high relief, two wells and pen wipe, c. 1900, $200.00 – 250.00, rare. Rodkey collection.

Plate 711
Sheet steel with polychrome decoration, stovepipe hat and umbrella, well lid is crown of hat, pen is umbrella handle, opaque glass insert, English, 4⅜" x 1⅝" x 1⅜", c. 1890 – 1900, $450.00 – 500.00. Rodkey collection.

Plate 712
Same as Plate 711.

Plate 713
Brass, cube-shaped with embossed Rococo scroll work on body, Renaissance high relief lid with central human figure, 1½" x 1⅝" high, c. 1880 – 1900, $200.00 – 300.00. Rodkey collection.

Plate 714
Sheet brass with brass covered wood base, cylindrical, champagne cork type lid, cast brass snap-lid, Art Nouveau influence, possibly American, 1⅜" x 2¼" high, c. 1900 – 1910, $150.00. Rodkey collection.

Plate 715
Silver-plated white metal with fine repousseé leaf design, heraldic symbol on inner cover, two spring-loaded covers with thumb release button and security catch, English, c. 1900, $100.00 – 150.00. Meyer collection.

Plate 716
Brass barrel-shaped, heraldic symbol with lettering "KKA" and "PRIV" on inner cover, two spring-loaded covers with thumb release button and security catch, Austria, c. 1890, $100.00 – 150.00. Meyer collection.

Plate 717
Hard rubber, two screw covers, Germany, c. 1920, $60.00 – 80.00. Meyer collection.

Plate 718
Sheet metal beer mug-shaped, top removes to reveal pen holder, pencil holder, and screw top inkwell, black lettering "MAINZ," Germany, c. 1890 – 1900, $200.00 – 300.00. Meyer collection.

Plate 719
Nickel-plated brass, "Beer bottle catch," impressed lettering "GMS," Germany, c. 1900, $130.00 – 150.00. Meyer collection.

Plate 720
Black leather cover on brass interior, violin case-shaped, brass carrying handle, two spring-loaded covers with thumb release button and security catch, case contains well and brush, possibly English, c. 1870, $300.00 – 350.00. Meyer collection.

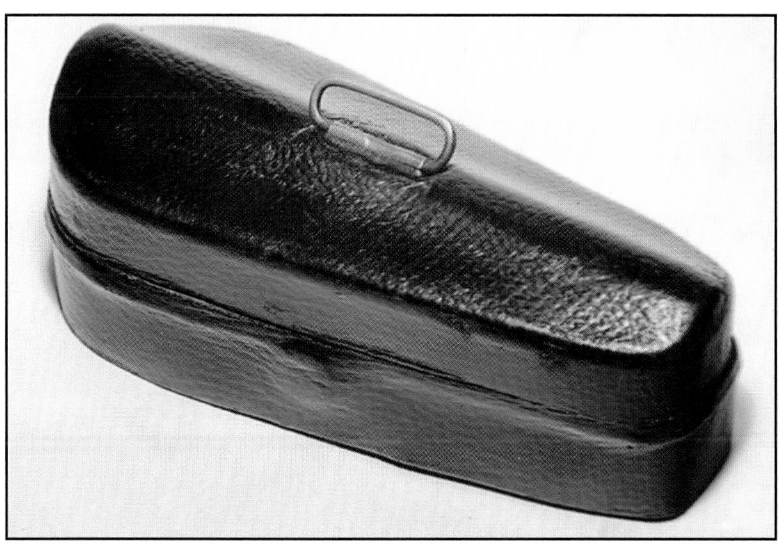

Plate 721
Same as Plate 720.

Plate 722
Genuine snake leather cover over brass interior, laundry basket-shaped, snake leather handle, two spring-loaded covers with thumb release button and security catch, American, c. 1870, $250.00 – 300.00. Meyer collection.

Plate 723
Black leather cover on brass interior, brass carrying handle, spring-loaded cover with unusual catch, England, c. 1900, $100.00 – 150.00. Meyer collection.

Plate 724
Black leather cover on brass interior, brass carrying handle, gold embossed lettering "PERRY CO LONDON," spring-loaded cover with thumb release button and sliding security catch, inscribed "DEPOSE," England, c. 1890 – 1900, $100.00 – 150.00. Meyer collection.

Plate 725
Nickel-plated brass, pressing the spring-loaded hinged cover of well opens the four sides of the container, England, c. 1900, $100.00 – 130.00. Meyer collection.

Plate 726
Same as Plate 725.

Plate 727
Stetson hat-shaped with leather brim and brass crown, brass interior, two spring-loaded covers with thumb release button and security catch, possibly English, c. 1870, $300.00 – 350.00, rare. Meyer collection.

Plate 728
Rosewood, cylindrical shape, bayonet locked cover, France, c. 1900, $80.00 – 100.00. Meyer collection.

Plate 729
Red leather cover on brass interior, binocular-shaped case, two spring-loaded covers with thumb release button and security catch, possibly English, c. 1870, $300.00 – 350.00. Meyer collection.

Plate 730
Burgundy leather cover on brass interior, chased decoration, contains well, stamp box, brush, and roller blotter, two spring-loaded covers with thumb release button and security catch, possibly English, c. 1870, $350.00 – 400.00. Meyer collection.

Plate 731
Same as Plate 730.

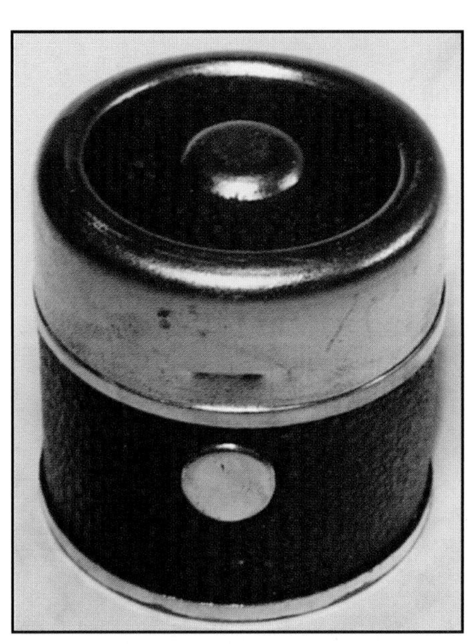

Plate 732
Black leather on plated brass interior, two spring-loaded covers with thumb release button and security catch, possibly English, c. 1900, $80.00 – 120.00. Meyer collection.

Plate 733
Rosewood barrel-shaped, bayonet locked cover, possibly French, c. 1900, $80.00 – 100.00. Meyer collection.

Plate 734
Burgundy leather cover on brass interior, engraved anchor with winding fish on inner cover, two spring-loaded covers with thumb release button and security catch, possibly English, c. 1900, $80.00 – 100.00. Meyer collection.

Plate 735
Burgundy leather cover on brass interior, chased decoration, embossed lettering "KPRI" and stylized bird on interior, two spring-loaded covers with thumb release button and security catch, Austria, c. 1870, $100.00 – 140.00. Meyer collection.

Plate 736
Wooden cover on plated brass interior, tree trunk shape, heraldic symbol with embossed lettering "K.K.PR." on inner cover, two spring-loaded covers with thumb release button and security catch, Austria, c. 1900, $300.00 – 350.00. Meyer collection.

Plate 737
Brass, chains anchor cover to base, c. early nineteenth century, $100.00 – 150.00. Meyer collection.

Plate 738
Cream-colored plastic cover over glass bottle with spring attached cork inside, inscribed "SWAN The Travellers Fountain Pen Ink Filler," England, c. 1920, $70.00 – 90.00. Meyer collection.

Plate 739
Polished solid brass, screw-on cover with gadroon trim, ⅜" central opening inside, American, 1⅝" diameter x 1¾" high, c. 1900, $110.00. Hummer collection.

Plate 740
Hard rubber with screw caps, right and left are black, center is brown, gutta-percha, all are 2" diameter x 1¾" high, c. 1900, $75.00 – 80.00. Hummer collection.

Plate 741
Leather covered brass, spherical shape, interior has brush, nib wipe, expandable pen, and insert, c. 1890, $175.00 – 200.00. Rodkey collection.

Plate 742
Dull silver finish, snap type hinged cover with woman's head in relief, beaded motif on shoulders, interior glass bottle, marked on base "PAT'D APPLIED FOR," 2¼" diameter x 1½" high, c. 1900, $90.00. Hummer collection.

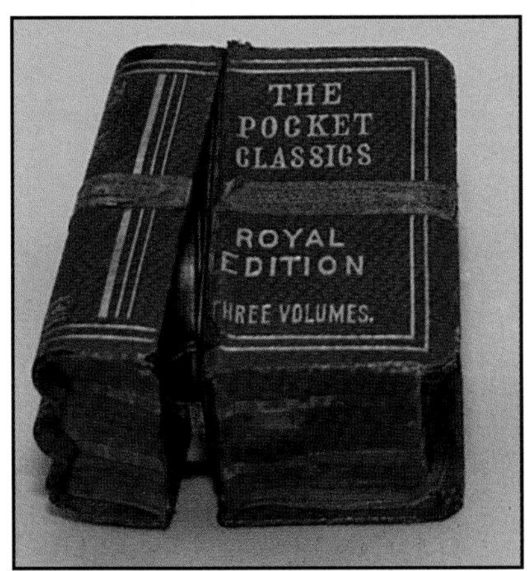

Plate 743
Red leather covered brass, book-shaped, two spring-loaded covers with thumb release buttons and security catch, glass bottle, marked "THE POCKET CLASSICS ROYAL EDITION THREE VOLUMES" plus "ESSAYS–TRAVEL–POETRY," 1³⁄₁₆" x 2³⁄₁₆" x 1⅞" high, c. 1890 – 1900, $140.00 – 160.00. Hummer collection.

Plate 744
Patinated brass with hinged snap cover with finial, glass bottle, marked on paper label on base "MADE IN AUSTRIA" plus marked on interior cover "KKA–PRIV" under anchor insignia, 2⅛" base x 2⅝" high, c. 1910 – 1920, $100.00 – 110.00. Hummer collection.

Plate 745
Brown leather cover on brass interior, chased decoration, two spring-loaded covers with thumb release button and security catch, England, c. 1870, $100.00 – 130.00. Meyer collection.

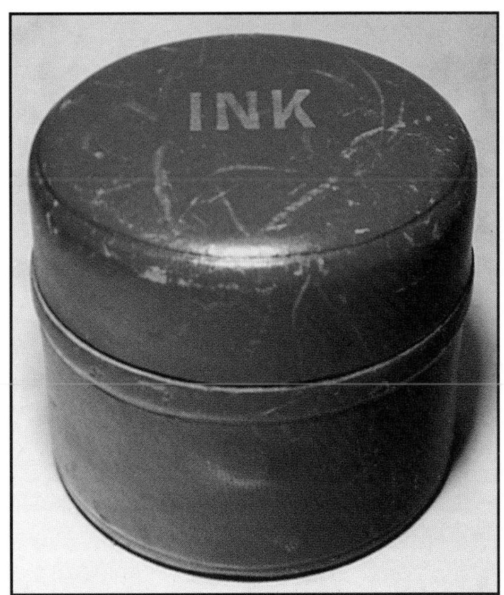

Plate 746
Red leather cover on brass interior, chased decoration, two spring-loaded covers with thumb release button and security catch, gold embossed lettering "INK" and "MADE IN AUSTRIA," c. 1870, $100.00 – 150.00. Meyer collection.

Plate 747
Brown leather cover on brass interior, hexagonal contour, chased decoration, two spring-loaded covers with thumb release button and security catch, gold embossed lettering "INK," England, c. 1870, $120.00 – 160.00. Meyer collection.

Plate 748
Red leather cover on brass interior, heraldic symbol on inner cover, two spring-loaded covers with thumb release button and security catch, England, c. 1900, $80.00 – 120.00. Meyer collection.

Plate 749
Nickel-plated brass traveler's writing equipment container, wave guilloche, contains pen knife (letter opener) with silver-plated fluted spiral body, silver-plated fluted spiral propelling pencil, and screw covered plated brass insert containing a miniature inkwell, England, c. 1880, $150.00 – 200.00. Meyer collection.

Plate 750
Rolled brass, square contour, leaf and stipple decoration, brass hinged spring lock cover, scrolled brass inner lid with spring lock, blown bottle with sheared lip, Chinese, c. 1840 – 1850, $125.00 – 145.00. Thorp collection.

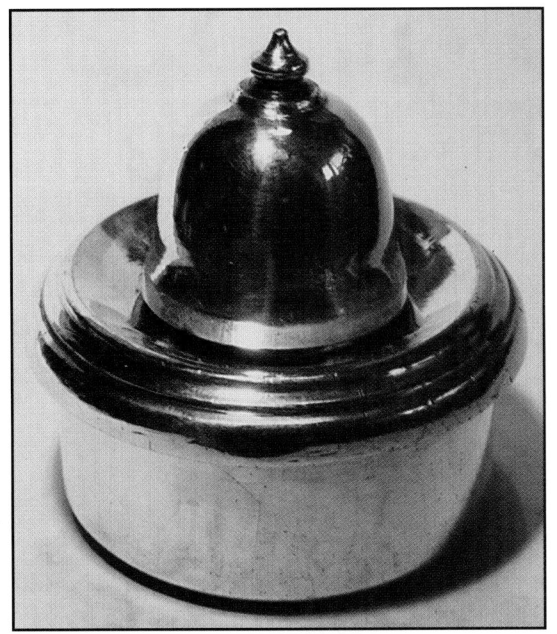

Plate 751
Silver-plated white metal, bell-shaped top over screw cover, England, c. 1880, $100.00 – 150.00. Meyer collection.

Plate 752
Silver-plated white metal traveler's writing equipment container, cigar-shaped, cable twist design, two covers and compartments, main compartment contains pen knife with silver-plated fluted spiral body and writing quill with black lettering "PATRICK THOMSON LTD. EDINB," main compartment cover contains second compartment with miniature inkwell, inkwell cover with security bar, Scotland, c. 1880, $150.00 – 200.00. Meyer collection.

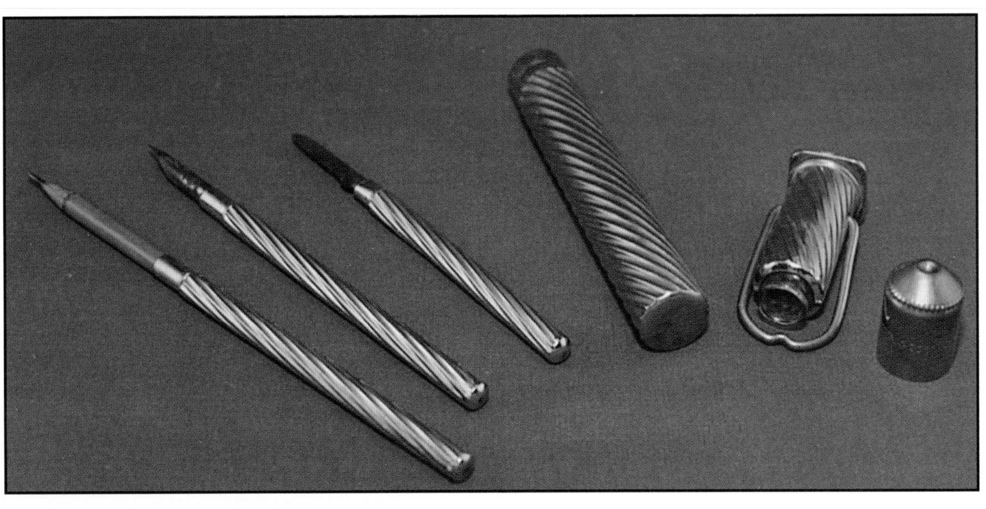

Plate 753
Silver-colored metal, twist design, case contains pen, pencil, and knife, top contains well, 4¾" long, c. 1900 – 1910, $150.00 – 200.00. Rodkey collection.

Plate 754
Stamped sheet metal, bottle-shaped, right: champagne bottle, 1⅛" x 3¾" high; left: cognac bottle, 1¼" x 3" high, c. 1900, $175.00 – 200.00 each. Rodkey collection.

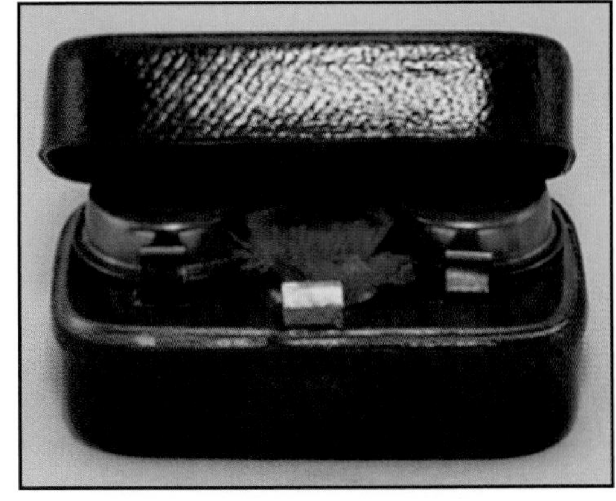

Plate 755
Red leather covered brass case, brass fittings and interior, two wells and red brush nib wipe, c. 1890 – 1900, $200.00. Rodkey collection.

Plate 756
Carved wood English walnut-shaped well attached to polychrome leaf with handle, hinged top lifts to reveal quill brush and well, glass insert, rustic style, Germany, 8½" x 5½" x 4" high, c. 1890, $150.00 – 200.00. Hummer collection.

Plate 757
Same as Plate 756.

Inkwell Inserts

What is an inkwell without an insert? Perhaps less attractive and definitely less valuable. We make porcelain inserts to fill this void. The cost is $14.00 each p.p.; 24 karat gold trim, add $2.00.

For complete details, write Veldon Badders, 692 Martin Road, Hamlin, NY 14464.

We would like to thank all the girls at the Briggs Pottery in Fairport, New York, for their cooperation in helping us with the resurrection of porcelain insert production.